Zora in Florida

Zora in Florida

Edited by

Steve Glassman and Kathryn Lee Seidel

University of Central Florida Press
Orlando

Photographs of Zora Neale Hurston reproduced in this volume courtesy of Special
Collections, University of Florida Libraries

Library of Congress Cataloging-in-Publication Data

Zora in Florida / edited by Steve Glassman and Kathryn Lee Seidel.
p.   cm.
Includes bibliographical references and index.
ISBN 0-8130-1050-0 (alk. paper). — ISBN 0-8130-1061-6 (pbk.:alk. paper)
1. Hurston, Zora Neale—Knowledge—Florida. 2. Afro-Americans—
Florida—Folklore.   3. Afro-Americans in literature.   4. Florida in
literature.   5. Folklore—Florida.   I. Glassman, Steve.
II. Seidel, Kathryn Lee.
PS3515.U789Z955   1991
813'.52—dc20   90-19551

The University of Central Florida is a member of University Presses of Florida, the scholarly
publishing agency of the State University System of Florida. Books are selected for
publication by faculty editorial committees at each of Florida's nine public universities:
Florida A&M University (Tallahassee), Florida Atlantic University (Boca Raton), Florida
International University (Miami), Florida State University (Tallahassee), University of
Central Florida (Orlando), University of Florida (Gainesville), University of North Florida
(Jacksonville), University of South Florida (Tampa), University of West Florida (Pensacola).

Orders for books published by all member presses should be addressed to University Presses
of Florida, 15 NW 15th St., Gainesville, FL 32603.

To Leslie Seidel and Alexis Wang and
Marguerite and Eugene Glassman

Contents

Introduction

One of the most enduring and romantic legends of American letters is that of the writer who toils long and difficult years in obscurity but who, after death, is recognized as one of the great interpreters of the age. Of the many candidates who are put forth for such literary canonization, Emily Dickinson was the real thing, as was her contemporary, Herman Melville. In our century Zora Neale Hurston, the central figure in this collection of essays, has only recently been recognized as a powerful and influential writer whose work deserves immediate recognition. In the first wave of the rediscovery of her work, readers and critics responded especially to her masterpiece, *Their Eyes Were Watching God* (1937). These essays represent a second wave of critical response that focuses on Hurston's less-known works, on her nonfiction, on gathering and preserving primary source materials, and on assessing the elements that allow her to enter the canon as a major figure.

Zora Hurston in her day was a writer of limited success because her work was not taken seriously by those who would have been most likely to appreciate it. In chapter 3 David Headon points out that Carl Van Vechten and Ralph Ellison, both noted black literary figures, dismissed Hurston as frivolous and insufficiently political. Part of the new appreciation of Hurston has to do with her use of her native place and her cultural traditions as the main ''stuff'' of her work. This volume focuses, therefore, on the place that gave her inspiration, the frontier wilderness of central Florida.

At the time of Hurston's birth, just before the turn of the century (the date of her birth is discussed in chapter 2), central Florida was still reeling from the Great Freezes of 1893–94, which devastated the nascent citrus industry and sent many recent immigrants fleeing north. At about the same time, it was discovered that the seemingly barren Florida sands were laden with phosphate. Some of the rowdiest mining towns in American frontier history replaced those blighted communities of former northerners founded with the possibility of liberal education and views. The already-existing sawmill and turpentine camps were almost as notorious in their lawlessness as the mining boomtowns. Often the black labor in these places was forced in a system known as debt peonage, embarrassingly similar to antebellum slavery, made acceptable by a thin legal sugar coating. The country was so wild and sparsely settled that cattle ranged freely throughout much of the Florida peninsula.

From this ostensibly unpromising soil, Zora Neale Hurston drew her nourishment and inspiration as a writer. Although it would be mistaken to claim that Hurston's hometown of Eatonville—the first community wholly organized and settled by blacks in the state and perhaps in the nation—was as wild as many of the others in the area, the violent and unsettled conditions of the peninsula affected it. Yet to Hurston, Eatonville did indeed seem to be an oasis, an Eden in the midst of a depressed economy. Hurston's strengths as a writer—and perhaps some of her idiosyncrasies as a person—can be traced in large part to her frontier roots. As she tells us in her autobiography, *Dust Tracks on a Road* (1942), and shows us in her novels—*Their Eyes Were Watching God* (1937), *Jonah's Gourd Vine* (1934), and her collection of folklore, *Mules and Men* (1935)— in Florida she heard and later recorded the speech of the common people, a group of African-Americans who were singularly interested in preserving their integrity as a community. Also, Hurston's fierce independence both as a person and as a writer can perhaps be traced to the egalitarianism that frontier conditions often inculcate. At a time when it was believed that "real" black writers should concentrate on the struggle with the white majority, Hurston concentrated on themes of self-discovery and African-American culture, which her contemporaries did not hold in particularly high regard. Almost sixty years later, feminist and African-American critics take issue with that assessment. They see, in Hurston's writings, black women characters who struggle to liberate themselves in a world dominated by men and their values. There is political content in her work after all.

Even today, more than thirty years after her death and a half century after her most influential work appeared, some critics are not sure what to make of Hurston's work—aside from a general belief that it is of enduring importance. (For instance, today some feminist critics feel that the view of Hurston adopted when she was rediscovered in the seventies was a bit too romantic.) Many undergraduate literature anthologies include a short story by her, and increasingly her books, especially *Their Eyes Were Watching God,* appear on required reading lists for the undergraduate and graduate specialist. However, in spite of this broad interest, critical attention, though by no means negligent or negligible, has been quite parochial. This collection of essays, for instance, is the first in which anyone seriously examines the contribution of Florida material to Hurston's work, apparent though it is at even a cursory reading.

The editors made a concerted effort to solicit at least one essay on each major phase of Hurston's literary career that was somehow bound up with Florida. For instance, this collection contains two essays devoted to her first novel, *Jonah's Gourd Vine,* which, except for several introductory chapters, is set wholly in Florida. (See chapters 7 and 8.) Previously, little critical attention had been paid to this seminal first book. In fact, a comprehensive computer search turned up mention of the book in exactly a dozen articles, only one of which was devoted totally to the novel.

Likewise, chapters in this collection discuss such critically neglected areas as Hurston's early nonfiction, her early short play *Color Struck* (chapter 11), and her work for the WPA Florida writers' project in the thirties (chapter 13). In addition, chapters are also included on Florida-based works to which scholars have devoted more attention, such as *Mules and Men* (chapters 4, 5, and 6), *Dust Tracks on a Road,* her autobiography (chapter 14), and her short fiction, such as "Sweat" and the "Spunk" complex (chapter 10). Other chapters are oriented toward the peculiarly Floridian elements in her work, such as her use of floral and faunal imagery in many of her works (chapter 1). Still others talk about the actual environment and conditions Hurston confronted in Florida. In chapter 15 Kevin McCarthy discusses her several legal entanglements with an eye to explaining the eclipse that befell her late in life, another area where critical attention has been minimal prior to the publication of this volume.

Although a concerted effort was made to cover all major phases of Hurston's Florida life, no effort was made to impose any particular critical orientation throughout this work. Serious study of Hurston dates back less than two decades. It is too early for a consensus to have formed—or at least one that has abided. The editors decided that the volume should speak to the largest possible community of Hurston scholars, both the professional student as well as the casual reader infatuated by the Zora mystique. Thus, some essays in this collection speak to a wide readership with facility and clarity; the focus of others narrows with the intensity and depth of their authors' vision. All are informed by a knowledge of contemporary critical debates regarding Hurston, and all treat new material regarding her life and her work and their relationship to her native state.

Hurston usually tendered a time around 1901 for her birthdate, but the evidence is mounting that she was actually born in 1890 or 1891—and likely not in central Florida. Robert Hemenway's groundbreaking biography of 1977 included only a few paragraphs on Hurston's life in Eatonville; however, scholars such as Anna Lillios have uncovered new evidence by speaking with contemporaries of Hurston who are still living in Eatonville (chapter 2). Hurston tells us in her autobiography that she had a generally pleasant childhood, playing and fantasizing in the pine barrens and oak scrubs of the lake district of what is called the central ridge in Florida, until her mother died (when Hurston was about nine, by her account).

The seventh of eight children, she attended schools in Eatonville and Jacksonville until she joined a Gilbert and Sullivan repertory company and moved north. In Baltimore, perhaps already in her late twenties, she attended Morgan Academy in 1918 (now Morgan State University). It was there that she became excited about literature, specifically a rendition of Coleridge's "Kubla Khan," as she reports in *Dust Tracks*. She was awarded a scholarship to Barnard College, becoming its first black student, and received a bachelor of arts degree in 1928. She married at this point, but the marriage lasted only a few years and we know little about it. Living in New York at the crest of the Harlem Renaissance was an exhilarating experience but one fraught with frustration as well. Her early work, such as "Spunk" and "Sweat," brought her to the attention of popular novelist Fannie Hurst, who hired her as a secretary in 1925. Other patrons soon followed, but her publications were often criticized as lacking in political content. Her two marriages were both short-lived, with one husband accusing her of threatening him with "voodoo" (as Hemenway reports).

During the 1930s and '40s, when Hurston was most productive, she frequently lived in New York and often traveled to the Caribbean but always returned to Florida. Sometimes financial exigency drove her back to her adopted home state. (Hemenway tells us her largest royalty was $943.75.) At various times she taught drama at Bethune-Cookman College in Daytona Beach and took a position with the Works Progress Administration (WPA), as Christopher Felker tells in chapter 13. At other times, Hurston seemed to come back to Florida simply because she liked the mild climate and enjoyed the fishing. Then in 1948 an incident occurred in New York that sent her back to Florida more or less for good. A ten-year-old boy accused her of sexual molestation. The charge was eventually dismissed, but the incident damaged her reputation and in great part prevented further publication prospects.

In spite of her connections with the best-selling Fannie Hurst and the Harlem Renaissance, Hurston's career as a serious writer was launched from provincial Florida. In 1933, a dozen years after she published her first piece in a student literary magazine and after she had already completed one book that no publisher wanted, Hurston sent a short story called "The Gilded Six-Bits" to Robert Wunsch, a professor at Rollins College in Winter Park. Wunsch liked the story and recommended it to the influential literary quarterly *Story,* whose editors agreed to print it. When "Gilded Six-Bits" came out later that year, it attracted the attention of Bertram Lippincott, who wrote to ask if Hurston had a novel for submission. According to Hurston, who sometimes liked a good story better than the literal truth, she sat down at a typewriter and six weeks later completed *Jonah's Gourd Vine,* which Lippincott published in 1934. (Chapter 12, by Maurice O'Sullivan and Jack Lane, tells this story in detail.)

The following year the same publisher brought out *Mules and Men,* Hurston's collection of folklore from Florida with additional material from points around the Gulf coast. The material from this book was gathered under the direction of Frank Boaz ("Papa Franz," as Hurston called him), one of the foremost anthropologists in the United States at the time. Hurston had studied under Boaz while at Barnard. Already a successful anthropologist who had published several papers in ethnographic journals, Hurston adapted the techniques of fiction to deal with her Florida data. *Mules and Men* can be regarded both as an anthropological text as well as a literary work, as Robert Hemenway hints in his excellent biography and as Dana Preu discusses in some detail in chapter 5.

Hurston's next book project, *Their Eyes Were Watching God,* generally considered her masterpiece, appeared in 1937. This novel plots the long and torturous life of Janey Crawford through several relationships and misfortunes, including the most calamitous natural disaster in modern Florida history, the drowning of more than two thousand persons on the south shore of Lake Okeechobee during the devastating 1928 hurricane. *Their Eyes Were Watching God* is a sort of picaresque novel turned inside out. While the traditional picaresque has a rogue for its central character, Janey begins as an innocent who is buffeted by human and natural forces but never gives up, even after her husband, Tea Cake, becomes rabid and Janey is forced to shoot and kill him. The structure of the novel, so criticized in the first wave of Hurston criticism, has been newly appreciated as a result of work by such critics as Henry Louis Gates; his book *The Signifying Monkey* (1988) gives a fine account of Hurston's central role in the creation of the African-American aesthetic.

Hurston's next major work, *Tell My Horse* (1938), is indicative of her breadth as a writer. It is a first-person account of her fieldwork in Haiti, where, among other things, she claimed to be the first person to photograph a zombie. Barbara Speisman, herself the author of the highly acclaimed play *A Tea with Zora and Marjorie* (*The Rawlings Journal* I [1988]): 67–100), points out the connection of Hurston's fieldwork in Haiti with her Florida-based novel in chapter 8. *Dust Tracks on a Road* (1942), Hurston's autobiography, which her publisher encouraged her to write, is generally regarded as the last of her major works. Although many critics have faulted the factual errors and omissions in this book, few deny its artistic strength. Like many autobiographies and all of Hurston's books, whether fiction and nonfiction, *Dust Tracks on a Road* should best be regarded as a literary work of high merit rather than a resource book of facts.

Hurston published two other books whose literary significance has yet to be determined. *Moses, Man of the Mountain* (1939) is a biblically inspired tale, and *Seraph on the Suwanee* (1948) is a saga of a white cracker family in Florida. In addition to her books, Hurston published many shorter works in a wide range of periodicals and anthologies. Some of her early short stories and nonfiction pieces that appeared in obscure publications are now considered some of her most important or illuminating shorter works.

Later in life, especially after her legal troubles in 1948, she turned away from the longer form except for an unpublished (and possibly unpublishable) historical novel set in the time of Christ. Her shorter nonfiction at this time appeared in such diverse places as the *American Legion Magazine, Negro Digest,* and local and special-interest newspapers. In recent years several of Hurston's anthropological essays have been collected into a volume entitled *The Sanctified Church* (Berkeley: Turtle Island, 1983).

The contributors to this volume reflect the growing diversity of scholarly interest in Hurston studies. As one might expect, most of the authors live in Florida, more than half are women, and many are black. Otherwise, the demographics of the authors and editors cannot easily be classified, nor indeed are they probably as easily summed up as the preceding sentence seems to indicate. One editor, Kathryn Seidel, is assistant dean of the College of Arts and Sciences at the University of Central Florida and has published widely in feminist studies; Hurston's hometown of Eatonville lies almost directly between Seidel's residence and her office. Steve Glassman, the other editor, teaches at Embry-Riddle Aeronautical University in Daytona Beach, a technically oriented university whose student population is almost 90 percent male. Some of the essays in this volume were originally read at "The Zora Conference," sponsored by Glassman's institution in November 1989. Glassman, the originator and institution in November 1989. Glassman, the originator and director of the conference, developed an interest in Hurston through his interest in Florida studies.

When Hurston died in 1960 in a nursing home in Fort Pierce, Florida, her literary career was at low ebb and she seemed all but forgotten. She was buried in an unmarked grave. Today the town of Eatonville has erected a memorial to her and has begun a campaign to return her remains to her home.

Acknowledgments

We would like to thank John W. Williams, academic vice-president at Embry-Riddle, for supporting the Zora conference that was the origin of several essays. At University of Central Florida John Schell, chair of the Department of English, and Interim Dean Stuart Lilie provided support. Lynn Prine created a selected bibliography of works. Beth Dold at Embry-Riddle and Karen Lynette at University of Central Florida typed the manuscript. Kevin McCarthy, Walda Metcalf, and Deidre Bryan made helpful suggestions throughout. The manuscript's readers, Kathleen Hickok and Carol Manning, made many astute recommendations. To all we give our gratitude.

CHAPTER ONE

Flora and Fauna in Hurston's Florida Novels

ANN R. MORRIS AND MARGARET M. DUNN

Zora Neale Hurston begins her autobiography, *Dust Tracks on a Road* ([1942] 1984), with the words "I have memories within that came out of the materials that went to make me. Time and place have had their say" (3). Zora's "place" was Florida, and, in the most literal sense, the flora and fauna of that state lend their colorful profusion to her fiction. In *Jonah's Gourd Vine* (1934), *Their Eyes Were Watching God* (1937), and *Seraph on the Suwanee* (1948), Hurston uses her knowledge of the plants and animals of Florida to provide realistic settings, to compose authentically natural speech for her characters, and to create central symbols.

Certainly the natural beauty of Florida has been celebrated by many writers. Perhaps the earliest well-known author to describe Florida flora and fauna was William Bartram who in his *Travels* (1791) wrote about a trip along the St. Johns River. The naturalist explored extensively along the river, and his impressions of the Florida landscape were well known by the English Romanticists Wordsworth and Coleridge. In the nineteenth century John James Audubon reported in words and pictures his investigations of Florida birds, and John Muir in *A Thousand Mile Walk to the Gulf* (1916) described his observations during a march from Fernandina to Cedar Key. Marjorie Kinnan Rawlings is probably the best-known describer of Florida plants and animals, beginning in 1933 with *South Moon Under*. Since then many other well-known writers have used Florida places and characters in their fiction: A 1989 collection entitled *Florida Stories*, compiled by Kevin McCarthy, includes such authors as Ernest Hemingway, Ring Lardner, Andrew Lytle, John D. MacDonald, and Isaac Bashevis Singer. Most came with notebooks ready to record their observations of the tropical world. Zora Neale Hurston, however, grew up unconsciously absorbing impressions about Florida's flora and fauna.

Hurston knew virtually all parts of her home state, for she had traveled the length and breadth of it gathering folktales and working in various capacities. However, it is Eatonville and its environs that she features most prominently in her fiction. In *Dust Tracks on a Road,* Hurston describes lovingly the big chinaberry trees that shaded the front gate of her family's home; she used to climb to the top of one of these trees to see the far horizon that she longed to explore. Close by, citrus trees and guava bushes broke the expanse of Bermuda grass. She also remembers palmettos and peach trees (both of which her mother used for switches), sandspurs that the eight Hurston children got in their hair when they played in the grass, and cape jasmine bushes with hundreds of "fleshy white fragrant blooms" (later she would learn in New York that people call these "gardenias" and sell them for a dollar apiece). Her favorite tree was one she called the "loving pine," a friend that, she insisted, "talked to her" as she sat beneath it.

On summer evenings she could hear the mockingbirds singing all night in the orange trees while alligators bellowed in nearby Lake Belle. Eatonville at that time was a frontier town where it was not unusual for the young Hurston to see alligators raiding hog pens, wildcats fighting yard dogs, and huge rattlesnakes lying across doorsteps. Nearby she could pick wild violets in the woods or play beneath the moss-draped oaks. After her mother, Lucy, died in 1904 and her father remarried, Hurston became acquainted with a different Florida, that of the St. Johns River up which she traveled in order to go to school in Jacksonville. During the boat trip on the sidewheeler *City of Jacksonville,* she was thrilled by the "smothering foliage that draped the river banks and the miles of purple hyacinths" (109). Along the shore she saw wild hogs, flocks of waterfowl, and gators slipping off palm logs into the stream. Peering into the dark waters she glimpsed schools of mullet and catfish "as long as a man."

In Jacksonville, however, she was homesick for Eatonville. As she wrote later in *Dust Tracks,* she missed "the loving pine, the lakes, the wild violets in the woods and the animals I used to know" (95). Apparently she never got over this homesickness, for she returned to Florida whenever she could: to marry twice; to collect folklore throughout the state; to teach school in Daytona Beach, St. Augustine, and Winter Park; and during her last years to work at whatever job she could get, mainly in Fort Pierce, where she died. According to Robert Hemenway in his introduction to the reprint of *Dust Tracks,* Hurston felt an intense pride in her home state (xxiv). In his biography, Hemenway describes her as having "the map of Florida on her tongue" (90), and he reports that one of the happiest periods in Hurston's life was the time spent in Eatonville in 1932 while she completed her revision of *Mules and Men* (1935). When she arrived in her hometown that spring, she immediately planted a garden—with black-eyed peas, watermelon, pole beans, and okra—and then sat on her porch each evening, listening to the mockingbirds and smelling the honeysuckle (162).

Hurston's description of the locales where her characters live shows her extensive knowledge of the flora and fauna of various parts of Florida. Both her first novel, *Jonah's Gourd Vine* (the barely fictionalized account of her parents' marriage), and her second novel, *Their Eyes Were Watching God,* are set mainly in central Florida where Hurston grew up. The action in the two texts is laced with references to trees and plants characteristic of central Florida. In *Jonah's Gourd Vine,* for example, when John Buddy Pearson and his wife, Lucy, arrive in Eatonville from Alabama, Lucy is captivated by the smell of night-blooming jasmine; later the family enjoys guavas and mangoes, and Pearson preaches in a church decorated with red hibiscus. Similarly, in *Their Eyes Were Watching God,* when Janie moves with her second husband, Jody Starks, from the Panhandle to Eatonville, she has a big yard with palm and chinaberry trees. At the corner of the house is a lemon tree from which, after Jody's death, Janie makes lemonade for Tea Cake.[1] Citrus trees are common in central Florida where Janie lives, so common, in fact, that she measures time by the citrus seasons. She says that in her first marriage she waited for love "a bloom time, and a green time, and an orange time" ([1937] 1978, 24).

Hurston's knowledge of citrus is never more apparent than in *Seraph on the Suwanee.* Here the protagonist, Arvay Meserve, moves from the town of Sawley in West Florida to Citrabelle, described as being "on the Florida ridge, south of Polk County" (1948, 64). Although both towns are apparently fictional, the description of the locale is realistic. As soon as Arvay and her husband, Jim, arrive in Citrabelle, he goes into the citrus business. Having bought some acreage, he chooses the sandiest part of the land for his grove because "the sandier the land, the thinner the skin, and the juicier the orange" (70). He plants both early and late oranges (the best moneymakers): Parson Browns, pineapples, temples, navels, and Valencias. Grapefruit and tangerines complete his grove because they too always bring good returns. Because Jim plants budded stock rather than seedlings, the grove begins to produce in just three years. Meanwhile Jim grows "black-eyed peas" (cowpeas) in the grove to feed the animals and people on his farm and to add nitrate to the soil.

Most of the trees, shrubs, fruits, and flowers that Hurston names in her three books are common throughout the South, but few writers mention so many of them. The chinaberries (which Hurston at one point calls "umbrella trees"), live oaks, scrub oaks, and pines throughout the state; the magnolias and dogwoods chiefly in north Florida; the bays and cypress in the swamps—all of these appear in her work. When Arvay and Jim Meserve live in west Florida, he is in the turpentine business, and Hurston gives a detailed account of gathering the "gum" (from the pines) for the "teppentine still" (*Seraph*, 38–39).

She shows, too, the Sunshine State's bountiful array of other fruits besides citrus, including figs, pears,[2] possum persimmons,[3] guavas, wild grapes, and mangoes. And she mentions a vast abundance of flowers, from the familiar crape myrtle and verbena to the less-known sawgrass bloom and Cherokee rose.[4] Some of the animals she mentions may also be unfamiliar to many readers. The "coudar," for example, is a striped, hardshell, freshwater turtle[5]; the "piney wood rooter" is a razorback hog; and the gopher is a land tortoise native to Florida. A "tusk hog," as a reader might guess, is a wild boar whose tusks make vicious weapons.

Sometimes Hurston characterizes the people of an area by the plants and animals around them. For example, in *Jonah's Gourd Vine* the conjure woman An' Dangie Devoe lives in a hut that "squats . . . behind a mass of Palma Christi and elderberry" ([1934] 1987, 199). The Palma Christi is more commonly known as the castor bean, a plant that grows throughout Florida and is known not only for its seeds, from which castor oil is made, but also for its poisonous qualities. In this case the natural setting is appropriate because An' Dangie is trying to "poison" the Reverend John Pearson's marriage. Hurston says in *Seraph*, "Trees and plants always look like the people they live with, somehow" (1). Apparently to support this, she has one character call the people of Sawley "dumb peckerwoods" (woodpeckers) (240), while she characterizes these people as ignorant, money-grubbing farmers. Appropriately these mercenary farmers grow mainly tobacco, cotton, and peanuts and only occasionally a few "bucket-flowers" (potted plants, often in tin cans).

In comparison, when Arvay and Jim reach Citrabelle they find people "powerful fond of painting houses and planting flowers." Arvay is non-plussed by the pleasantness of this life: "Things had a picnicky, pleasury look . . . . It was the duty of man to suffer in this world, and these people . . . were obviously shirking their duty. They were living entirely too easy" (64). Years later, after Arvay has finally perceived the ugliness of life in Sawley and decided to join Jim in New Smyrna where he has now become a commercial fisherman, she is shocked again by a new world, this time the beautiful inland waterway with its groves of leaning palms, flowers, pleasure boats, and happy-looking people. Even the birds and fish are different in this part of the state. Instead of the Leghorn pullets that people raised in Sawley, herons roost like "great white blooms" among the dark leaves of the mangrove swamps. Instead of the Suwannee's bream, perch, catfish, and black bass (which Hurston says are "locally known as trout"), exotic creatures such as octopi, sea nettles, and Portuguese Men-o-War abound in the waterway (296–98). Arvay learns that because of an abundance of food to be reaped from the sea, and because of the many dangers that remind commercial fisherman of their mortality, they spend freely and enjoy life vigorously when they can. So they "bought likker and loved recklessly" (285), much like the people whom Janie Crawford meets in the Everglades when she goes there with Tea Cake.

These Everglades people work on "de muck" planting stringbeans and tomatoes, then harvesting these and sugarcane from the rich black earth near Clewiston and Belle Glade. For meat they shoot rabbits; for practice they shoot alligators. Janie finds the life there easy because crops are plentiful, and as Tea Cake says, "Folks don't do nothin' down dere but make money and fun and foolishness" (*Eyes*, 192). Yet even the foolish have a profound respect for nature. The migrant workers on the muck govern their lives by the crops; the Seminoles in the glades watch the earth for signs. When the sawgrass blooms, banana trees blow in the wind, and snakes, raccoons, possums, deer, and panther move east, the Indians know that a hurricane is coming and stolidly head for the Palm Beach road. These Floridians, like others whom Hurston describes in her three novels, are influenced by their local flora and fauna.

One of the more obvious ways that Hurston makes apparent this influence of plants and animals on characters is in the way they speak. A southern child, Hurston says, is "raised on simile," and many of the figures of speech that they use come from the plants and animals they know. She comments, "It is an everyday affair to hear somebody called a mulletheaded, mule-eared . . . hognosed, gatorfaced, shadmouthed . . . goatbellied so-and-so." In other words, she continues, because southerners are "not given to book reading, they take their comparisons right out of the barnyard and the woods" (*Dust Tracks*, 135–36). This background, then, was part of the "time and place" that "had their say" in Hurston's life and fiction.

When Hurston says that southerners "take their comparisons out of the barnyard and the woods," she is suggesting a major way in which her characters use their familiarity with plants and animals; they make similes. For example, one character says, "I sure hope you ain't lak uh possum—de older you gits, de less sense yuh got" (*Eyes*, 170). Another comments, "De only difference 'tween him and uh mule is, de mule got four good foots" (*Jonah*, 74). Yet another, promising not to spread gossip, says, "Ah just lak uh chicken. Chicken drink water, but he don't pee-pee" (*Eyes*, 173). Some of the comparisons express disgust. For example, when John Pearson tries to make excuses for an extramarital affair, his wife, Lucy, tells him, "Big talk ain't changin whut you doin'. You can't clean yo'self wid yo' tongue lak uh cat" (*Jonah*, 204). And when John's congregation gets tired of his philandering, his friend comforts him with this scathing description: "'Tain't de sin so much, John. You know our people is jus' lak uh passle uh crabs in ah basket. De minute dey see one climbin' up too high, de rest of 'em reach up and grab 'em and pull 'im back. Dey ain't gonna let nobody git nowhere if dey kin he'p it" (263). Again, when Tea Cake leaves Janie alone in Jacksonville and she cannot find the money she had hidden in case anything went wrong, she runs around the room "like a horse grinding sugar cane"— in other words, getting nowhere (*Eyes*, 177). And most scathing of all, when Arvey has failed to come to Jim's defense against a huge rattler, he chides her, "You love like a coward. . . . Just stand around and hope for things to happen out right. Unthankful and unknowing like a hog under a acorn tree. Eating and grunting with your ears hanging over your eyes, and never even looking up to see where the acorns are coming from" (*Seraph*, 230).

Hurston also uses references to animals and plants in other figures of speech characteristic of the Floridians she is describing. For example, when John Pearson boasts of what he has accomplished, a competitive friend calls John "uh wife-made man" and adds metaphorically, "If me and him wuz tuh swap wives Ah'd go past 'im so fast you'd think it wuz de A.C.L. [Atlantic Coast Line railroad] passin' uh gopher" (*Jonah*, 184). Lucy also uses a metaphor when she tells her daughter Isie (as Hurston's mother had told her), "Always strain tuh be de bell cow, never be de tail uh nothin'" (206). Several of the characters remark that "God don't eat okra," a metonymy that apparently refers to the slickness of cooked okra and thus means that God doesn't like slick, crooked ways.

Such figures of speech came naturally to Hurston. As Barbara Johnson has pointed out, Hurston "cut her teeth on figurative language during the tale-telling or 'lying' sessions that took place on a store porch in Eatonville" (208). Henry Louis Gates, Jr., sees such use of figurative language as part of the signification common in Afro-American culture, and he mentions Hurston as one of the earliest writers to define the term "signify" and to use "signification" in her fiction.[6] Gates defines the term signifying to mean "punning . . . troping . . . embodying the ambiguities of language" (286). An example might be John Pearson's description of how he will escape the sheriff when in trouble. "Ah'll give mah case tuh Miss Bush and let Mother Green stand mah bond.'' But he adds, having tired of that subject, "Les' squat dat rabbit and jump uh 'nother one" (*Jonah,* 157). Or consider Jim's courting of Arvay, who is acting coy. One of Jim's friends cheers him on with these words: "Go Gator, and muddy the water" (*Seraph,* 20).

Perhaps the best example of signifying in the three books is the description in *Their Eyes Were Watching God* of the last days and the "draggin'-out" of Matt Bonner's old yellow mule. After taking pity on the mistreated mule and buying him from Bonner, Jody Starks sets the mule free. Hurston remarks that the "free mule" was usually around the store "like the other citizens" and that new lies sprang up daily about his "free-mule doings." When the old mule finally dies, the townspeople drag him some distance out of town and make "great ceremony" over him. Mayor Jody delivers a eulogy over the "distinguished citizen," and someone preaches on the joys of mule-heaven, which is "a pasture of pure bran with a river of molasses running through it." Finally the mule is left to the impatient buzzards, but the "stoop-shouldered" birds won't eat until Parson Buzzard flies in to conduct his own ceremony over the dead beast (92–97). All of this is clearly satirizing the so-called freeing of the slaves and the pretense that they are treated as equals by society; then the satire itself is ridiculed by having the buzzards mimic the actions of the townspeople. Reading such passages led Sherley Anne Williams to observe, "In the speech of Hurston's characters I heard my own country voice and saw ... my own country self" (quoted in Mitchell, 59).

Flora and fauna not only lend authenticity to settings and dialogue; they also provide a central symbol for each of the three novels. Lillie P. Howard has pointed out that in *Jonah's Gourd Vine* "snake symbolism abounds" in the form of whips, literal snakes, and trains (84–85). Clearly, from the beginning of the book, John Pearson's interest in women is likely to land him in trouble. Appropriately, his temptations are imbued with snake imagery. In her afterword to the reprinted edition of the novel, Holley Eley explains that its title refers to Jonah 4:6–10, which Hurston loosely interpreted in these words: "You see the prophet of God sat up under a gourd vine that had grown up in one night. But a cut worm came along and cut it down" (322–23). John Pearson too is finally cut down, though he has earlier overcome the snakes he encounters. Early in the novel his mother warns him, "Look out under foot so's yuh don't git snake bit" (27), and he successfully kills a big cottonmouth that threatens him and Lucy (67). Though he can conquer the literal snake, however, he cannot overcome the symbolic one, the train. When as a young man he first glimpses a train, he is fascinated by the power of the "fiery-lunged monster" (34–35), not knowing that this will eventually destroy him. On the way to his destruction, Pearson becomes involved in a series of sexual dalliances, and even while happily married to and in love with his wife, Lucy, he carries on a torrid affair with a woman named Hattie. The "Hattie affair" is in fact such a scandal that Pearson might lose his church over it. In a sordid climax to a tawdry episode, Lucy on her deathbed pleads with him to end the affair, and he, in a rage, slaps her. Determined to begin again, John flees to Plant City and tries to become a better man. Somewhat redeemed, he is invited to preach again in Sanford. Prophetically, however, in this sermon he pictures Christ as struck down by "de damnation train," and when he leaves the church he rushes into the arms of a prostitute. Immediately repentant, he starts home for Plant City, but he never reaches it. John's car is struck by a train and he is killed. The snake has finally triumphed.

In *Their Eyes Were Watching God* the central symbol is a pear tree. When Janie is sixteen and living in west Florida, she spends one spring day under a blossoming pear tree near her home. Watching the "snowy virginity of bloom . . . she saw a dust-bearing bee sink into the sanctum of a bloom; the thousand sister calyxes arch to meet the love embrace. So this was a marriage!" (24). From that moment Janie longs to find a bee for her blossom. When her grandmother insists that Janie marry the elderly Logan Killicks, Janie has a vision of Killicks desecrating the pear tree (28). Janie gives in, however, until fast-talking Jody Starks comes along. Though he does not represent "sunup and pollen and blooming trees," he speaks "for far horizon" (50), and Janie hopes that he may fulfill her longings. However, after seven years of marriage, Janie realizes that Jody only wants her to be Mrs. Mayor Starks, an attractive possession. From that point on, she is no longer "petal-open" with him (111). After Jody dies, Janie finally meets the man who "could be a bee to a blossom—a pear tree blossom in the spring" (161). Throughout the novel, Janie's relationship with this man called Tea Cake (his real name is Vergible Woods) is associated with nature and springtime. He brings Janie strawberries, takes her fishing, and introduces her to the joys of planting and growing vegetables in the Everglades. In short, instead of treating her like "de mule of de world" (Janie's grandmother's description of the black woman's role in life), Tea Cake treats Janie as an equal. She learns, in Cyrena Pondrom's words, "to rejoice in the creative forces of the universe, the forces that animate the plants of the fertile muck" (192). Although the exuberant lovers have only two years of happiness together before the storm in the Everglades and Tea Cake's death, Janie has had her blossom time. When she returns to Eatonville, she brings with her a packet of seeds that Tea Cake had left when he died; these she will plant, for "the seeds reminded Janie of Tea Cake more than anything else" (283). These seeds fit into the pattern of springtime fertilization and new growth carried throughout the novel by the bee-blossom imagery. Although Janie has had to kill her lover because he had been bitten by a rabid dog, she has known with him a self-fulfillment much more desirable than the security and status provided by her first two husbands. And as Barbara Christian has pointed out, "The blossoming pear tree is the image of Janie's sensuality and of her desire for completeness" (60).

Just as Janie sees herself as a "tree in bloom" with "glossy leaves and bursting buds" (25), Arvay Henson Meserve's image of herself centers around a tree, in this case a mulberry tree that grows behind her home in Sawley. In contrast with Janie, Arvay's relationship with her tree changes as her image of herself changes in *Seraph on the Suwanee*. When a young woman, Arvey thinks of the big mulberry as "a cool green temple of peace" (34). She hides from her poor white family within the "green cave" made by low-hanging, supple branches, and when she had decided to marry Jim Meserve she takes him to this "green tent" (44). Here she loses her virginity to him in a scene that is more rape than seduction, after which he takes her off to the courthouse to marry her. This early description of the tree and what happens there establishes Arvay's desire for protection and her passivity; she is not as openly sensual as Janie, and unlike Tea Cake, Jim does not treat his fiancée as an equal. Even after Arvay has lived in Citrabelle for years and has had three children, she still sees the tree as a "leafy haven" (119). By this time, however, Arvay and Jim have grown apart. She disapproves of his moon-shining business and his friendship with black Joe Kelsey; he is disappointed that Arvay won't acknowledge that their first child, Earl, has dangerous violent outbursts and needs to be institutionalized. This is the situation when Arvay returns to Sawley for a visit and walks out under her mulberry tree. High in the tree a small screech owl is sleeping, and she identifies with this "lonesome creeture" that cries for "someone to come and drive away the lonesome feeling from its heart" (119). Looking at the sleeping owl, Arvay wonders if she would even have escaped from this "ugly and lonesome place" if Jim had not arrived to carry her away. Clearly, now the tree is a lonely place to escape from rather than a "cool green temple."

Arvay's final return to the tree does not occur until many years later. By this time Earl has attacked a young woman and been killed by a posse, the other children are grown, and Jim has left Arvay. The couple's alienation from each other has climaxed in an incident with a rattlesnake, an incident in which Jim nearly loses his life while Arvay stands and gawks instead of trying to help her husband. Jim is rescued but decides to leave Arvay because, as he tells her, he is tired of her "stand-still... kind of love" and wants "a knowing and a doing love" (140). After Jim leaves, Arvay is called home to see her dying mother. She finds her mulberry tree leafless, for it is late February. But she knows that, before long, "tender green leaves would push out of those tight little brown bumps" and "green knots... would turn out to be juicy, sweet, purple berries." She realizes that this "great, graceful green canopy... was a sacred symbol... her tree of life," and that "here, in violent ecstasy, had begun her real life" (268–70). At last Arvay sees how life-denying and restrictive her family home had been and realizes that she should be actively involved in pursuing life rather than expecting Jim to shelter her as the mulberry tree did when she was a child. What Lillie P. Howard calls "Arvay's grail-like quest for self-actualization" (136) has at last been completed. She goes to Jim, ready to be an equal partner and to protect him as the mulberry tree had protected her. Clearly the tree symbolized the haven that the weak, whining Arvay needed at first as a young girl and later as a lonely owl-like woman. By the end of the novel, the tree has become a symbol of her strength. When she cradles the sleeping Jim to her in the novel's last scene, she realizes that "he hungered for her hovering... so helpless sleeping there in her arms," and she knows that no woman could do "more mothering and hovering than she could" (310). Although this change in Arvay is unconvincing, clearly she is intended to be portrayed here as someone who at first lacks confidence and needs the tree's protection. Later Hurston portrays her as a woman who is like the strong, vigorous mulberry tree that is the central symbol of the book.

Hurston herself was such a woman—strong, vigorous, confident. When Alice Walker traveled to Fort Pierce in 1973 to find this "boda-cious" woman's grave, she was continuing a quest for "the secret of what has fed that... often mutilated, but vibrant, creative spirit that the black woman has inherited" (239). Walker found in Fort Pierce the unmarked grave in a field of weeds; she also found an old man who had lived near Hurston during her last years. The one thing Walker wanted to ask the man was whether Hurston liked flowers. His reply was "She was crazy about them. And she was a great gardener. She loved azaleas, and that running and blooming vine (morning glory), and she really loved that night-smelling flower (gardenia). She kept a vegetable garden year-round, too. She raised collards and tomatoes and things like that" (114). This reply should not startle anyone familiar with Hurston's Florida novels.

Undoubtedly, as Hurston foresaw they would, time and place "had their say" in her work. In the lyric descriptions of settings, the lucid and realistic dialogue, and the haunting simplicity of symbols, her knowledge of the Sunshine State is evident. Marjorie Kinnan Rawlings once wrote to Maxwell Perkins that Hurston "is proud of her blood and her people" (293). Rawlings should have added "and of her state," for Hurston's fiction shows that she recognized the profuse natural beauty of the Florida countryside. Hurston once described herself as a person who loved "magnificence, beauty, poetry, and color so much that there can never be too much of it" (quoted in afterword to *Jonah's Gourd Vine*, 319). In the Sunshine State that she knew so well, Hurston lived with magnificence, beauty, poetry, and color. More important, she brought it all to her depiction of flora and fauna in the Florida novels.

Notes

1. This was possibly a "rough" lemon, a variety that was widely grown in Florida during the time Hurston was writing. These lemons are larger, juicier, and thicker-skinned than the Lisbon, Eureka, and Villafrance varieties grown in southern California and sold throughout the United States.

2. Hurston does not name the variety of pear tree she refers to in several of her fictional works, but she does comment in *Seraph on the Suwanee* that the pears were "only good for preserving" (8). Such pear trees—probably a variety of sand pear—were fairly common in the north and central regions of the state until a bacterial infection known as fire blight began to reduce their number. The most common varieties of sand pear were Hood and Pineapple, still grown for canning today. Compared to the Bartlett pears commonly available in supermarkets today, these varieties are very hard and less succulent. Nevertheless, when cooked with plenty of sugar, they are often used in pies and preserves.

3. Possum persimmons are apparently the wild persimmon common in Florida pinelands and fields. The trees often grow to be fifteen to twenty feet tall. The name comes from the fact that the fruit is eaten by possums.

4. The Cherokee rose that Hurston speaks of (89) is a wild rose found in low woods and along roadsides in a number of southeastern states. It is a lush, hardy rose that sends out long shoots that are thornier than those of the average rose. The small white flowers are not numerous. Because the Cherokee rose grows so well in sand, resists the summer heat, and continues to bloom for more years than most varieties, Florida rose growers have recently begun using the Rosa Fortuniana (Double Cherokee) as root stock on which to graft tea roses.

5. In *Jonah's Gourd Vine* Hurston describes the good meals that could be made from turtles that are stewed, fried crisp and brown, or boiled. She adds that Floridians often caught turtles on a hook baited with "white side-meat" (2).

6. Gates points out Hurston's use of the term "signify" in *Mules and Men*, where she also defines it as "to show off" (161). In addition, writes Gates, *Their Eyes Were Watching God* is a "paradigmatic signifying test . . . because it uses signifying both as thematic matter and as a rhetorical strategy of the novel itself" (290).

Works Cited

Bartram, William. *Travels*. 1791. Reprint, edited by Mark van Doren. New York: Dover, 1951.

Christian, Barbara. *Black Women Novelists: The Development of a Tradition, 1892–1976.* Westport, CT: Greenwood, 1980.

Gates, Henry Louis, Jr. "The Blackness of Blackness: A Critique of the Sign and the Signifying Monkey." In *Black Literature and Literacy Theory,* edited by Henry Louis Gates, Jr., 285–321. New York: Methuen, 1984.

Hemenway, Robert. *Zora Neale Hurston: A Literary Biography.* Urbana: University of Illinois Press, 1977.

Howard, Lillie P. *Zora Neale Hurston.* Boston: Twayne, 1980.

Hurston, Zora Neale. *Dust Tracks on a Road.* 1942. Reprint, with introduction by Robert Hemenway. Urbana: University of Illinois Press, 1984.

———. *Jonah's Gourd Vine.* Philadelphia: Lippincott, 1934. Reprints, with afterword by Holly Eley. London: Virago, 1987.

———. *Mules and Men.* Philadelphia: Lippincott, 1935.

———. *Seraph on the Suwanee.* New York: Scribner's, 1948.

———. *Their Eyes Were Watching God.* Philadelphia: J. B. Lippincott, 1937. Reprint. Urbana: University of Illinois Press, 1978.

Johnson, Barbara. "Metaphor, Metonymy and Voice in *Their Eyes Were Watching God.*" In *Black Literature and Literary Theory,* edited by Henry Louis Gates, Jr., 205–19. New York: Methuen, 1984.

McCarthy, Kevin, ed. *Florida Stories.* Gainesville: University of Florida Press, 1989.

Mitchell, Leatha Simmons. "Toni Morrison, My Mother, and Me." In *In the Memory and Spirit of Frances, Zora, and Lorraine,* edited by Juliette Bowles, 58–60. Washington, D.C.: Howard University Institute for the Arts and the Humanities, 1979.

Muir, John. *A Thousand Mile Walk to the Gulf.* Boston: Houghton Mifflin, 1916. Reprint. Boston: Houghton Mifflin, 1981.

Pondrom, Cyrena N. "The Role of Myth in Hurston's *Their Eyes Were Watching God.*" *American Literature* 58 (May 1986):181–202.

Rawlings, Marjorie Kinnan. *Selected Letters of Marjorie Kinnan Rawlings,* edited by Gordon E. Bigelow and Laura V. Monti. Gainesville: University of Florida Press, 1982.

———. *South Moon Under.* New York: Charles Scribner and Sons, 1933.

Walker, Alice. *In Search of Our Mothers' Gardens.* New York: Harcourt Brace, 1983.

CHAPTER TWO

Excursions into
Zora Neale Hurston's Eatonville

 ANNA LILLIOS

Eatonville . . . . a city of five lakes, three croquet courts, three hundred brown skins, three hundred good swimmers, plenty guavas, two schools, and no jailhouse.   —Zora Neale Hurston, *Mules and Men*

Maitland is Maitland until it gets to Hurst's corner, and then it is Eatonville. Right in front of Willie Sewell's yellow-painted house the hard road quits being the hard road for a generous mile and becomes the heart of Eatonville. Or from a stranger's point of view, you could say that the road just bursts through on its way from Highway #17 to #441 scattering Eatonville right and left.
    —Zora Neale Hurston, "Eatonville When You Look at It"

"In a sense, everything Zora Neale Hurston wrote came out of her experience of Eatonville," Alice Walker says of the writer who inspired her. Eatonville provided Hurston with folktales, personalities, and events, which later appeared in her novels, *Jonah's Gourd Vine* (1934) and *Their Eyes Were Watching God* (1937); her collection of folklore, *Mules and Men* (1935); and her short stories, most notably "The Eatonville Anthology" (1926) and "Sweat" (1926).

Unfortunately, the people of Eatonville who told Hurston their folktales have nearly all died, the buildings with which she was familiar no longer exist, and the rural landscape has been transformed by commercial districts and housing developments. Less than thirty years after her death, most of the physical traces of the Eatonville that Hurston knew as a girl have vanished. Walker's search for Hurston's unmarked grave in Fort Pierce in 1973 typifies the elusive quest for Hurston's presence in her hometown. Nevertheless, some landmarks in Eatonville closely associated with Hurston can be identified.

According to Eatonville residents, the Hurston family home was located on Taylor Street, behind the police station. The Orange County Indexing Department records that Hurston's father, the Reverend John Hurston, bought parcels of land from Joe Clarke on January 15, 1901, and April 14, 1910. This property fell in the block bounded by West, Lawrence, People, and Lord streets. (No one in town today has heard of Lawrence and Lord streets, which have long been renamed. The Hurston property most likely fell in the block bounded by present-day Lemon, People, Lime, and West streets.) In *Dust Tracks on a Road* (1942) Hurston describes her family home as a kind of Florida paradise:

> We lived on a big piece of ground with two big chinaberry trees shading the front gate and Cape jasmine bushes with hundreds of blooms on either side of the walks. I loved the fleshy, white, fragrant blooms as a child but did not make too much of them. They were too common in my neighborhood. When I got to New York and found out that people called them gardenias, and that the flowers cost a dollar each, I was impressed. . . . There were plenty of orange, grapefruit, tangerine, guavas and other fruits in our yard. We had a five-acre garden with things to eat growing in it, and so we were never hungry. ([1942] 1984, 18)

When Hurston was a girl she would cross the street and listen to "the big picture talkers" who "painted crayon enlargements of life," as they hung out on the front porch of Joe Clarke's general store. Clarke, the man after whom Jody Starks in *Their Eyes Were Watching God* was modeled, owned at least a dozen parcels of land, including the forty acres comprising Eatonville. He had purchased this land from Josiah Eaton on November 1, 1884. Clarke's store, which also included a U.S. Post Office, was located on the northeast corner of West Street and Kennedy Boulevard and faced West Street. Clarke's home was next door to the store. The R & R Grocery Store is currently located on the site. In her autobiography, Hurston describes the store's atmosphere: "There were no discreet nuances of life on Joe Clarke's porch. There was open kindnesses, anger, hate, love, envy and its kinfolks, but all emotions were naked and nakedly arrived at. It was a case of 'make it and take it.' You got what your strengths would bring you. This was not just true of Eatonville. This was the spirit of that whole new part of the state at the time, as it always is where men settle new lands" (62).

Hurston's father was a moderator of the South Florida Baptist Association and preached in the Macedonia Missionary Baptist Church, located in the early days of the century on the south side of Eaton Street, between West and East streets. The Macedonia Baptist Church is now located in a new building on Calhoun Street and East Kennedy Boulevard. The Reverend Hurston also served as the mayor of Eatonville from 1912 to 1916. According to Eatonville's town historian, Frank M. Otey, the reverend was "a vocal and knowledgeable politician" who formulated some of the town laws and emphasized education. He encouraged the town's citizens to send their children to school rather than to work. Otey notes that the Reverend Hurston set an example with his own children: "Ben became a pharmacist, Clifford Joe was a principal in a school in Alabama, and John ran a market in Jacksonville, FL. Both Dick and Everette became postal clerks, Dick as a railroad employee and Everette in New York. Of the two girls, Sara married and raised a family, while Zora became a renowned writer" (Otey 1989, 18).

Hurston attended the Robert Hungerford Normal and Industrial School, which was modeled on the Tuskegee Institute and considered one of the best southern black schools at the time. The school was built in 1899 by Russell C. Calhoun and endowed by E. L. Hungerford in memory of his son, who died of yellow fever while caring for blacks in the bayou region of Louisiana. Besides the typical academic subjects students were also taught vocational and domestic skills. None of the original buildings exists. The school was given to Orange County as a public trust on May 6, 1950. Today the school is called the Wymore Career Educational Center, a vocational-technical institution for 480 students in grades 7 to 12. The Hungerford Elementary School also occupies part of the property.

Several women still alive recall Zora Neale Hurston in Eatonville. In the winter and spring of 1989–90 I interviewed Clara Williams, Hoyt Davis, Annie Davis, Mattie Jones, Jimmie Lee Harrell, and Harriet Moseley, all of whom knew Zora Neale Hurston in their hometown. Except for Clara Williams, who resides nearby in Orlando, they still live in Eatonville. My questions focused on the women's memories of Hurston as well as of life in Eatonville during the 1920s and 1930s. I also wanted to see if I could clear up some mysteries surrounding Hurston, such as her date of birth and her whereabouts when she returned to Eatonville, as well as get some sense of the townspeople's regard for her.

The accepted date of Hurston's birth, which appears in Robert Hemenway's biography (1977), is January 7, 1901. But legal documents indicate otherwise; her death certificate gives January 7, 1903, as her birth date, and the marriage certificate that Sandy Shuler discovered in St. Augustine records that Hurston was twenty-eight years old when she married Herbert Steen on May 19, 1927. Cheryl Wall of Rutgers University has located census records in the National Archives that indicate that Hurston was nine years old in 1900. Two of the people I interviewed led me to believe that Hurston was indeed born in 1891. Mattie Jones, born in 1903, said that Hurston was a "grown woman" when she was a girl, that Hurston was of her parents' generation. Clara Williams said that her father was born in 1890, and he told her that Hurston was one year younger than he. This information is corroborated by Everette Hurston, Sr., Zora's brother, who showed Robert Hemenway his family genealogy in 1976 (1977, 32). Perhaps Hurston moved her birth date into the twentieth century in order to appear more modern, though future scholars may discover other motives.

When Hurston returned to Eatonville as an adult, she would stay in a great variety of places. Usually she would reside with friends, notably Armetta Jones and Matilda Moseley. Basically, she would come and go like a free spirit, appearing and disappearing with little notice, according to the women I interviewed. But in the 1930s she apparently lived in a little house on a lake, possibly Lake Hungerford. Hurston wrote about her house in a short essay, "Eatonville When You Look at It," dated October 1, 1938; this essay may have been written in connection with her work for the Federal Writers' Project. Hurston describes her home as "the last house in Eatonville," "a big barn on the lake." She says, "and west of it all, village and school, everybody knows that the sun makes his nest in some lonesome lake in the woods back there and gets his night rest." She concludes that another lake, Lake Belle, is the home of Eatonville's "most celebrated resident, the world's largest alligator" (2).

Another author in the Federal Writers' Project, Paul Biggs of Lakeland, Florida, writes of visiting Hurston's home, which he locates on Lake Buck (perhaps an earlier name for Lake Hungerford): "The house in which Miss Hurston occupies is located close to Lake Buck. It is a weather-boarded house, very spacious, and comfortably arranged in the interior. Around the house will be found games for recreational amusements, such as: badminton, croquet, and holes for golf putting. Which makes its physical setting ideal for a country lodge" (1938, 1).

In the interviews I also tried to determine the townspeople's regard for Hurston. Two potentially alienating factors surround her presence in her hometown. One has to do with her education at Barnard and her acquaintanceship with famous scholars and artists in New York. The other has to do with Hurston's sometimes harsh portrayal of Eatonville folk such as Joe Clarke in her fiction.

Clara Williams, the daughter of Rosa and Enoch Nixon, was born December 25, 1924. She has many memories of Hurston, whom she laughingly told me had been interested in her father. She confirmed the

1891 birth date. Her father, born in 1890, told her that Hurston was one year younger than he.

AL: What do you remember about Zora?

CW: You wouldn't want me to tell my favorite memory of her. (Laughs)

AL: You don't want to tell it?

CW: Well. . . . I have a lot of memories about Zora Neale Hurston, but one. . . . She used to come up on what they call a hill where my grandmother lived, and talk to us, you know, tell stories to the children there. One day she came up, and without asking my grandmother—people in those days didn't care, as long as somebody they knew had the childrens. She took us to her house and she had this photographer with her and he was taking pictures. They had all this watermelon—these long watermelons—and she quartered them and gave each one of us a piece of this watermelon for this photographer to take our picture. And, of course, being children we went to eating it, while he was steadily taking pictures. We thought nothing of it. My dad came to pick us up that Friday, 'cause mother was coming home from summer school. My youngest brother told daddy, "We went to Miss Zora's house the other day, Daddy, and she gave us a long piece of watermelon and told us to eat it and this man was taking our picture and we was just going up and down that watermelon, chomp, chomp chomp." My daddy got us back in the car. He told us to stay there until he came back. He disappeared and then he came back and carried us home, back to Orlando. But we didn't think anything of it. You know, somebody taking your picture. First of all, feeding you . . . watermelon that was good and cold and it was summertime. But he didn't want those pictures in a book.

AL: Did you ever see those pictures?

CW: We've never seen them. Never heard anything else about them. . . . I'm sure she kept them. Then I met her again at Florida A&M when I was a junior in college. She was there promoting some of her books, and she recognized me because I look so much like my daddy. She told the people there that she saw somebody that she recognized (*laughs*), but I don't think I saw her after that. She spoke—she was a member of my sorority and she spoke for the sorority that day—and she had her books and everything.

AL: What year was that?

CW: It must have been . . . I graduated in 1946 . . . so it must have been in 1945, late, probably.

AL: What was she like as a person?

CW: As far as I knew her she was all right, because, see, I was a child growing up and anytime somebody comes up and gives you something, you think, that's a good person. I didn't know her as an adult, so I can't say.

AL: Can you describe her personality?

CW: She had a very outgoing personality and as far as children were concerned she was a very nice person because whenever she came up the hill she always had something to give us.

AL: She loved the kids. . . .

CW: Yes. She'd sit down and she'd tell us stories and things about places she had been and something like that. She just had everybody's attention when she came.

AL: Did she tell stories about the community or were they about her life?

CW: No, she would just tell us stories, but I can't remember her saying anything about anyone in the community. I mean, she was just talking to us. But she would say things just to hold our attention. I guess to see our reactions.

AL: Do you remember any of these stories?

CW: No. But, you see, I have read all of her books now so if I were to say I remembered anything she told, it would be probably something from her books—which would not be right. She never said where the stories were from. When she would come up, we knew she was going to tell us a story and everybody just sat on the ground, cross-legged, and listened.

AL: Was she a great storyteller?

CW: She could hold your attention.

AL: Did she sing to you?

CW: No, she didn't sing to us, she just told us stories. And then she'd jump up and say, "Well, I've got to go," and everybody would be, "Bye, Miss Zora, bye, Miss Zora, bye, Miss Zora," until she got out of sight. And, then back up the trees we'd go (*laughs*) or back around the fields or somewhere like that. But I can't remember any of them.

AL: Did you have any sense how old she was at the time?

CW: She was an adult and in those days children respected adults. Nobody ever worried about how old anybody was. And you said miss, and that was it.

AL: Were times tough during the depression?

cw: Everybody had gardens, you grew chickens. If your neighbors needed something, they just came over and said, I need something, and they got it. We didn't have money. But money meant nothing, because we didn't need it. We had plenty to eat. We wore clothes made of feedbags. We bought beautiful feedbags and they made beautiful clothes. What difference did it make? We'd go to the feedstore and take a quarter—a quarter was a lot of money—and buy you some bags . . . panties to match your dress. That's true. We had a good time. We didn't realize we were poor. We were, but we didn't realize it, because everyone else was in the same condition.

AL: What kind of work did the men do?

cw: Most of them worked in the orange groves. My father worked in a packing house. My grandfather worked in a hotel. Now they have torn it down and built a new one. There is a marker in front of it on Highway 17–92, just before you turn to go to Eatonville. At the time it was a big old-fashioned hotel. What he did, other than cleaning up and cutting the yard, I don't know. My grandmother took in laundry from different people around in Maitland. But she stayed home—she didn't go out—and did it.

AL: What other jobs did women do?

cw: That's all I know they did . . . cleaning houses. Very few of them that I know of went off to school. At Hungerford they taught them how to keep house, wash, and take care of children—along with the lessons. Very few of them were fortunate enough to read and go to college.

AL: What kinds of food did people cook?

cw: Everything. You name it, they cooked it. But they didn't have all this fancy stuff like today. They just had regular food. They'd have chicken, fish, beef, pork, pigs' feet, chitlins, potatoes, tomatoes, okra, peas . . . 'cause they grew most of their own vegetables. Somebody grew pigs, had cows and milk. They shared.

AL: How did the townspeople feel about Zora?

cw: She'd written some things about Eatonville and when she came back, they said they were going to fix her. (*Laughs.*) They didn't like some of the things she said or the way she said them.

AL: Were they joking?

cw: I don't know whether they were joking or angry. You just hear as a child in passing. This goes on over you. But I heard them say, You just wait till she comes back home.

AL: Did anyone ever confront her?

CW: I don't know. I heard my grandmother say something about, yeah, I saw that in the book. (*Laughs.*) I don't know if anyone else said anything. When she was in town, they didn't discuss it. People just didn't sit down in those days and talk about people like we do now. (*Laughs.*) I was a child and she didn't associate with us, other than to tell us stories. Naturally, we wouldn't hear anything negligent about her or negative, because they wouldn't tell us that. They would just tell us where she was, if she was telling stories somewhere, and we'd go to listen to her. That's it.

Hoyt Davis, born June 7, 1903, was close to Hurston in age but does not remember playing with her as a child. Her first contact with Hurston came when she was an adult and Hurston would come to town. Mrs. Davis would visit her at Lula Moseley's house. She would go over to say hello but never had time to visit. Mrs. Davis did domestic work in Maitland, beginning when she was around nineteen years old. Her memories of Hurston are dim, but she does remember that "everyone liked her, that she was a kind-hearted person. She fit in with people just as if she was living here. They were so glad to see her." The questions that I asked Mrs. Davis had to do with life in Eatonville during the 1920s and 1930s.

AL: Tell me about your job.

HD: I did domestic work. I began around nineteen. The first job I had I was helping a woman over in Maitland. I would do the dishes and do the bathrooms. In the wintertime when I was going to school, I would go in the afternoons. In summertime I'd go in the mornings. After I got older I started working for another woman in Maitland. She had boarders and she needed someone to help her in the kitchen because she did the cooking. She hired me to do that. I started cleaning vegetables and washing dishes. She taught me how to cook, she taught me how to set up the table correctly, she taught me how to serve correctly. As time passed by, she knew that I was capable of really cooking, because she had trained me to do it. She had cookbooks there—the Fanny Farmer and the Boston cookbooks, they were the leading cookbooks. Then she just turned the cooking over to me.

AL: What about your child? Who took care of him?

HD: My aunt took care of him.

AL: Was it hard to leave him?

HD: *Yes,* it was hard, but I had to do it. My husband and I had separated.

AL: Did many other women work outside the home?

HD: Yes. They did the same type of work I did—some of them were cooks, some of them did maid work.

AL: Was it common for women to work outside the home?

HD: Oh, sure.

AL: Did you experience hard times during the 1930s?

HD: No, I didn't because I was working on this job. And my father and my brother, we all lived together right here on the same property. And, of course, they were working in the citrus groves. With me working we made it all right. We were never hungry, not even a day. My father always had a garden. He grew chickens and they'd lay eggs. So we got along pretty good. To tell you the truth, I don't know of one person being hungry at that time in Eatonville. Everybody out here planted gardens and they grew chickens. They could eat chickens whenever they wanted and they fished. So I never heard of anybody asking for food.

AL: What was Eatonville like in the 1920s and '30s?

HD: It was a quiet little town. Wasn't too much going on. Nothing like today. The people then they shared and cared. That made it nice. One person had maybe a cow. They'd milk the cow and they'd send the neighbors milk and butter. It was like one big family. There weren't too many people out here when I was a girl. People started coming in to Eatonville in the 1950s.

AL: Were the churches the center of life?

HD: Yes. Both of the churches were very active. Everybody went to church. Everybody took their children to church.

AL: Every Sunday?

HD: *Every.* My father and mother, they went every Sunday. A lot of people here went every Sunday. They never missed a Sunday unless they were sick.

AL: Did you ever hear Reverend Hurston preach?

HD: I don't remember him. My father used to tell me about Reverend Hurston, but I don't remember him. He said he was a good preacher and a good man. To tell you the truth, all the men out here were just hard-working, good men.

AL: Tell me what you remember about your girlhood.

HD: Every Friday we had to rake yards so we could go to the penny party on Saturday afternoon. The woman who sponsored the party was Mary Weston. Some of the kids wouldn't have any pennies, some of them would. They would turn them over to Miss Weston. She would make cookies and lemonade and that's what she'd serve. That was just wonderful for us and we'd enjoy it so much. She would take these pennies that she collected on Saturday and on Sunday morning she'd turn them over to her class in the church. The money went to the church.

We used to go to Lake Sybelia and we would swim. The boys and the girls, we would all be together. Sometimes on holidays the women and the men would get together and have this picnic. After the picnic there would be a baseball game. We enjoyed it. Eatonville would sometimes be playing Winter Park, sometimes Oviedo. The men were all young. The girls didn't play. We played hopscotch and things like that.

Another thing that children would do this time of year [spring] . . . Mr. Sam Moseley, he grew sugarcane. He had a cane grinder. I guess it was one he made himself. It looked like he might have made it. He had a horse to grind the cane. The kids would all be around in the daytime. He had cups there and he would give all the kids a cup of cane juice. Then he would make syrup and he sold the syrup. People all bought the syrup. On Saturday nights, the adults would have what they called a candy pulling. And all the kids would be at that.

AL: Do you have any more memories of enjoyable childhood experiences?

HD: Some of the women who lived in Eatonville worked at the Park House. It was a big hotel and they had to have help. I don't know who owned it at the time. Sunday afternoons some of us—just would be girls, wouldn't be any boys with us—would get together. We would go and pick violets, wild violets. We would wash them up and we'd go to the Park House. Those people there were northern people, down here for the winter. They would give us ten cents a bunch.

I interviewed Annie Davis, who knew Hurston in the 1940s, on September 29, 1989. Mrs. Davis's father was Will Davis, whose second wife was Armetta Jones (the woman Hurston visits in *Mules and Men*). Mrs. Davis lived in Jacksonville, Florida, during the time that she had contact with Hurston.

AD: Every time she'd come back she would come to my mother and father's house. I don't know if she was the oldest or I was the oldest. I don't know anything about her age. I think she had done finished college up North. I know she would come home and have a lot of little books, a lot of papers. She had wrote and taken notes because she was writing about here from her childhood. Some liked it and some didn't. My mother and daddy knowed all of her people, all about her. But I didn't hear all that much ... you know, from the ending up to the beginning. I just know her by them. She'd always come to my mother and father's house and stay. She'd stay there till she was ready to go back.

I spent a lot of time with her. We'd just get together and talk. I wasn't here that long. I was back and forth from Jacksonville. [Davis was married and living in Jacksonville at the time.] Most of the time when I come home, she'd be here and she'd talk about her childhood days. She was trying to write books. I never had a chance to read her books. My mother's niece, she had a lot of her books and papers, but when she died the niece ... we don't know which way those papers and books and things went. We was trying to get a-hold of them but we never did.

AL: Your mother's name is in one of her books.

AD: Yes, and Matilda Moseley.... There's a lot of names in those books.

AL: How did she fit in when she came back? Was she like one of you?

AD: Yes, that's right. She was just Zora. She never looked over none of her people because she had more education. She never looked over the lower class that was under her. She never did. She was always Zora. She was always happy. She was always rejoiced. She didn't care what you had to sit down to eat. She always made herself welcome. She wasn't one of those high-class people. To look at her, the type of woman she was, you could never tell by the way she treated you. She always was nice. She was always kind. When she spoke to any of her people she always spoke nice. She just wanted to put in her book her childhood on up.

AL: How did other people like her?

AD: Some liked her. Some loved her. Some didn't. They didn't want her to write in this book.

AL: Did they feel she told too much about Eatonville?

AD: Yes. Some didn't like what she was saying. She wasn't doing nothing but telling the truth. You know how these slums and places are ... outdoor toilets, pumps in the backyard, chickens, hogs, and cows and everything. She come out of a slum. I read some of that in her books.

AL: Did she have any relatives here?

AD: No. She wouldn't stay with nobody if she wasn't with Mrs. Moseley and them or she was to my mother and father.

AL: She writes a lot about the men sitting around Joe Clarke's store, telling stories. Did you ever hear these stories?

AD: No. At least I wouldn't *dare*. (*Laughs.*) I wouldn't dare to be out where the mens would be telling these things. That's something the women would never do. My mother and dad were alive. When I come here I was young. The only time I'd be with her was when she was home to the house, but not to go out with her. I know she was a sweet person, that's all I know about her. She was just regular. Digging up her background from her childhood, I couldn't tell you anything like that.

AL: What kind of stories would she tell?

AD: She never would tell any stories . . . just ordinary talking. She'd go off and be on the side porch. We had an open porch and then a screened-in porch. She'd always go off and be by herself and she'd be writing, humming little songs. She was just a nice, quiet person.

Mrs. Mattie Jones was born on February 28, 1903. She came to Eatonville in 1916, but she does not recall much contact with Hurston at that time. She got to know Hurston in the 1930s and 1940s. Her husband's brother was Ellis Jones, Armetta Jones's first husband.

AL: Were you the same age as Zora?

MJ: She was older than I. She was a good ways older than I was. I was just a young girl when I came.

AL: I've seen her birth date listed as 1901 and 1891. When you came to Eatonville in 1916, how old do you think she was? Was she a teenager or a woman?

MJ: She was older than I. I was a teenager then. She was a woman.

AL: Have you read her books?

MJ: I haven't read up nothing about her in a long time. I don't go out nowhere.

AL: What kind of person was she?

MJ: She was nice and friendly. She'd take so much patience with you. I can remember that about her. She was real nice. Other than that, I don't remember. She did a lot with the children when she came to Eatonville. All the children would be around.

AL: Did people like her?

MJ: Oh, yes. Everybody as far as I know liked her very much. She was real good as far as I can remember.

AL: Was she writing books then?

MJ: Yes. There was an old lady here at that time, named Miss Henderson, and she hadn't seen her people in Georgia for fifty years. Her people all thought she was dead. Zora wrote a book about her and put a picture in the book. That was the way her people in Georgia found out that she was still living.

AL: Did she fit in with the community?

MIRIAM BAKER (DAUGHTER): She was just one of them. It wasn't until I got grown in these late years that I really realized how famous and great she really was. All I ever heard or remember of her was that she was just one of the people here.

Jimmie Lee Harrell, born June 7, 1905, remembers spending one evening with Hurston in 1934. Harrell's brother, John C. Hamilton, married Hurston's niece, Winifred, and lived with Harrell's parents on Eaton Street; Hurston was visiting them at the time.

AL: What were your impressions of Zora?

JLH: She was friendly and a writer, I heard her telling my mother. I thought she was a schoolteacher. She [looked] like a businesswoman. She knew what she was doing.

AL: What happened on the evening that you spent with her?

JLH: I cooked the food and waited on the table. Then I was dismissed.

AL: But you were a woman then . . .

JLH: Oh, yes. I was a woman at that time. I had four children.

AL: Why didn't you sit at the table?

JLH: I couldn't sit at the table and wait on the table. I cooked all the time.

AL: Do you remember Zora as a kind person?

JLH: She *was*. She was just kind and friendly.

AL: Some people in town disliked the fact that she put them in her books. Did you hear anything about this?

JLH: The background of their inheritance is just like myself. They didn't have much schooling. But Zora was one, from what I can understand, who had been to school long enough to know what she was saying and doing. I imagine there was some jealousy. Zora was well educated. The people who were living here at the time weren't making too much of their lives. I think they were just jealous. But they don't talk like they hated her or nothing.

Harriet Moseley's great-great uncle was Joe Clarke, and her grandmother, Matilda Moseley, often hosted Hurston when she visited Eatonville. Hurston baptized Harriet Moseley in 1928.

AL: Do you have any memories of your godmother?

HM: I was a little bitty girl. I can't remember all that stuff way back then. We were all small kids . . . kids from the community that she carried over to Rollins College [probably around January 5, 1934, when Hurston staged *All De Live Long Day* at Rollins College]. She had all the children hopping on the stage, dancing and doing little things.

I remember one morning, Grandmama asked Zora what did she want for breakfast. "Tillie, make me some of them pancakes." Grandmama said, "Well, Zora, I ain't have no syrup." "Well, Tillie, make some of that homemade syrup you make." You see, my grandmom used to make syrup out of sugar—plain old sugar. She [Zora] loved pancakes. She was just like one of the family, like she was related to us—but she wasn't. If she had lived, she and my grandma would have been the same age. My grandmama passed in 1980, and she was eighty-nine. Mama said they were the same age. She and my grandma were just like sisters.

AL: You mentioned that your godfather, Ellis Jones, got angry at Zora for using his name in a book. . . .

HM: He told me everyone was mad at her . . . all the citizens around here. She would do all her writing up at Joe Clarke's store and she would talk about the citizens. Instead of using fictional names, she would use their ordinary names. My godfather got highly mad with her, because she used his name in one of her books.

AL: Did he confront her with a gun?

HM: Yes. She jumped up and left. She ran in the house, got her bag, and left. If she hadn't, he was going to kill her.

AL: Are there any family stories about Joe Clarke? Did he beat his wife?

HM: I don't know anything about Joe Clarke.

AL: Why did Zora name you Harriet?

HM: My grandmother said she believed Zora got the name from Harriet Tubman. I hated that name. Zora used to send me cute little dresses. She sent me clothes. I was the only one around here with a parka and boots. Zora used to send me all that stuff. She always sent me something.

Eatonville has grown tenfold since Hurston's time. It is now a town of three thousand residents, who celebrated its hundredth anniversary on August 18, 1987. Since Hurston's death in 1960, the town has undergone two very different phases of development. The first phase involved the improvement of its water and sewer system, the paving of its roads, the construction of a public pool and a community center, the creation of a parks and recreation system, the construction of a fire station, the expansion of the police department, and the beginning of an interstate park with one hundred acres for business sites.

The second phase in Eatonville's recent history focuses on preserving its unique past. The Preserve the Eatonville Community, Inc., committee was formed in 1987 under the direction of N. Y. Nathiri. The largest project thus far with which this committee has been involved was the first annual Zora Neale Hurston Festival for the Arts, which took place on January 25–28, 1990; the guest speaker was Alice Walker. The committee is involved in a number of other activities, including trying to prevent the widening of Kennedy Boulevard, the main thoroughfare through the town; commissioning Eugene Fry to conduct a historic survey of the town, in order to justify Eatonville's inclusion on the National Register of Historic Places; lobbying the post office for a Zora Neale Hurston commemorative stamp; planning to create a town archives; and dedicating a memorial in town in honor of Hurston. Hurston's niece, Lucy Hurston Hogan, will authorize that Zora's remains be moved from Fort Pierce to Eatonville in 1990.

Works Cited

Bigg, Paul. "To the House By the Lake." Written for the Federal Writers' Project, September 22, 1938. State Historical Society, Tampa, FL.

Hemenway, Robert. *Zora Neale Hurston: A Literary Biography.* Urbana: University of Illinois Press, 1977.

Hurston, Zora Neale. *Dust Tracks on a Road.* 1942. Reprint. Urbana: University of Illinois Press, 1984.

———. "Eatonville When You Look at It." Written for the Federal Writers' Project, October 1, 1938. State Historical Society, Tampa, FL.

———. *Jonah's Gourd Vine.* Philadelphia: Lippincott, 1934.

———. *Mules and Men.* Philadelphia: Lippincott, 1935.

———. *Their Eyes Were Watching God.* 1937. Reprint. Urbana: University of Illinois Press, 1978.

Otey, Frank M. *Eatonville, Florida: A Brief History.* Winter Park, FL: Four-G Publishers, 1989.

Walker, Alice. *I Love Myself When I Am Laughing and then Again When I Am Looking Mean and Impressive: A Zora Neale Hurston Reader.* Old Westbury, NY: The Feminist Press, 1979.

CHAPTER THREE

"Beginning To See Things Really": The Politics of Zora Neale Hurston

⚘ DAVID HEADON ⚘

When Zora Neale Hurston, all youthful confidence and swagger, addressed the issue of race in her 1928 essay "How It Feels To Be Colored Me," she placed herself in a developing tradition of African-American social commentary stretching back to the slave narratives. Perhaps the most contentious expression of this issue before that of Hurston, Alain Locke, and Langston Hughes in the 1920s had been made by W. E. B. DuBois in his *Souls of Black Folk* (1903). DuBois suggested that the "Negro" was "a sort of seventh son, born with a veil, and gifted with second-sight in this American world,—a world which yields him no true self-consciousness, but only lets him see himself through the revelation of the other world. It is a peculiar sensation, this double-consciousness, this sense of always looking at one's self through the eyes of others" (364). Hurston, a quarter of a century later, identified no such dilemma. No "double consciousness" for her, no measuring of oneself with the tape of the white world. She declared: "I am not tragically colored. There is no great sorrow dammed up in my soul, nor lurking behind my eyes. I do not mind at all. I do not belong to the sobbing school of Negrohood who hold that nature somehow has given them a lowdown dirty deal and whose feelings are all hurt about it" (1928 [1979], 1652).

The parameters of the debate, then, had been established. In the decades to follow, Hurston's persistent expression of personal liberation from what she considered the misconstrued issue of race—in fiction and nonfiction alike—would ensure her a controversial status among her contemporaries. She would be resented—sometimes for good reason—and misunderstood. Richard Wright, reviewing *Their Eyes Were Watching God* (1937) shortly after its publication, anticipated the waning critical and community interest in Hurston in the later 1940s and 1950s when he alluded to her simple minstrel characters who "swing like a pendulum eternally in that safe and narrow orbit in which America likes to see the Negro live: between laughter and tears" (Hemenway, 241). It was not accurate criticism, but it was damning. And prophetic. When Hurston died in 1960, she was separated by at least a generation from her halcyon days of literary status and success. Her work, it seemed, did not reflect the growing politicization of the black community.

Not unexpectedly, during the revival of critical interest in her in the last fifteen years—a rediscovery led by Alice Walker, Robert Hemenway, and Larry Neal, among others—Hurston's personal politics have continued to present a problem, a nettle not easily grasped. The paradoxes and contradictions, the rash generalizations and occasional braggadocio, still cannot be overlooked or ignored. How to deal with a black writer whose characters steadfastly refuse to acknowledge DuBois' "veil," characters who celebrate instead of plotting revenge, characters who want to love, discover, and transcend, rather than commit murder? How to deal with a writer whose conservatism led to an almost doctrinal anti-Communist article in the repugnant McCarthy era published in, of all places, the *American Legion Magazine*? And, most difficult of all, how to deal with a vibrant, intelligent African-American woman who, in the last pages of her 1942 biography, *Dust Tracks on the Road*, could sum up the immense human tragedy of centuries of slavery, and its particular relevance to her, in these terms: "I see nothing but futility in looking back over my shoulder in rebuke at the grave of some white man who has been dead too long to talk about. That is just what I would be doing in trying to fix the blame for the dark days of slavery and the Reconstruction. From what I can learn, it was sad. Certainly. But my ancestors who lived and died in it are dead. The white men who profited by their labor and lives are dead also. I have no personal memory of those times, and no responsibility for them" (290). The insensitivity and culpable naïveté, even callousness, of this passage are obvious. It is devoid of a sense of history and current affairs. The cockiness is at best misplaced; at worst, it is a gross misreading of the priorities and aspirations of the black community at the time.

Little wonder that the critics, rediscovering Hurston in the 1970s and 1980s, have recoiled from her politics and her apparent lack of political acumen. Alice Walker suggests that "we are better off if we think of Zora Neale Hurston as an artist, period—rather than as the artist/politician most black writers have been required to be" (1979, 3). For Walker, Hurston is a "*cultural* revolutionary" (1983, 89). Larry Neal, in his 1974 profile of Hurston, summarizes the consensus critical case with this simple assertion: "One thing is clear ... unlike Richard Wright, [Hurston] was no political radical" (161).

I want to take issue with this prevailing interpretation of Zora Neale Hurston. I propose to revise the conventional wisdom regarding the broad range of her writings, both fiction and nonfiction from 1924 to about 1950, in order to demonstrate her evolving political consciousness—individual and eccentric on occasion, yes, but perceptive and lucid, ahead of its time also. I want to show that the cutting edges of Hurston's thought have more in common with the directions of radical African-American literature of this century than has previously been recognized. While Hurston was never interested in the role of public iconoclast, her writings from 1927–28 onward confirm a steadily more trenchant awareness of the ambiguities of black/white relations, especially as this applied to the concept of "civilization." In this evolution of her political consciousness, Florida and its black population played *the* seminal role. When Hurston left Barnard to collect folklore in her home state, she had, without realizing it, embarked on a personal odyssey that would eventually lead to the adoption of a stance as potentially revolutionary in its way as that of the most militant black activist.

There are four distinct chronological stages in Hurston's development. First are the years of the young writer and scholar up to 1927, which do not show us much more than a simple joy in creation and positive sense of community. Second are 1927 and 1928, the early years of Hurston's folklore gathering in Florida, when interest in literature gives way to the excitement and discovery of the cultural mother lode confronting her in the rich imaginative lives of black people in the South. Third is the period from 1931 to 1935, when Hurston could assess more maturely the worth of her source material. Delight turns to hardened resolve and bold assertion. Political awareness ripens. In the early 1930s Hurston had the very nature and operation of Western "civilization" firmly in her sights. And fourth are the years from 1945 to 1950, Hurston's last important period of creativity, when she produced a few essays that, in their clarity and skepticism, confirmed and enlarged on the most penetrating aspects of her social critique. In my discussion I will include a cross-section of the important, but lesser known, nonfiction essays.

In "Profile" Larry Neal suggests that a "truly original" black literature will require "some new categories of perception; new ways of seeing a culture" (162). This is a helpful starting point. Hurston does create with freshness, vigor, and originality. As I work through the stages of her political and literary development, I will make passing reference to what emerge as the six most important "new categories of perception": her recognition and celebration of the quality of black communal life— what Alice Walker in *In Search of Our Mothers' Gardens* calls her "racial health" (1983, 85); her emphasis on the poetry and creativity of black

English; the significance she attaches to notions of personal identity and self-worth; her emergent feminist aesthetic, in natural opposition to what Walker has labeled the "Great White Western Commercial of white and male supremacy" (1979, 4); her suspicion of Western civilization and its machinery of cultural appropriation; and her eventual realization and articulation of the inadequacies of Western anthropological methods.

In the mid-1920s, shortly after Hurston's arrival in New York, two documents were published, less than a year apart, that were destined to assume an honored place in the literary history of this country: Alain Locke's *The New Negro* (1925) and Langston Hughes's landmark essay "The Negro Artist and the Racial Mountain" (1926). Both would have their passionate admirers and adherents, Hurston no doubt among them, and both would ultimately be accorded the prestigious title "manifesto" of the Harlem Renaissance (Hemenway, 1977, 39). Significantly, both men advocated the literary potency of the black folk heritage—Locke suggesting that the folk gift could be carried "to the altitudes of art" because it did not need to fight "social battles" and right "social wrongs" (1925, 39) and Hughes pointing to the "great field of unused material," the black "heritage of rhythm and warmth" ([1926] 1970, 161).

Hurston's writing at this time—short stories, prose sketches, and poems—tends to reflect the aesthetic philosophy of Locke and the passion of Hughes. The stories "Drenched in Light," published in 1924, and "Spunk," her contribution to Locke's *New Negro* anthology, are cases in point. Isie Watts, the central character in "Drenched in Light," is incorrigibly joyful. Her happiness is infectious. "Spunk," on the other hand, opens with the protagonist Spunk Banks sauntering and strutting with his married companion, Lena Kanty. Together they are, in Elijah Mosley's words, as "big as life an' brassy as tacks" ([1925] 1925, 105, 111). Joe Kanty, Lena's humiliated husband, "that rabbit-foot colored man," is killed by Spunk, but eventually returns as a big black bobcat to haunt Spunk and finally cause his death. The fickle Eatonville townspeople, devourers of the gossip of the love triangle, figure in the story's concluding paragraph, the women eating heartily of the "funeral baked meats" and the men "[whispering] coarse conjectures between guzzles of whiskey" (106–7, 111). Eatonville life is crude, slow, deliberate; it is also a little intoxicating. But, as in the series of sketches in "The Eatonville Anthology," Hurston is content nostalgically to recall her happy childhood. Not even the death of Joe and Spunk can undermine the warm glow of memory. At this stage of her literary career, as Hurston would later state in the introduction to *Mules and Men*, her Florida background "was fitting me like a tight chemise. I couldn't see for wearing it" (1935, 17). She was still satisfied with the surface of things, content faithfully to reproduce the flavor of black communal life and speech. She lacked artistic—and moral—direction.

Of all the material published before Hurston's first Florida folklore-gathering trip in early 1927, the only story that anticipates the political range and achievement of her later works is the sketch entitled "Sweat," published at the end of 1926. In "Sweat" Delia Jones, a washwoman, toils relentlessly to remain with her husband, Sykes, and keep them both in food. Delia, when first married fifteen years earlier, "wuz ez pritty ez a speckled pup" ([1926] 1979, 200). As we begin the story, Delia has sweated and slaved for too many years; there is now too much "debris" cluttering "the matrimonial trail" (199). Husband Sykes has taken a lover, whom he flaunts; he beats Delia and enjoys taunting her and playing on her fear of snakes. But he does this once too often. Revenge figures in the story's conclusion, as Sykes is killed by his own rattlesnake.

Robert Hemenway, in his fine biography of Hurston, calls "Sweat" "a story remarkably complex at both narrative and symbolic levels" (70). He enlarges on the Freudian and Christian symbolic structure, the sophistication of the "literary design." It is a convincing interpretation, providing we endorse the tools of New Criticism. Hemenway places his emphasis where Alain Locke might have located his in the 1920s. I feel the story works more meaningfully—is more political—at the narrative and folk levels.

"Sweat" seems to be, in part, Hurston's response to Langston Hughes's imprecation to black writers in his "Racial Mountain" essay to change the old whisper " 'I want to be white,' hidden in the aspirations of the black middle class of the twenties, to 'Why should I want to be white? I am a Negro—and beautiful' " (163). Delia Jones is beautiful—and dignified and, above all, courageous. She will not, finally, be cowed by Sykes's physical and verbal coercion. He assaults her and calls her an "ole snaggle-toothed black woman" (199). Eventually Delia's "habitual meekness" disintegrates. Her verbal tirade, a statement of liberation, is the emotional climax of the story: " 'Ah hates you, Sykes,' she said calmly. 'Ah hates you tah de same degree dat Ah *useter* love yuh. Ah done took an' took till mah belly is full up tuh mah neck . . . Ah don't wantuh see yuh 'roun' me atall. Lay 'roun' wid dat 'oman all yuh wants tuh, but gwan 'way fum me an' mah house. Ah hates yuh lak uh suck-egg dog' " (204).

In "Sweat" Zora Neale Hurston forcefully establishes an integral part of the political agenda of black literature of this century. She places at the foreground feminist questions concerning the exploitation, intimidation, and oppression inherent in so many relationships. It is not the civil rights of Du Bois and *Crisis*, but it is civil rights nonetheless. One of Hurston's wonderful Eatonville cameo characters in "Sweat," a man named Clarke, provides the philosophical overview: " 'Taint no law on earth dat kin make a man be decent if it aint in 'im. There's plenty men dat takes a wife lak dey do a joint uh sugar-cane. It's round, juicy an' sweet when dey gits it. But dey squeeze an' grind, squeeze an' grind an' wring tell dey wring *every drop* uh pleasure dat's in 'em out. When dey's satisfied dat dey is wrung dry, dey treats 'em jes lak dey do a cane-chew. Dey throws 'em away' " (201).

"Sweat" is, in fact, protest literature. Published just before Hurston's first Florida excursion, it foreshadows, also, the far wider range of her second stage of writing—one where moral concerns take root. In a letter written in March 1927, Hurston expresses real concern at the decline of folk life and traditions in Florida's rural black communities. "Negroness," she writes "is being rubbed off by close contact with white culture" (Hemenway, 1977, 91). Her revitalized interest in Florida folk life had prompted her to question the coziness and tidiness of the discourse of academic life. Assumptions were no longer clear-cut, as she had been taught; she was now in the field, on the muck in Florida experiencing some of the less visible but still pervasive by-products of Western cultural appropriation.

The essay "How It Feels To Be Colored Me," published in 1928, is interesting in this context. It is almost as controversial now as when first written. One sentence in particular continues to be offensive to Hurston's readership: namely, "Slavery is the price I paid for civilization" (1652). Even Alice Walker reacts to this statement with bitter disappointment: "We can assume this was not an uncommon sentiment during the early part of this century, among black and white; read today, however, it makes one's flesh crawl" (151). The problem, obviously, is the word "civilization." Isolated from the larger context of the essay, "civilization" appears to represent Hurston's coveted target, the implied goal of the black community at large. Up from slavery to embrace the rewards of white society. Yet, one page later in the same essay, as Hurston sits in the New World Cabaret whooping to the tempo of the "narcotic harmonies" and dancing "wildly" inside herself, she remarks that, having experienced the ecstasy of enjoyment in the music, "I creep back slowly to the veneer we call civilization. . . . " "Civilization" is now used pejoratively, connoting boredom, conservatism, apathy, and, by implication, pitifully limited cultural range.

Hurston subtly undermines rather than promotes the grand myth of Western culture—its "civilization"—the concept used most commonly to justify the barbarous excesses of European imperialism for over five hundred years. Many years later, motivated by frustration to write "My Most Humiliating Jim Crow Experience" ([1944] 1979), she would take the opportunity to add her most telling remarks on this question. A white doctor treated her in a demeaning, insulting manner, prompting Hurston to reflect, rather than angrily react: "I went away," she says, "feeling the pathos of Anglo-Saxon civilization. . . . And I still mean pathos, for I know that anything with such a *false foundation* cannot last. Whom the gods would destroy, they first made mad" (164).

Hurston had come a long way from the hero worship she accorded to some of her university professors of the mid-1920s. It was the myth of Western civilization, of course, that had constituted the very foundation stone of Papa Franz Boas's anthropology courses at Barnard.

Freeing herself from the conditioning of the white community, she began her lone journey of personal, moral, and political discovery. It was only fitting that the catalyst should be her own turf, Florida. Letters that she wrote during the months of March and April 1928 reflect a sensibility excited and profoundly aware of the importance of her mission. She radically altered her research technique between 1927 and 1928. In her first trip, she had, as she recalled in *Dust Tracks*, "[gone] about asking, in carefully accented Barnardese, 'Pardon me, but do you know any folk-tales or folk-songs?' The men and women who had whole treasures of material just seeping through their pores looked at me and shook their heads" (183). Hurston, the Barnard anthropologist, was fortunate enough to have been raised in the region. She knew of the existence of the treasures and could make appropriate adjustments. Margaret Mead, in Samoa, would not have the same good fortune. Nor indeed would Western anthropologists in the deserts of Australia who, thinking they were getting the words for "tree," "star," and "rock," were in fact being tricked and supplied with words describing parts of the male and female genitalia. They simply were not aware of their vulnerability; Hurston was. So she changed and began to give more of herself, be less academic, less objective. Success almost immediately followed. On March 8, 1928, she wrote a letter describing the thrill of heightened perception: "I am getting inside of Negro art and love. I am beginning to see really. . . . This is going to be big" (Hemenway, 112). A month later she referred to "the greatest cultural wealth of the continent" when describing black folk life (113). The stage was set for the stunning achievements of her third and most significant stage of writing.

Hurston outlined the essence of her new perceptions and insights of these years in the seven essays she included in Nancy Cunard's *Negro: An Anthology* (1934). She recalled in *Dust Tracks* her youthful need to "stretch her limbs in some mighty struggle" (64). In the early 1930s the struggle had at last been clearly identified. The Cunard essays, on the surface detailing the originality of black art forms, go much further. At stake, for Hurston, is the crucial issue of black identity itself: self-image. So she discusses the "drama" that permeates a black person's "entire self," along with the "will to adorn," to beautify (Cunard, 39); in addition, she specifies a range of black cultural heroes and heroines. Her last essay in the group, "Spirituals and Neo-Spirituals," opens with an assertion (359): "The real spirituals are not really just songs." They are in fact about a whole rich, complex way of life, ranging from "sorrow songs" to celebration. Spirituals are not about glee clubs, concerts, tuxedoes, and audience hype. As Hurston points out, "The real Negro singer cares nothing about pitch. The first notes just burst out and the rest of the church joins in—fired by the same inner urge. Every man trying to express himself through song. Every man for himself" (360). Spirituals are not entertainment, they canvas notions of freedom, confidence and self-revelation.

One of the inevitable corollaries of Hurston's promotion of the inherent quality of black life was the need to sharpen the attack on those blacks who rejected their own cultural forms, individuals who, as she put it, "ape all the mediocrities of the white brother" (Cunard, 43). In 1934 she wrote an article for the *Washington Tribune* entirely devoted to the ways of the so-called black-fur-coat peerage (*Dust Tracks*, 242): "Fawn as you will. Spend an eternity awe struck. Roll your eyes in ecstasy and ape the white man's every move, but until we have placed something upon his street corner that is our own, we are right back where we were when they filed our iron collar off" (quoted in Hemenway, 206). Hurston had finally given her political ideas prominence. It remained only for her to place something of lasting quality on art's street corner. Between 1934 and 1937 she did exactly that, in the form of one memorable short story, one extensive work of nonfiction, and one great novel. Together they comprise her most extensive political, moral, and artistic statement. The works in question are "The Gilded Six-Bits," *Mules and Men*, and *Their Eyes Were Watching God*. All three works reflect her Florida roots.

Missie May and Joe in "Six-Bits," Janie and Tea Cake in *Their Eyes Were Watching God*, the riches of folklore and hoodoo in *Mules and Men*, along with the tour-de-force description of Polk County—all exemplify Hurston's claim in *Mules and Men* concerning the "wealth and beauty of her material" (202). She had discovered ways to combine her literary aspirations and highly individual sense of social commitment. If her popularity declined for a couple of decades, Alice Walker pinpoints why: "It seems to me that black writing has suffered, because even black critics have assumed that a book that deals with the relationships between members of a black family—or between a man and a woman—is less important than one that has white people as a primary antagonist" (Walker, 1973, 202).

Zora Hurston confronted, ultimately, the complex politics of self. In her 1945 article "Crazy for This Democracy" she attacked the hidden aspects of the Jim Crow laws: psychological manipulation (that is, whites being conditioned into believing their right to be "first by birth") and the fact that "darker people" are taught to suffer their "daily humiliations" (Walker, 1973, 163). The carefully crafted ending of "Six-Bits" exposes the complete absurdity of stereotyping; Janie's quest for self-fulfillment in *Their Eyes Were Watching God* does the same.

This is the revolutionary message of Hurston's writing: Liberate the self, and all else follows. Never succumb. In 1943 and 1950 Hurston wrote two more essays on this subject—"The 'Pet Negro' System" and "What White Publishers Won't Print"—so dominant had it become in her thinking. Her mother exhorted her when she was young to "jump at de sun" (*Dust Tracks*, 29). Hurston, at the peak of her artistic powers in the 1930s (and with her fertile Florida of the imagination to call on), encouraged all blacks to do the same.

Works Cited

Baraka, Amiri. Foreword. Langston Hughes, *The Big Sea—An Autobiography*. 1942. Reprint. New York: Thunder's Mouth Press, 1986.

Cunard, Nancy, ed. *Negro: An Anthology*. London: Wishart, 1934.

Du Bois, W. E. B. *The Souls of Black Folks*. 1903. Reprinted in *Writings*. New York: Library of America, 1986.

Hemenway, Robert. *Zora Neale Hurston: A Literary Biography*. Urbana: University of Illinois Press, 1977.

Hughes, Langston. "The Negro Artist and the Racial Mountain." 1926. Reprinted in *On Being Black*, edited by Charles T. Davis and Daniel Weilder, 161. New York: Fawcett, 1970.

Hurston, Zora Neale. "Characteristics of Negro Expression." In *Negro: An Anthology*, edited by Nancy Cunard. London: Wishart, 1934.

———. "Crazy for This Democracy." *Negro Digest* 4 (December 1945). Reprinted in *I Love Myself . . .* , edited by Alice Walker. New York: The Feminist Press, 1979.

———. "Drenched in Light." *Opportunity* 2 (December 1924): 37–74.

———. *Dust Tracks on a Road*. Philadelphia: Lippincott, 1942.

———. "How It Feels To Be Colored Me." *World Tomorrow* 11 (May 1928). Reprinted in *The Norton Anthology of American Literature*, edited by Nina Baym et al. 2d ed. New York: Norton, 1979.

———. "Mourner's Bench, Communist Line: Why the Negro Won't Buy Communism." *American Legion Magazine* 50 (June 1951): 19–25, 55–60.

———. *Mules and Men*. Philadelphia: Lippincott, 1935.

———. "My Most Humiliating Jim Crow Experience." *Negro Digest* 2 (June 1944). Reprinted in *I Love Myself* . . . , edited by Alice Walker. New York: The Feminist Press, 1979.

———. "The 'Pet Negro' System." *American Mercury* 56 (May 1943): 593–600.

———. "Race Cannot Become Great Until It Recognizes Its Talent." *Washington Tribune*, December 29, 1934.

———. "Spirituals and Neo-Spirituals." In *Negro: An Anthology*, edited by Nancy Cunard. London: Wishart, 1934.

———. "Spunk." *Opportunity* 3 (June 1925). Reprinted in *The New Negro*, edited by Alain Locke. New York: Albert and Charles Boni, 1925.

———. "Sweat." *Fire!!* (November 1926). Reprinted in *I Love Myself* . . . , edited by Alice Walker. New York: The Feminist Press, 1979.

———. "What White Publishers Won't Print." *Negro Digest* 8 (April 1950): 85–89.

Locke, Alain, ed. *The New Negro: An Interpretation*. New York: Albert and Charles Boni, 1925.

Neal, Larry. "A Profile: Zora Neale Hurston." *Southern Exposure* 1 (Winter 1974): 161–66.

Walker, Alice. *I Love Myself When I Am Laughing . . . And Then Again When I Am Looking Mean and Impressive—A Zora Neale Hurston Reader*. New York: Feminist Press, 1979.

———. *In Search of Our Mothers' Gardens*. New York: Harcourt Brace Jovanovich, 1983.

———. "Interview." In *Interviews with Black Writers*, edited by John O'Brien, 202. New York: Liveright, 1973.

CHAPTER FOUR

Through the Prism of Africanity: A Preliminary Investigation of Zora Neale Hurston's *Mules and Men*

⬤— BEULAH S. HEMMINGWAY —⬤

Zora Neale Hurston—novelist, folklorist, feminist, anthropologist, and playwright—was a seminal figure in the Harlem Renaissance. Nowhere is this more evident than in her *Mules and Men*, published in 1935. Viewed superficially by early critics as a quaint collection of black folklore from simple black rural southerners and valued chiefly for entertainment, *Mules and Men* has experienced a revival as more sophisticated scholars from interdisciplinary backgrounds examine its content. Newer interpretations salute Hurston's presentation of black creativity and spontaneity and her celebration of the exuberance of black life. But *Mules and Men* is much more. This slender volume symbolizes Hurston's acceptance of the Africanity portrayed in its pages by illiterate black people, who protested the sterility of Western culture through imaginative folklore rooted in Africa, but adapted to the American environment.

Hurston's choice of rural black southerners as griots and tale-tellers was both deliberate and correct. Because blacks were isolated in Eatonville, a small town in central Florida, and in sawmills and lumber camps of the deep South, oral tradition remained strongest among them, and most were uninfluenced by standard American paradigms for thinking and acting. Thus, African survivals were more prevalent among people separated from the common influences of urban life. Although poor and illiterate, Hurston's characters are a clever, dignified, proud people who are spunky enough to parry harsh insults from other blacks and glaring disrespect from whites. Collectively they shared an ethos by which their souls lived, readily defended their humanity, and shaped and controlled, more than is commonly recognized, their own world and destiny.

These blacks experienced freedom in its truest sense. They lived from the inside out, fashioning and developing a value system that whites could neither constrict nor control. For them, as for Hurston, black life was more than a response to white injustice. They lived by their own yardstick and measure of their own worth, while rejecting white definitions for their humanity and capabilities. Thus, spiritualism occupied a central role in their worldview, as did cooperation, communalism, group survival, respect for nature, the celebration of life, and an uncommon resilience. Considered escapism by some critics and politically naive by others, this worldview, while incomplete and unbalanced in an industrialized world, was tailored to the needs of the black masses who lacked political power.

Illiteracy is not necessarily a synonym for ignorance. Hurston's characters knew their limitations. Whether they accepted them or not is another question; they were knowledgeable about their environment and struggled to fashion a better way of life. Robert Hemenway's introduction to the reprint edition of *Mules and Men* affirms this view. "*Mules and Men*," he writes, "refutes the pathological view of uneducated rural black people. . . . Even in the face of an historically brutal experience, black people affirmed their humanity by creating an expressive communication system that fostered self pride and taught techniques of transformation, adaptation and survival" (Hurston, [1935] 1978, 20). Such creativity proved an invaluable tool for black survival and softened the effects of racial discrimination and poverty.

Folklore occupied a special place in the lives of such people, for it was more than entertainment. Folklore was their novel. Thematically legends, myths, proverbs, and games in *Mules and Men* represent a satirical description of the world and the inter- and intragroup relations of its people. Functionally such folklore educated and inspired blacks while defending their humanity and preserving African culture. No claim is made here that all Hurston's folklore originated in Africa, only that its use and content served an African function. But in tone, style of delivery, themes, and content, *Mules and Men* reflects African creativity in the use of language as symbolic action and the manipulation of oral tradition to redefine the world for blacks in accordance with their needs.

The folklore of *Mules and Men* follows most African-American tales in form and function. Thematically, animals dominated trickster tales, which emphasized small, weak, unimposing animals that consistently outwit and outmaneuver strong animals to obtain their desired goals. Tricksters considered such action proper and good, even if the means were immoral. For them, the end justified the means. Though small and weak, tricksters possessed an arsenal of weaponry. Most were plucky, proud, brave animals filled with audacity and egoism that rarely tired of overcoming natural and artificially imposed limitations to achieve desired goals.

The world of the trickster is explored in Robert D. Pelton's *The Trickster in West Africa: A Study of Mythic Irony and Sacred Delight.* Pelton describes the trickster as a study in ambiguity and complexity. In his view, the trickster personified the human personality: The trickster is at once noble and foolish, heroic and cowardly, daring and deceitful, often beaten, but never defeated. Religion was important to the trickster, but not in a fixed, unchanging way. Most tricksters accepted the gods as beings not to be served but to be conquered. For them man was the measure of things, especially in his use of the mind to transcend life's difficulties (1–24).

Rural black Floridians, like their forebears elsewhere in the South, employed such tales symbolically to control and manipulate a hostile social environment. Accordingly, trickster tales, an embodiment of wish fulfillment and role inversion, dominated and turned society upside-down. Tricksters rarely obeyed laws, ignored society's norm of decency, and waged a constant war of rebellion. Lawrence Levine in *Black Culture and Black Consciousness* relates the saying of a slave: "Well you know what was de fust stealin' done? Hit was in Afriky, when de white folks stole de niggers je' like you'd get a drove of horses and sell 'em." This South Carolina slave (a Gullah preacher) articulated a common feeling when he asked in one of his sermons: "Ef buckra neber tief (thief), how come yer here" (124). For them, survival by any means necessary was legitimate and practical.

But tricksters did not always win. Sometimes they were tricked by smaller, weaker animals or people. Such tales were not the childish, simple entertainment early collectors thought them to be; instead, these tales represent human behavior, emotions, and character. Indeed, Hurston's characters metamorphosed into humans at will but retained animal features and qualities. Such abilities allowed her characters the best of all worlds. Alternating between fact and fantasy, they both satirized and protested society's constraints. Psychologically this ploy reinforced black spiritualism, thereby strengthening black resolve.

Florida's natural environment provided the wildlife for the animal tales in *Mules and Men.* Alligators, panthers, bears, rabbits, gophers, raccoons, opossums, and squirrels are prevalent, but domestic animals, such as dogs, cats, mules, and cows, are prominent as well. Trickster tales are represented in this collection, and tricksters also experience dilemmas in many of these tales. Collectively the tales are educational, emphasizing the value of self-reliance while warning against entrusting one's welfare to another. In the tale of the ox and the mule, for example, the ox feigns illness to avoid work, thereby forcing the mule to perform all labor. The mule tires of his role and informs the owner of the ox's trick. Thereafter, the owner butchers the ox who had sworn revenge on the mule. While this tale clearly is demonstrative of a trickster who is tricked, conversely it reveals the importance of self-representation in an environment controlled by others (126).

A more classic animal trickster tale is Hurston's retelling of the story of the dog and the rabbit who struggle to gain the favored role in the courtship of a beautiful maiden. When the dog gained the advantage by singing, Brer Rabbit resolved to neutralize his voice. He pretended to aid the dog in sweetening his voice, but split his tongue instead and ruined the dog's voice. The rabbit never capitalized on his feat, because the dog has been chasing him ever since. The rivalry eventually resulted in a dog convention, which issued a moratorium on chasing rabbits and invited the rabbit to dinner to celebrate the truce. Brer Rabbit was cautious and feared trickery. After several warning signs, he declined the invitation, explaining "but all de dogs ain't been to no convention, and anyhow some of dese fool dogs ain't got no better sense than to run all over dat law and break it up. De rabbits didn't go to school much and he didn't learn but three letter, and that's trust no mistake. Run every time de bush shake" (119). On that note, the rabbit parted company with the dogs.

Inequality breeds suspicion and distress in societies permeated with ethnocentric and racial biases. These factors combined in Florida to foster black skepticism relative to the judicial system's impartiality and the ability of whites to treat blacks fairly. These concerns are related in Hurston's tale about the gopher in court: "De gopher come in and looked all around de place. De judge was a turtle, de lawyers were turtles, de witnesses was turtles and they had turtles for jury-men.

"So de gopher ast de judge to excuse his case and let him come back some other time. De judge ast him how come he wanted to put off his case and de gopher looked all around de room and said, 'Blood is thicker than water,' and excused hisself from de place." Clearly, the gopher's doubt rested not only on suspicion but on historical experience as well. He is willing to assume responsibility for his welfare in the absence of demonstrated concern by the court (129).

Hurston's most noted trickster tales involved the relationship between John, a slave, and massa, his master, or the struggle between black and white people. Role inversion and wish fulfillment dominate such tales. John is portrayed as a wise, cunning figure who not only outwitted whites, but on occasion tested God and the Devil. John's trickster tales symbolized hope and faith on one level, but inspired, motivated, and provided a role model for the downtrodden on another plane. In short, John was the personification of human potential; his character reflected the range of human behavior. John's environmental difficulties, at once both cruel and kind, normally dictated his behavior, which was at all times controlled by the will to survive.

John the Conquerer portrays this range of behavior best. A symbolic, legendary figure in black folklore, John roamed all the plantations, sawmill camps, and railroads, answering the needs of slaves and their descendants. John was a bearer of gifts: laughter, hope, inspiration, all manifestations of the soul, advantages gained from the inside, gifts by which the soul lived. Such qualities lifted the spirits of the downtrodden and allowed them to "keep on trucking," "make a way out of no way," "hit a straight lick with a crooked stick."

Hurston's characters uniformly believed that John (blacks) was smarter than massa (whites). John's tales symbolized as much. In the tale of "Ah'll Beatcher Makin' Money," John, a slave, is given one of the two horses that massa owned. When John abused massa's horse, informants told on him, and his owner promised to kill the horse if the trend continued. John disobeyed the warning and massa killed his horse, whereupon John promised to beat him making money. This tale symbolized the rapacity of southern culture, illustrating that materialism occasionally warped one's judgment so extensively that the quest for wealth made the rational irrational. In the end, John outmaneuvers massa at every turn and drowns him in a nearby river after stating that he hopes massa finds all he's looking for (45).

Black intelligence, likewise, is exalted in the tale "First Colored Man in Massa's House." John, the slave, "didn't know nothin' mo' than you told him and he never forgot nothin' you told him either" (85). After guiding the slave on a tour of his house and identifying furniture and other household items in sterile, superficial language, massa retired for the night. Thereafter, John accidentally set the house afire. When he related the events to massa in his (the master's) own language, the slave's master was slow to understand. Impatient, the slave then related the scenario in plain English. Such a tale refutes white stereotypes of black intelligence and satirizes whites' pretentiousness and penchant for mystification of the simple.

John's tales symbolize the legendary strength and bravery of blacks and contradict the effeminate, weak, cowardly image projected by whites. Confrontations with both natural and supernatural forces demonstrated John's masculine qualities. Hurston's characters were staunch supporters of John, whom they believed more deserving of the "king of the world" title than either the lion or the grizzly bear. John soundly defeated both animals in bitter and bloody battles for the title, eliciting from both an admission of their inferiority (140–43). Interestingly enough, John gained his advantage in the conflict through the adroit use of a razor and a gun, weapons often identified with "bad Negroes." These conventional law-breakers lived on the fringes of society, as members of the proletariat.

But neither God nor the Devil was John's equal. Big Sixteen, a legendary powerful slave, was able to perform any feat of strength or to meet any challenge posed by massa. Accordingly, Big Sixteen was ordered to catch the Devil. Whereupon the slave promptly dug a hole to Hell, knocked on the door, and slew the Devil with a nine-pound hammer, a feat that astonished massa. When Big Sixteen died, he went to Heaven, but St. Peter rejected the slave out of fear of his power and his (St. Peter's) inability to control him. Because Big Sixteen had to go somewhere, he went to Hell, where the Devil's wife likewise refused to accept him. "You aint coming in here," she said. "Here, take dis hot coal and g'wan off and start you a hell uh yo' own" (170–73).

John's tales clearly reject the myth of the helpless, effeminate black man emasculated by the slave experience. Hurston's characters, like other blacks, considered and understood such hype or propaganda projected by slave owners, pseudoscientists, or scholars. This psychological ploy was used to deny blacks the basic privileges to which they were entitled. Conversely, John's tales accomplished the opposite result. They aided in the reemasculation of black men by projecting powerful role models who, stripped of the advantages bestowed by money, race, and power, were clearly superior to whites. More important, such characters were worthy role models or precursors of imaginary heroes such as John Henry or Shine, both of whom demonstrate the superiority of man over machines or technology.

John's tales corrected alleged distortions of slaves by masters and scholars alike. Far from the faithful, loyal, mythological slave portrayed in literature and history, John was that "troublesome property" Kenneth Stampp alludes to in *Peculiar Institution*. In Hurston's "The Fortune Teller" (87–90), John, a loyal, trusted slave, reveals his clairvoyant powers to his master, who feigns disinterest but passes the secret to a neighboring planter. When a dispute between the men arose over John's alleged powers, the neighbor wagered his plantation and worldly goods and secured a notary public to legalize the bet. Meanwhile, John's master promised him wealth if he succeeded but death if he failed. The neighboring planter captured a raccoon, placed it under a washpot, and ordered John to guess its contents; John guessed right, made his master wealthy, and gained more trust. When massa left for a northern trip, he put John in charge. He returned to check his possessions only to find John had planned a party. The angry master decided to hang John, but the slave outwitted massa and gained his freedom.

The quest for freedom is a central theme in *Mules and Men* folklore as blacks struggled against an omnipresent, oppressive society. Rural African-Americans, illiteracy aside, were familiar with that oppression, its infrastructure and maintenance mechanisms. Hurston also portrays the quest for freedom, illustrated in the tale of the slave who was promised his freedom if he made a good crop. John produced and massa grudgingly kept his promise, but only after attempting to dissuade John from accepting manumission. But John ignored massa's entreaties relative to familial ties and his request that John remember "youse a nigger, tho?" Confident, self-reliant, and hopeful for a better tomorrow, John strode toward Canada (97–98).

John's tales, as noted, symbolized wish fulfillment and role inversion but were often based on truth. The struggle for freedom, status, power, and self-esteem was always hazardous, and failure invited certain destruction. Thus, blacks learned to be circumspect in their actions, silent about their thoughts, self-reliant, and distrustful of others' motives. In an oppressive society bent on the control of its underclass, such actions are seen as positive attributes in the struggle to survive. Thus, the trickster role was complex and fraught with danger. Consider, for example, the tale of "Big Talk" (83–86), where two ex-slaves exchange trickster roles. One slave claims to have cursed massa and escaped punishment. His comrade repeated the identical action and is severely punished. Afterward he confronts the first slave, who later informs him that he cursed the master from a distance. The second slave swears revenge and concocts a story about looking under missy's dress and escaping harsh treatment. When the first slave repeats this action, massa almost kills him. Angry, he confronts his friend, who, in turn, informs him that "Ole Miss's drawers they wuz hangin' out de clothes line.... It's uh wonder the [massa] didn't kill yuh dead" (84–85).

The tale of "High Walker and Bloody Bones" relays similar lessons. High Walker was a powerful, fearless black man who encountered a talking skeleton that informs him, "My mouf brought me here and if you don't mind, yourn will bring you here" (185). Frightened, High Walker repeats the event to a white man and foolishly promises to forfeit his life if the skeleton didn't talk. But High Walker couldn't force the skeleton to talk, and lost his life. Thereafter, the skeleton spoke: "Ah told you dat mouf brought me here and if you didn't mind out, it'd bring you here" (185).

A more critical examination of *Mules and Men* will no doubt reveal a system of cultural values predicated on an African worldview. This frame of reference promoted group cohesiveness, strengthened black resolve, and fueled the will to survive. These factors generated a sophisticated protest mechanism that resisted American definitions of black humanity and racial stereotypes. While seen as simple, happy-go-lucky, childlike figures by some early and modern folktale collectors, Hurston's characters are instead sophisticated people who conjure up the memory of an old black saying: "A heap sees, but a few knows," or the admonition of Robert D. Pelton that warns against "mistaking the shallowness of our own understanding for the shallowness in the people we study" (21).

Works Cited

Hurston, Zora Neale. *Mules and Men*. 1935. Reprint, with introduction by Robert Hemenway. Bloomington: Indiana University Press, 1978.
Levine, Lawrence. *Black Culture and Black Consciousness*. New York: Oxford University Press, 1977.
Pelton, Robert D. *The Trickster in West Africa: A Study of Mythic Irony and Sacred Delight*. Berkeley: University of California Press, 1980.
Stampp, Kenneth M. *The Peculiar Institution: A Slavery in Antebellum South*. New York: Vintage, 1956.

CHAPTER FIVE

A Literary Reading of *Mules and Men*, Part I

&ᴦ— Dana McKinnon Preu —ᴦ&

It is now a cliché to speak of Zora Neale Hurston as a woman several decades ahead of her time, yet the current strength of the renaissance of interest in her works indicates we have yet to satisfy our desire to know and understand this complex creator and curator of black culture. Her dual role as literary creator and anthropological curator is, for some, a problem and for others, including me, the fascination in approaching the first part of *Mules and Men* (1935). Without the creativity that Hurston used to present her collection of black folklore, *Mules and Men* would probably be in deserved oblivion, along with other folktale collections of the 1920s and 1930s. Indeed, current scholarship has consistently validated the authenticity of Hurston's portrayal of her black culture—that of poor, mostly nonliterate, central Florida blacks.

In at least three ways, Hurston anticipates current scholarship, and thus our understanding of these elements enhances our appreciation of her writing. The first example of her foreshadowing of contemporary scholarship is her inclusion of a prayer and a sermon, both recorded in poetic form. This awareness of black prayers and sermons as oral poetry has been fully documented by Bruce Rosenberg in *The Art of the American Folk Preacher*. While Hurston implies that the sermon and prayer are types of black American folklore, Rosenberg's analysis of sermons by black American folk preachers places the sermons/poems in the oral narrative tradition of Homeric and Anglo-Saxon epic poetry (3–5). Of greater importance, and now generally recognized, is Hurston's unique position during her lifetime of advocating the beauty, dignity, and wholeness of the isolated poor, black, oral culture. Of course, the purpose of her record was to show and preserve all these positive characteristics ignored by the white and literate black cultures. Further, she ignored all cross-cultural aspects, including segregation and racism, to focus upon an independent, self-created, and self-sustaining black culture (Hemenway, 1978, xxvi).

Hurston developed a unique format for presenting her view of black culture. In contrast to other anthropologists of the 1930s who dealt essentially with folktales isolated from the communal environment in which they were told, Hurston dramatically creates the communal context of the folklore. In fact, she anticipates Robert A. Georges' method of a holistic study of storytelling events "to appreciate their true significance as communicative events, as social experiences, and as unique expressions of human behavior" (1969, 328). Her literary creation of community and of communal behavior patterns allows for character revelation necessary for her purpose. For a people, like individuals, must have beauty, dignity, and a sense of wholeness within the group, as symbiotically separate individuals and the group give and receive identity. Most crucially, Hurston's dramatized record, or literary reconstruction, of "the between-story conversation and business" creates a vital world into which she invites the reader to experience anagogically the fullness and complexity of black oral culture (Hemenway, 1978, XXIV–XXV). Thus, in *Mules and Men* curator/anthropologist and literary creator merge.

Two approaches allow us to appreciate the complexity of "the between-story and conversation business." One is to contrast Hurston's oral literature techniques and point of view with a work treating similar subjects that uses fully literate personal-essay techniques and point of view, in this case, Marjorie Kinnan Rawlings's *Cross Creek* (1942). The other more fundamental way to understand Hurston's orality is to recognize the characteristics of an oral culture and oral literature, for a world of orality uses a different set of mental processes and behavioral patterns from those in our world of literacy. In fact, our literate expectations can prevent us from perceiving "the true inner life of the Negro," to use Franz Boas's phrase, or "that which the soul lives by," to use Hurston's own phrase. Fortunately, contemporary scholarship aids us in understanding what *orality* means in a practical way of individual behavior and group dynamics as well as in a theoretical way of defining such abstractions as *culture*. I am basing the remainder of my analysis of orality primarily on Walter J. Ong's 1982 synthesis of scholarship in this area, *Orality and Literacy*.

These key terms in the title call for a brief clarification. *Orality* or *nonliterate* carries no pejorative connotation. In fact, the scholarship and Ong's presentation stress through examples from a wide historical and geographical range the practical and artistic accomplishments of oral cultures. Nevertheless, literacy—the use of writing, of printing, and of this century's electronic communication methods—expands human mental capabilities, and oral cultures are thus limited when they are juxtaposed with literate ones. Ong also stresses the complexities inherent in a contrast of the two cultural states. However, informed contrasts need to be made: first, to avoid the error of dismissing an oral culture as "primitive," "simple," "quaint," or "inferior," and, second, to appreciate an oral culture positively as an earlier or different state of human consciousness (1–3, 174–75).

Certainly, Hurston's purpose was to give readers of *Mules and Men* a positive experience with black oral culture in three distinct black communities: her home of Eatonville, a sawmill camp at Loughman, and a phosphate mining camp in Pierce. Her purpose in creating to preserve literately these pockets of black orality affects her stance as narrator. To put herself in the oral setting as narrator without violating the authenticity of the setting, she had to forgo the literate techniques of analysis, classification, presentation of objective data and introspection of the self-conscious narrator (Ong, 49–57). The stance she assumes may be described in one of Ong's phrases for a characteristic of orality: "empathetic and participatory rather than objectively distanced" (45). In light of her extroverted nature and forceful personality, Hurston is unusually successful in submerging herself within the group. She consistently allows the tellers, audience participants, and the conversational groups their individual voices. With a few brief lapses, such as her classification of Eatonville's tales (*Mules and Men,* 21), her analysis of black men's laughter (67–68), and her explanation of the white law's attitude toward black women killers (65), she maintains her persona of an orally oriented member of the group.

. In her introduction, Hurston indicates her conscious assumption of her role, one that is defined in the immediate situational environment of Eatonville (Ong, 49ff). She explains, "I didn't go back there so that home folks could make admiration over me because I had been up North to college. . . . I was just Lucy Hurston's daughter Zora" (*Mules and Men,* 3). Her accounts of the various communal settings and the indigenous folklore can easily be analyzed according to the characteristics of authentic oral cultures and the communal performances provided by Robert Kellogg in his article "Oral Literature" and by Ong. Such analysis validates Hurston's stance as narrator and her accounts.

Just as she accepts her role as an orally oriented narrator, Hurston likewise accepts the characteristics of the oral or residually oral communities she records. The designation of "oral" implies isolation within a few square miles, a present-tense frame, and specificity rather than generalization or abstraction. These characteristics of oral communities also tend to give a romanticized picture of subjects, a charge that has been made against *Mules and Men* (Hemenway, 1978, xxvff). Certainly Hurston was fully aware of the problems of extreme depression, poverty, segregation, and the deprivational consequences of these conditions; however, the natural limitations of orality cause the community's unawareness, or very vague awareness, both of the outside economic and social influences and also of the historical influences upon their immediate conditions. Hurston does not impose a literate analysis upon her material. She does, however, present three specific functioning black communities in the immediacy of the weeks or days of her visits.

The structure of her presentation of the communities is literary, despite the seemingly natural chronological progression of her travels between the communities and within each one. The residual oral communities of Eatonville and Pierce frame the more authentically oral community at the sawmill camp at Loughman. While Hurston, Lucy's daughter, takes home-girl pride in the formally incorporated Eatonville, Hurston the anthropologist, by juxtaposing her hometown and the sawmill camp, reveals her awareness of the dilution of black culture in communities civically organized according to white, literate patterns. The brief return to the sawmill camp at the end of her trip serves as a startling coda to emphasize the contrasting communities.

Beginning at Eatonville, Hurston establishes for the reader her point of reference, her roots. In her introduction, she provides a physical description of Eatonville: "a city of five lakes, three croquet courts, three hundred brown skins, three hundred good swimmers, plenty guavas, two schools, and no jail-house" (6). Later, with pride of a literate citizen, she emphasizes Eatonville's formal civic organization when she describes Wood Bridge, a nearby black community: "No enterprising souls have ever organized it. They have no schoolhouse, no post office, no mayor. It is lacking in Eatonville's feeling of unity" (15).

The citizens of Eatonville and Wood Bridge are portrayed as having a sense of social grace and manners. A popular social event was the toe-party, a gathering sponsored by a community organization to raise money. The women at the party stand behind a curtain, exposing only their toes. Each man pays to choose a set of toes, then treats their owner to dinner (17). The toe-party to which Hurston goes in Wood Bridge with Eatonville friends is indeed lively, and there is coon dick, a raw "likker," as well as Coca-Cola. However, social propriety is observed throughout the evening. Later in her visit, when some of the men in Eatonville are coming to tell Hurston their lies, her hostess makes gingerbread for a refreshment. Hurston's portrait of Eatonville's communal behavior pattern includes several examples of agonistically toned verbal exchanges, all characteristic of oral cultures (Ong, 43–45). However, in Eatonville these verbal battles for superiority are generally done in good humor, or when there is evidence that the verbal exchange might evolve beyond a stylized game into a serious, perhaps physical, exchange, someone in the group can interrupt the combatants. Hurston also shows the internal function of the church in the community. During a lull in one lying (storytelling) session, the group hears the concluding prayer from a meeting at the Baptist church, and Hurston records it as a natural part of the cultural environment (27). The ritual poetry of the prayer contrasts with the high-spirited narrative of the tales, yet both are integral parts of the unified culture.

A brief note on the content of the folktales is necessary. With the stories told in Eatonville and in the other two communities, Hurston gives concrete examples of major points of Ong's analysis of storytelling within the communal setting. The basic point is that while the tales are traditional, the teller's art is shown by his ability to fit his story into the social context of the moment and engage his immediate audience. Hurston shows the recognized importance of the traditional or established tale as authority when Gene accuses his wife, Gold, of making up a story just to get at him. He fails to discredit Gold only because Armetta and Shoo-pie, two ladies of authority, insist they both know the "ole tale" (33).

Hurston's tales are, as Ong describes other oral tales, close to the human lifeworld of the culture. Perhaps of most significance for experiencing the black culture of Eatonville is Ong's explanation of the homeostatic characteristic of oral cultures. As he explains, "Oral societies live very much in a present which keeps itself in equilibrium or homeostasis by sloughing off memories which no longer have present relevance" (46). If we view the content of the stories as reflecting community thought, we see in some stories a culture that is able to view itself with a high degree of mature, comic detachment and a healthy skepticism; "How the Brother Was Called to Preach" and "How the Church Came to Be Split Up" are two such tales. These examples, like many others, also show the creation of lore to cover contemporary situations. Both stories occur when the group hears activity in the two churches of the town. After noting the activity in the first, Gold comments, "Hard work in de hot sun done called many a man to preach" (22). This observation introduces a story about a man who thought he heard God's call. After years of failure, he realized he mistook the mule's bray for God's voice (22–24).

After the group hears Pa Henry's prayer from the other church—one of Hurston's records of oral black religious poetry—Hurston comments,

"It's too bad that it must be two churches in Eatonville" (28). Charlie patiently explains that Peter himself is to blame for the divisions. He implies that there is no way to change the original situation, and Armetta reenforces the recognition of the irreconcilable split: "Baptis' and Methdis' always got a pick out at one 'nother" (31).

Banter, stories, and a song are the oral weapons used by those in Eatonville to fight the battle of the sexes. Gold changes the subject and takes jabs at her man Gene, and the two have heated banter on who is blacker. Gold finally sidesteps the argument with a tale explaining that "niggers" got black because they misunderstood when God said "Get back!" They dutifully got black (33). A comment by George Thomas that "Her tongue is all the weapon a woman got" (33) occasions Mathilda's tale of how women got God's keys to the kitchen, bedroom, and cradle to offset men's superior physical strength (33–38). Despite the women's assertions, a young man recites, "Sue, Sal and That Pretty Johnson Gal," the story of a young man's simultaneous affairs with the three girls (39–40). Another couple takes up the game, and the sexual banter concludes when the male contender falls asleep because of the effects of coon dick (40–41). This verbal agonistic behavior in the residually oral community contrasts with the physically violent agonistic behavior of the more exclusively oral sawmill camp.

Several stories and the song "John Henry" all celebrate the wit and cleverness of blacks to be masters of their own situations. In "Ah'll Beatcher Makin' Money" (45–49), the traditional hero John gets, by his wits, justifiable revenge on Ole White Massa, and in another story the equally traditional hero Jack outwits the Devil ("How Jack Beat the Devil," 51–58). These two heroes, along with "John Henry," represent the poetic role of the marvelous heroes who must be type figures and whose deeds must be remembered easily. Of course, "John Henry" reflects the extraordinary physical strength of a tragic black hero; but, in addition, this song and the story "How to Write a Letter" show black oral heroes up against the technology of power-driven machinery and writing. Although the nonliterate father in the story momentarily holds his own against his literate daughter, his tale along with "John Henry" may well reflect blacks' awareness of different types of outside technology threatening their established oral culture. It would be typical of these blacks to externalize such awareness, because self-analysis and introspection are characteristics of literate cultures.

While this analysis is far from complete, it will perhaps suggest a people who have used the full resources of their oral environment to establish a communal cohesion that provides group and individual identity and dignity. Folklore provides a reality that supplies positive psychological elements for the physical security and mental well-being of the group. The literate outsiders who enter Eatonville on the community's terms can perceive a beauty that transcends their perception of poverty and oppression.

The black community at the Loughman sawmill camp has an atmosphere and physical characteristics different from those in Eatonville and, thus, provides elements of black culture not seen there. The camp community includes the jook joint, which features blues, corn likker, and jook women like Ella Wall, whose reputation was known in Eatonville. Life here is harsher even though the men are employed. Certainly it embodies the physically violent side of the oral cultures, a characteristic that is an extension of the "agonistically toned" oral characteristic (Ong, 43). More than one woman in the camp had shot or knifed a man (*Mules and Men,* 69), and Box-Car, who introduced Hurston to a chain-gang song, had learned the song on the gang (163; also see 133). The harshness of white law had intruded upon this community, yet it was a refuge from that law. Hurston finally wins acceptance here when she explains that her $12.98 dress, which contrasted with the $1.98 mail-order dresses of the other women, and her car were gifts from her bootlegging man and that they had split up to run from the law (66, 68–69). It is not surprising that several tales of John getting the better of Massa came from this community. On one occasion Eugene Oliver exclaims, "Go 'head and tell it, Cliff. Ah love to hear tales about Ole Massa and John. John sho was one smart nigger" (75, also see 85). Other incidents of note that occur in this community are the visits of an itinerant preacher whose sermon Hurston records as oral poetry (148–51) and examples of ritual verbal combat.

Two purely ritualized forms of verbal combat contrast with the agonistic banter recorded at Eatonville. The first is called woofing. A form of flirting, it calls for quick, witty repartee. An excellent example is Pitts's woofing of Hurston at a dance shortly after her arrival at Loughman. She plays willingly and well. After she has passed this test, the men are comfortable with her (68–70). The second is a form of "can you top this?" and the content provided by several participants is a series of outlandish one-liners on such subjects as the ugliest man. In the incident Hurston records, Clifford Ulmer's contribution is "Ah knowed one so ugly till you could throw him in the Mississippi river [*sic*] and skim ugly for six months." The ritual combat of this incident is evidenced when Jim Allen, the patriarch of this community, declares Cliff the winner (73). Interestingly, this form of verbal combat can be adapted situationally in a tale, as in "What Smelled Worse" (86–87).

One characteristic of orality not explicit in Eatonville is explicit at least twice in Loughman; this is, the members of an oral culture take their identity from the group, externally rather than internally; a person's position in the group is his identity (Ong, 69). The first incident of someone's asserting his identity and responding to what he considers a challenge occurs on the fishing trip. In the playfulness of the occasion, young Arthur Hopkins refers to Mr. Jim Allen, the patriarch, as "Jim." Mr. Allen responds:

"Don't you be callin' me by my first name. Ah'm old enough for you' grand paw! You respect my gray hairs. Ah don't play wid chillun."

"Ah didn't mean no harm," Arthur said.

"Dat's all right, Arthur, Ah ain't mad. Ah just don't play wid chillun. You go play wid Cliff and Sam and Eugene. They's you' equal." (*Mules and Men,* 104)

The second incident of asserting one's position involves the physically violent behavior pattern in the community. Enmity existed between Big Sweet who befriends Hurston and Ella Wall before Hurston's arrival, but her presence increased the tension. The women almost have one fight and later actually start a community brawl. The physical strength and violence celebrated in folktales of the culture thus become reality. These incidents may serve as other examples of the "agonistically toned characteristic of orality" (Ong, 1982, 44–45). But for all the harshness of this community, there is here, as in Eatonville, a culture that fosters communal cohesion and, thus, security and self-realization for the individual within the group. The jook joint fosters a reflection of black culture that Eatonville denies.

After the highly charged atmosphere of the sawmill camp, in the black quarter of the phosphate mining camp in Pierce, Hurston found a community much like Eatonville. Though the mining company provided relatively good living conditions, the black culture remained an independent, self-sustained one. Hurston records here only the evening of a lying contest, but this account is unusually rich because of the high degree of interaction within the group. Also, because Hurston concentrates all the tales into the one incident, this episode emphasizes the purely literary functioning of the group. Basically, the Pierce storytelling event enriches the accounts of the other two communities rather than adds new dimensions to the portrait of black oral culture.

While Hurston has created three easily distinguishable communities, each with its memorable characters, they share the verbomotor life-style described by Ong (68–69). For good and bad, orality forces close, personal, and frequent, if not continuous, interaction upon community members. Establishing an order and group identity is necessary for the individuals' physical and psychological survival. Hurston has shown how the lore and tales intricately woven into all facets of community activities enforce group order and cohesion to provide physical security and provide a reality for group identity and dignity that enhances psychological well-being.

A final way to appreciate the full import of Hurston's accomplishment in the dramatization of her oral world and to appreciate the dimensions of orality in her world is to contrast *Mules and Men* with a somewhat similar work. Marjorie Kinnan Rawlings, a white Florida writer of about the same period, presents her adopted central Florida home in a book of personal essays entitled *Cross Creek* (1942). Rawlings describes a small oral or residually oral community of citrus groves and fishing areas. The inhabitants include five white families, including Rawlings, and two black families, though other blacks and whites temporarily in the area and also those from peripheral areas significantly interact with the core community. Of course, with the personal essay form, Rawlings is the self-conscious, literately oriented narrator throughout (Kellogg, 59). She is the analytical, objective reporter *par excellence.* She is even objective when she presents her own emotions. And it is well to remember that her almost scientific concern for the accuracy of geographical and biological details makes *Cross Creek* and her novels a naturalist's reference source. On completing *Cross Creek,* the reader knows the community and its people from the limited point of view of the literate ''I'' narrator. The ''I'' narrator is the constant, interpretative tour guide for the reader through her world.

For contrast with Rawlings's presentations, I am limiting discussion to Hurston's presentation of the sawmill camp. This material may be effectively separated from *Mules and Men* to form a small oral epic, with the tales themselves secondary to action and characterization through the character's actions. Hurston's role as the participating, unanalytical ''I'' narrator in the context of oral literature has already been established. In turning to specific aspects of these works, I would emphasize that the contrast I am making is comparative only in terms of orality and literacy; the separate merit of both works is well established. The two points of contrast are, first, Rawlings's and Hurston's presentations of information about animals common to both communities and, second, the contrast in the characterization of Rawlings's 'Geechee and Hurston's Big Sweet. Rawlings's titles for the chapters on animals, insects, and snakes are ''Toady-frogs, Lizards, Antses and Varmints'' and ''The Ancient Enmity.'' The first title suggests the inclusion of oral animal lore, but the only significant element of orality is the definition of *varmint* given by

Martha Mickens, the black matriarch of Cross Creek: "Why a wild cat be's a varmint, Sugar.... Skunks be varmints, an' 'coons an' foxes an' 'possums. Minkses, too. A panther be's a varmint, an' a bear. All them wild things, Sugar, out in the woods" (1942, 156). This quotation could well be added to Ong's examples showing that orally oriented people define in terms of specific examples, not by a series of abstracted characteristics (53). However, Rawlings uses this and other quotations from orally oriented neighbors to establish the quaintness or strangeness of the backwoods people she had chosen to live among. Her presentation includes mainly her firsthand experiences with and observations of these creatures. Interspersed are only a little local lore and some scientific information. When we read Rawlings's account, we are in our comfortable literate reality and can objectively enjoy the trials and tribulations of the city lady's battles with uncivilized creatures that infested rural Florida.

On the other hand, Hurston's information on wild creatures is presented mainly in the folktales. Twenty-one are told on a fishing trip at Loughman where the men work in the cypress swamps most of the time. In the episode, there is much "in-between conversation" that includes animal lore not formalized into tales. Most significant about this extended storytelling event is that it clearly exemplifies Ong's reference to oral states of consciousness that contrast with literate states of consciousness (174). Robert E. Hemenway has already noted such a contrast in an analysis of fiction by Hurston and other Afro-American writers. Specifically he notes the fusion of the psychological reality of black folklore and objective reality in Afro-American fiction (1982, 28–35). In addition, Hemenway contrasts the "heuristic function" of the animal tales of black culture with the tales' reduction to "pediatric literature" in either Joel Chandler Harris's or Walt Disney's literate Uncle Remus setting (35–38). During the Loughman fishing trip, we hear the tales in an authentic communal setting. Thus, we can experience the complex role the tales play in the functioning and the reality of the community.

The fishing activity occasions a community gathering; men, women, single, married, young to old—all exchange information and opinions, teach and learn, assert individuality and reinforce group order and/or personal relationships. As I have already noted, tales are told because they contribute to the group's functioning, or their telling meets the psychological needs of the teller. Hurston's "between-story conversation and business," with additional folklore matter, indicate the relevance and function of each tale from the speaker's view and the listeners' views. In short, in black oral culture the tales are a complex, specialized communication system. Hemenway describes the tale as "coded cultural messages preserved and passed by word of mouth from generation to generation'' (1978, xxiii). Only a partial analysis of the fishing episode is given here.

Some of the tales reflect the oral culture's use of artistic ''logic'' to order the natural world. For example, Patriarch Jim Allen tells how God came to give ''de snake poison in his mouf and a bell on his tail'' (104–6). By extension, the long story affirms God's fair order as the Creator balances the powers of man and snake. ''How God Made Butterflies'' and ''Why the Waves Have White Caps'' also help explain the workings of God and natural forces. In answer to Jim Presley's question about what God changed after creation, Floyd Thomas explained that God created flowers because He got tired of looking at the bare ground and, in turn, made butterflies to keep the flowers company (129–30). In ''Why the Waves Have White Caps,'' Cliff Ulmer personifies the elements as women; the white caps are Mrs. Wind's children trapped by the jealous Mrs. Water (138–39). Cliff, Jim Allen's grandson, is one of the young men establishing for himself an independent identity among the men.

Like Cliff, other young men, especially Joe Wiley and Jim Presley, are establishing their identities not only by engaging in the combative game of topping others' assertions but also by creating their individual artistic reality; at this point they are exploring the elements of fire and water, albeit in terms of catfish and snakes. They get so farfetched that Mr. Allen gently chides them, ''Y'all done quit tellin' lies. Y'all done gone to moldin' em'' (104).

Tolerance and compassion, qualities necessary in the closebound oral community, are part of the theme of ''Why the Mocking Bird Is Away on Friday.'' This tale is also, in part, a statement defining bad behavior and showing its consequences, as is the tale of the man who went catfishing on Sunday. Some tales have the theme of change, for example, ''How the Possum Lost the Hair Off His Tail.'' Others justify a behavior, as in the case of Lonnie Barnes, who tells ''How the Woodpecker Nearly Drowned the Whole World'' to justify his desire to shoot woodpeckers. The final tale of this series, ''How the Lion Met the King of the World,'' affirms man's control over creation.

In this impromptu verbal jam session, we see the culture exploring and creating its specific integrated form of cosmic and physical reality. The group collectively through its lore has come to comfortable terms with the nature of God, man, and universe—and with each other. The power and various functions of the spoken word in the absence of writing are amply demonstrated. While Rawlings and her literate neighbors could not function with the sawmill's oral store of information, the oral sawmill community would find her abstractions, classifications, other scientific lore, and personal realistic experiences equally useless.

The second informing contrast between Rawlings's literate techniques and Hurston's presentation of black oral culture and its literature is the characterization of 'Geechee in *Cross Creek* and that of Big Sweet in *Mules and Men.* Of course, inherent here is also the contrast of a white writing about blacks in an essentially white setting and of a native black writing about blacks in an all-black setting. Naturally, this contrast emphasizes the unique record *Mules and Men* provides. Rawlings's characterization of 'Geechee must be seen in contrast with her characterizations of other blacks. In a chapter entitled "Black Shadows," Rawlings states, "I am not of the race of Southerners who claim to understand the Negro" (180). She goes on to state her realization that Negro behavior described by whites as "childish, carefree, religious, untruthful and unreliable" is "a defense mechanism as ingrained as the color of his skin" (181). In this chapter she recounts her relationships with a series of female and male employees. Her original readers, almost all of them white, could certainly share the frustrations she reveals in this chapter. Yet her attitude is sympathetic toward the blacks, and her underlying frustration is that her white, literate logic fails her in these relationships.

It is significant that 'Geechee is completely separate from the characters in "Black Shadows" for two reasons: First, 'Geechee is a woman with whom Rawlings develops close emotional ties and, second, while the characterizations in "Black Shadows" are in a comic mode, 'Geechee is cast in a tragic mode. In "'Geechee" Rawlings reveals the pain of a memorable, proud, capable woman whose tragic mistake was to give her heart to an unworthy man. In addition, she reveals her own pain at seeing her friend suffering and being powerless to help. Rawlings unconditionally accepts 'Geechee—something she did with few others—although she could not change 'Geechee's behavior, which forced their separation.

Rawlings presents a character who might be a spiritual cousin to Big Sweet, Hurston's friend and protector at the Loughman sawmill camp. Both are awesome in their physical strength, their dignity, and their actions to be masters of their fate. However, 'Geechee is seen in a literate tragic mode in the isolated setting of Rawlings's house at Cross Creek. The literate narrator freely uses abstraction and introspection with a resulting emphasis on internal action and conflict. In contrast, Hurston places Big Sweet in an oral folk epic mode. Thus, she is in a world of physical action in which she becomes an oral-literature hero, as Ong describes, "a person whose deeds are monumental, memorable and commonly public" (70).

Let us look first at 'Geechee. In one of Rawlings's most successfully dramatized incidents, she shares her initial encounter with 'Geechee. Analytically, Rawlings describes 'Geechee, whose physical and psychological strengths are overpowering: "She looked capable of murder. It would be like having a black leopard loose in the house. . . . It was her eyes that frightened me. One was blind and white fixing me with an opaque, unseeing purpose. I felt dazed and foolish, as though I had been hypnotized by a grotesque idol" (82–83). Rawlings's fear soon turns to trust and dependence as she experiences the excessively thorough work, devotion, and loyalty noted among 'Geechee's regional group, the blacks from the tidal waters of the Ogeechee River in Georgia (84). In time Rawlings learns that 'Geechee came to her because she felt the white woman could get her man, Leroy, out of prison. Admiring 'Geechee's determination, Rawlings does. However, to both women's distress, Leroy proves to be a hateful, menacing ingrate. Initially 'Geechee's conflict is between her devotion to Rawlings and to the worthless Leroy. Rawlings enjoys a brief victory over Leroy, but she loses 'Geechee to the maid's dependence on alcohol because of her despair over not freeing herself from an abusive lover and/or not being able to deal adequately with her loneliness.

'Geechee has tragic stature because we see her crucial moments of introspection as she voices her self-awareness and, even in her weakness, her determination to control her destiny. In her weakest moments, she retains a dignity that defies pity.

The breaking point with Leroy comes when he attacks Rawlings verbally after she has been extremely generous to 'Geechee and him. 'Geechee explains, "I don't mind him doin' me wrong. He ain't never done anything but wrong to me. But nobody ain't done for him what you done. He ain't worth killin' the way he talked to you. I wanted to die" (88–89). 'Geechee's second tragic awareness is voiced after a final drinking bout while she was working for Rawlings. With dignity and a sense of her own destiny, she says, "I know I got to go. I ain't no use to nobody. It comes over me and I can't help it. No use foolin with me, I won't never be no different" (95). In contrast, Big Sweet has no such moments of introspection.

About their relationship, Rawlings concluded with a personal moment of introspection, "No maid of perfection . . . can fill the strange emptiness she left in a remote corner of heart" (95). With her empathy, respect, and deep feelings for 'Geechee, the white writer has provided a touching yet limited sketch of her friend from a different ethnic background and with an oral societal orientation Rawlings never fully understands. Her hints at 'Geechee's fuller life are provocative: the violence of her society in which she lost an eye, the other women in Leroy's life, her willing acceptance of Leroy's mistreatment of her, his actions and place in the black urban society of Jacksonville, her relations with other blacks of the Hawthorne/Cross Creek area. But then we are asking the author to write a different story in another mode.

Hurston's story of Big Sweet at the almost all-black sawmill camp gives us a tale in an oral, not literate, mode. When we juxtapose 'Geechee with Big Sweet, we can observe the same strong qualities of a black woman, but now within the oral black community. However, we must adjust to Hurston's oral epic style of phsyical action, a style without introspection by the characters and without introspection or analysis by the narrator participating in the communal activity. The literate reader may make his own analysis after the excitement of the action.

Befitting the oral heroic mode, Big Sweet is monumental in her physical presence and in her actions, and we never see her outside the communal setting. In contrast to Rawlings, Hurston never gives an objective description of Big Sweet. She does identify Big Sweet among "the well-known women" of the area (*Mules and Men,* 67), and from what we later learn of her, this description might be an example of epic litotes. Of course, her name suggests a heroic epithet. In addition are her references to other women and the women's references to her. For example, she refers to Hurston, no small person, as "Little-Bit," and Ella Wall, her adversary, calls to Big Sweet, "Hey, bigger-than-me" (160).

Her actions among the men—black and white—portray her fearlessness and psychological strength as well as her physical strength. Significantly, she is the only woman to tell tales during the fishing trip; she tells "Why the Mocking Bird Is Away on Friday" and "How the Gator Got Black" with no objections from others. In fact, she forestalls an interruption by Sam Hopkins: "When Ah'm shellin' my corn, you keep out yo' nubbins, Sam" (115). Further, on the fishing trip before the whole community, she chides and challenges her man, Joe Willard, for fooling with Ella Wall. She cuts in a discussion about cats to pronounce "And speaking about hams, if Joe Willard don't stay out of dat bunk he was in last night, Ah'm gointer sprinkle some salt down his back and sugar cure *his* ham" (133). None of the men defends Joe.

In the jook joint, she is even more powerful. She first eyeballs down a half-drunk tenor because his noise interferes with her card game. More important, she challenges Ella Wall, who dared appear, to the point where both women open knives. Most important, when the white Quarter Boss steps in to stop the imminent battle between the women, she stands up to him. When the Boss demands her knife, she declares, "Naw suh! Nobody gits *mah* knife. Ah bought it for dat storm-buzzard over dere and Ah means tuh use it on her, too. . . . Don't you touch me, white folks" (161). The best he can do is take Ella's knife and make her leave the camp. When the Boss and Ella leave, Joe Willard proclaims, "You wuz noble!" "You wuz uh whole woman and half uh man" (162). In epic fashion we see the progression of three increasingly difficult challenges met and mastered by the hero. Indeed, her acts are easily remembered, a requirement for oral heroic deeds.

Like 'Geechee, she is loyal to friends, and, as we have seen, she directs her destiny. Loyalty to one she accepts is seen in her relation with Hurston and, of course, in her effort to keep her man. She successfully protects Hurston from Lucy, who is jealous because her man, Slim, plays and sings for Hurston, and possibly from Ella during their first encounter at the jook joint and later at Cliff Ulmer's wedding. Because Hurston had to leave in the middle of the melee following the wedding, we are not sure who survived, but I would bet on Big Sweet. In any event, she controlled not only her own destiny but also that of her community in several ways.

In contrasting the presentations of Big Sweet and 'Geechee, we see that one does not have to argue the effectiveness of orality or literacy. While it is true that Rawlings, the writer in the literate mode, frequently includes dramatizations of physical, public actions along with private and internal actions, she less frequently achieves the level of the marvelous and bigger-than-life aspects of oral literature. Rawlings shows us that a character in a literate mode of literature does not have to have a complete world/culture created in order to function publicly. The development of concern with the private life, with introspection and interior, and with psychological action came within the literate world. Nevertheless, the literate reader can still be moved by the oral hero's adventure stories of power and daring action in the public arena of perhaps a small but complete cultural world. Hurston's little epic places Big Sweet beside John, Jack, and John Henry as black folk heroes. Telling Big Sweet's story, Hurston shows us how the African griot creates a hero and serves the community.

All in all, we have seen that *Mules and Men* is unique not only because it preserves oral literature, but because as a literate writer, Hurston has created an authentic oral world/culture as the context for the literature.

In his conclusion Ong states, "Study of the contrast between orality and literacy is largely unfinished business" (156). And more specifically, he notes, "Literary history on the whole still proceeds with little if any awareness of orality-literacy polarities, despite the importance of these polarities . . . in the relationship of literature to social, intellectual and psychic structures" (157). Because of Hurston's fusion of anthropological research and literary creation, *Mules and Men* is unique in preserving a vital recording of a functioning Afro-American oral culture. As our study of orality continues, we are in debt to Zora Neale Hurston for providing not artifacts to be dissected, but a means whereby we may positively experience orality.

Works Cited

Georges, Robert A. "Toward an Understanding of Storytelling Events." *Journal of American Folklore* 82 (1969):313–28.

Hemenway, Robert E. Introduction to *Mules and Men,* by Zora Neale Hurston. Bloomington: Indiana University Press, 1978.

———. "Hurston's Buzzards and Elijah's Ravens." In *A Rainbow Round Her Shoulder,* edited by Ruthe T. Sheffey, 28–41. Baltimore: Morgan State University Press, 1982.

Hurston, Zora Neale. *Mules and Men.* 1935. Reprint, with introduction by Robert Hemenway. Bloomington: Indiana University Press, 1978.

Kellogg, Robert. "Oral Literature." *New Literary History* 5 (1973):55–66.

Ong, Walter J. *Orality and Literacy: The Technologizing of the Word.* New Accents series. New York: Methuen, 1982.

Rawlings, Marjorie Kinnan. *Cross Creek.* New York: Charles Scribner's Sons, 1942.

Rosenberg, Bruce A. *The Art of the American Folk Preacher.* New York: Oxford University Press, 1970.

CHAPTER SIX

Subversive Female Folk Tellers
in *Mules and Men*

&— MARY KATHERINE WAINWRIGHT —&

During the Great Depression, Zora Neale Hurston served as general editor of and a contributor to the Florida volume of the Federal Writers' Project American Guide Series. Robert Hemenway devotes only two paragraphs of his 1977 biography on Hurston to describing her brief tenure with the Federal Writers' Project, and other scholars and devotees of Hurston have also tended, as I had, to ignore or forget this detail of her life.

Several years ago, however, I happened quite by accident on a library copy of the 1939 *Florida: A Guide to the Southernmost State.* One sleepless night I discovered the following unauthored passage in the midst of what is, for the most part, an encyclopedic survey of Florida's history, agriculture, business, tourism, and education. In the description of the unincorporated town of South Bay, located on the banks of Lake Okeechobee, readers are told of the town's partial destruction during the 1928 hurricane (the same hurricane that Hurston describes in *Their Eyes Were Watching God*). Inserted into the otherwise dry, prosaic writing style that typifies this volume is this paragraph: "A Negro field worker who passed unscathed through several hurricanes has graphically described the velocity of a tropical gale: 'One day the wind blowed so hard, it blowed a well up out of the ground; blowed so hard, it blowed a crooked road straight. Another time it blowed an' blowed, an' scattered the days of the week so bad that Sunday didn't come till late Tuesday mo'nin' "
(*Florida*, 477). This voice I recognized; this voice, in fact, I knew well. And, despite the lack of evidence to suggest the author, I heard, without a doubt, the folkloric voice of Zora Neale Hurston speaking from these pages. Even when she was responsible for simply accumulating and recording data and statistics, Hurston, it seems, could not resist spicing up her prose with a bit of "lying."[1]

While we know that Hurston drew literary inspiration from her varied experiences and travels from Harlem to Haiti, her early childhood exposure to the wit, wisdom, drama, and hidden messages of Eatonville's folktales and folk life, as the preceding passage illustrates, clearly inspired her strongest literary voice and defined her goals as an African-American woman writer. In both major and minor texts, in her creation of literary characters, plots, themes, narrative techniques, and even statistical information about Florida, Hurston's dominant discursive voice is the voice of the Eatonville folk teller. As Hemenway has argued, "Zora Hurston was struggling to make literature out of the Eatonville experience. It was her unique subject, and she was encouraged to make it the source of her art" (1977, 19–20).

In exploring Hurston's literary use of her Eatonville experiences, scholars today recognize that folktales and glimpses of folk life do not appear in her texts as mere "structural blunder," as Darwin Turner claimed in 1971 (107). Instead, following the lead of Hemenway's 1977 critical biography, most scholars of the eighties, including Hemenway, Alice Walker, and Mary Helen Washington, understand that Hurston used her "folkloric ethos" (Neal, 162) as a way of "liberating rural black folk from the prison of racial stereotypes and granting them dignity as cultural creators" (Hemenway, 1977, 329–30). Or, in Alice Walker's words, the use of folktales allowed Hurston to emphasize "racial health, a sense of black people as complete, complex, *undiminished* human beings, a sense that is lacking in so much black writing and literature" (85). Certainly as we read and reread the stories in *Mules and Men* (1935) of John's outwitting "Ole Massa," of how objects in nature have acquired their distinctive characteristics, and of African-American creation stories, we begin to recognize the ways that African-American folk culture has functioned historically as a kind of literary underground railroad, preserving and transmitting positive racial images and alternative records of the African-American experience.

While agreeing with Hemenway and other scholars that the folktales serve as "the tradition-bearers for an Afro-American world view" because they refute the "pathological view of uneducated rural black people" (Hemenway, 1978, xix xx), my own study of Hurston's folkloric voice and vision suggests that she had another agenda, one that has been overlooked by the majority of scholars: to liberate black women, the "mules of the world" as she labels them in *Their Eyes Were Watching God* ([1937] 1978, 29), from historically sexist stereotyping. A careful analysis of both the structure and the themes of her collection of Eatonville folktales in *Mules and Men* suggests that Hurston's folkloric voice is embedded in this text for purposes even more subversive than have previously been recognized.

At the same time that she celebrates the life of the folk in *Mules and Men,* Hurston illustrates black women's vigorous defiance of conventional gender expectations and male authority. Using her folkloric sensibility to subvert the dominant culture's ideology regarding African-Americans, she adds a politics of gender to her politics of race by subtly employing the voice of the *female* folk teller to undermine negative assumptions about black women held by both black and white cultures. Although this simultaneous indictment and celebration is exemplified in various ways throughout this work, in this chapter I explore the ways that privileging men's views and values affects women's discourse; how men silence women's voices and texts; how women, in turn, fight for and eventually employ their own discourse; and how that discourse functions as a subtext that alters cultural assumptions and provides us with a different way to view the black cultural experience—from a woman's perspective. This subtle undermining encoded as a subtext in *Mules and Men* holds the key to Hurston's subversive use of the voice of the female folk teller.

One of the most important thematic threads in *Mules and Men,* Part I (the folktales), is the way that language functions as a source of power. Dr. Asa Hilliard maintains that power is the ability to define reality and have others agree with that definition, while Robert Hemenway believes that "whoever attempts to control language, the naming process, attempts to control our understanding of who we are, our definition of reality" (1978, xxiii). On the surface, *Mules and Men* suggests that men hold the power in the black community because they control its language. Divided into ten chapters that contain a total of seventy folktales, *Mules and Men* resounds with male voices. The seventy tales form the portion of the book that Cheryl Wall has called the "texts," and they are told from a male perspective: Twenty-eight of the storytellers are men while four are women; moreover, sixty-five of the tales are told by the male storytellers, but only five are told by women. Of these five, only one, Mathilda Moseley's "Why Women Always Take Advantage of Men," relates to experiences of black women from a woman's perspective. The tales from *Mules and Men* thus confirm what folklorist Roger Abrahams has noted about black folktales: an "invisibility" of female "images and values" (58). They also illustrate what Hortense Spillers has identified as a "theonomy," a view of human history that is "shot through with a male-engendered Divine Presence" (299) because both the tales and the practices they report are governed by male perspectives of history, society, folk life, and racial conflict.

But one of Hurston's major objectives in *Mules and Men* (and *Their Eyes Were Watching God*) is to replace the white and black male "theonomy" with a black female "matrinomy." Although only one of the five folktales told by a woman is specifically related to gender concerns, it leaves us with a powerful message of ways in which women assume power in situations that traditionally have rendered them powerless; moreover, the tale serves as a sharp contrast to some of the stories told by the men in which women are seen as prizes for men to win, as community peacemakers, as love and sexual objects, and as temptresses.

The only positive woman's tale in *Mules and Men* is prompted by George Thomas's trivialization of women. When he says "Don't you know you can't git de best of no woman in de talkin' game? Her tongue is all de weapon a woman got. . . . She got plenty hips, plenty mouf and no brains," Mathilda Moseley "jumps in" to protest: "Oh, yes, womens is got sense too. . . . But they got too much sense to go 'round braggin' about it like y'all do" ([1935] 1978, 33). She then proceeds to tell her tale.

Mathilda Moseley's folktale seems to reinforce a fairly conventional domestic role for women. According to the storyteller, in the beginning God created both men and women equally strong in physical powers and authority. But man got tired of this balance and desired domination. Therefore, he approached God to ask for "mo' strength than dat woman you give me, so Ah kin make her mind" (34). God granted man this strength, which the man then used to subdue the woman physically. Indignant, the woman went to God and begged for the "strength and power Ah useter have." But God refused her request, saying that he could not take back something that he had already given. Angry at God's refusal, the woman went immediately to the devil, who told her that she could have the advantage over man if God would give her the three keys hanging on his mantelpiece. This time God granted her request, and the devil explained to her their significance and their power: "Now dis first big key is to de do' of de kitchen, and you know a man always favors his stomach. Dis second one is de key to de bedroom and he don't like to be shut out from dat neither and dis last key is de key to de cradle and he don't want to be cut off from his generations at all" (36). Woman's strength, the devil goes on to say, will come if she will lock everything up and not open anything "until he use his strength for yo' benefit and yo' desires" (36). The woman did what the devil advised, and the resolution of the conflict was man's learning that he "had to mortgage his strength to her to live" (38).

This folktale discloses several important traditional cultural assumptions about women. It appears that the tale points to the dominant culture's deeply embedded belief that woman's domain lies in the private sphere of the home—the kitchen, bedroom, and nursery. The tale also points to ways that black women negotiate the private sphere in order to attain power in the public sphere. For example, in many black folktales, God is portrayed as the deity responsible for authorizing white supremacy. But in this tale, according to Mathilda Moseley, he is the deity responsible for authorizing *male* supremacy. By seeking an alternative and subversive authority, the traditional trickster figure of the black folk cosmos (the devil), women regain power; not the physical power of men, but the authority of their own female-centered experiences. By holding the keys to the kitchen, bedroom, and cradle, women in this folktale redirect a male-centered hierarchy of physical authority originated by God to a female world of domestic authority that usurps the power of men; man uses "his strength for yo' benefit and yo' desires." Another important message of this tale is God's initial equal creation of men and women, a motif Hurston expands in the "Adam's Rib" sermon in chapter 8. Finally, while men in this tale receive their strength from God, the conventional giver of gifts and power, women, by receiving their power from the devil, repeat a tradition established by Eve and Pandora, thus implicitly reinforcing the notion of women as usurper of male authority and disturber of men's power.

While this one folktale out of seventy suggests an alternative way to view the black cultural experience from a woman's perspective, we find further and more persuasive evidence of Hurston's feminist message in *Mules and Men* in what Cheryl Wall has called the "context," the narrative frame that introduces the setting from which the seventy formally structured tales emerge. Learning well from her childhood in Eatonville, Hurston knew that the occasion for "lying," usually as it was illustrated by the banter of the porch sitters at Joe Clarke's store, was as important to oral folktales as the tales themselves. It is this narrative frame, which replicates many of Eatonville's cultural rituals and community events (fishing trips, card games, backyard barbeques, trips to the jook and sawmill camps), that sets up the "lying sessions," the opportunity for telling folktales. One of the many thematic threads that runs through the narrative context is the struggle between black men and women over who has the right to speak, to be a user of language. Thus, the texts, the seventy folktales listed in the table of contents (with the exception of Mathilda Moseley's tale), are dominated by male discourse. In contrast, the context of the tales (Hurston's narrative frame) provides a view of the gender struggle, particularly the way women's discourse challenges men's by demanding that women have equal access to language use and the storytelling ritual. Through their words, by insisting on the right to be creators of texts, in the narrative context women gain control, esteem, and respect in their communities. Until chapter 10, the narrative frame also undercuts the male-as-norm motif of traditional folklore as well as Hurston's recorded tales.

The narrative context of *Mules and Men* thus portrays an alternative to the domestic power suggested by Mathilda Moseley's tale and offers another source of power for women, linguistic authority. Linguistic authority is most clearly exemplified by the character of Big Sweet, the woman who befriended Hurston and saved her life as she gathered folk-tales in the sawmill camp in Polk County, Florida. Big Sweet can also be seen as a prototype of the female artist, Janie Crawford, in Hurston's *Their Eyes Were Watching God,* one who has found the ability to reclaim the authority of language assumed by the male. In her autobiography, *Dust Tracks on a Road,* Hurston tells us that Big Sweet came to her "notice" the first week of Hurston's arrival at the sawmill camp: "I heard somebody, a woman's voice 'specifying' up this line of houses from where I lived" ([1942] 1984, 186). Big Sweet's "specifying," so Hurston reports, had gathered an audience of about four or five hundred people, who listen to her "giving her opponent lurid data and bringing him up to date on his ancestry, his looks, smell, gait, clothes, and his route through Hell in the hereafter.... Big Sweet broke the news to him, in one of her mildest bulletins, that his pa was a double-humpted camel and his ma was a grass-gut cow, but even so, he tore her wide open in the act of getting born, and so on and so forth. He was a bitch's baby out of a buzzard egg" (186–87).

Hurston repeats this view of Big Sweet talking "smart," using language as a way to assert her identity and to win community esteem, in her presentation of Big Sweet in the narrative context of *Mules and Men* as one who earns the privileged status of folk teller by verbally competing with the male storytellers. In chapter 6, for example, Big Sweet tells "Why the Mockingbird Is Away on Friday," but her position of storyteller is immediately usurped by the men in the group, who continue to expand on the theme of how animals have come to be as they are. Later in the chapter Big Sweet wants to tell her gator tale, but, as before, she is interrupted by Sam Hopkins. This time Big Sweet is determined not to lose her position as storyteller, so by asserting herself and talking smart to Sam—"When Ah'm shellin' my corn, you keep out yo' nubbins, Sam" (115)—she is able to retain her position.

Other verbal battles in which women triumph linguistically over the men occur in the times and spaces between the tales proper. For instance, in chapter 2 Gold, Shug, and Armetta debate gender roles with Gene Brazzle, responding to his comment that "women ain't good for nothin' exceptin' readin' Sears and Roebuck's bible and hollerin' 'bout, 'gimme dis and gimme dat' as soon as we draw our pay.'' Gaining the upper hand in this verbal match, Shug quickly replies, "We don't git it by astin' you mens for it. . . . you mens don't draw no pay. You don't do nothin' but stand around and draw lightnin','' while Gold quips, "Aw, shut up, Gene, you ain't no big hen's biddy if you do lay gobbler eggs. You tryin' to talk like big wood when you ain't nothin' but brush'' (26).

This verbal play between the men and women continues throughout the narrative context until, after a strategically placed sermon at the end of chapter 8, narrative power shifts to women's actions and discourse. In chapters 9 and 10 Big Sweet dramatizes the way that women reclaim the power of their own experience by insisting on joining their community's game-playing and oral rituals and, in Susan Willis's words, by reversing the community's accepted "systems of domination'' (43). Structurally, the Adam's Rib sermon preached by the traveling preacher in chapter 8 deserves consideration, as Cheryl Wall claims, because its emphasis on the equality of men and women "prepares the reader to accept and approve Big Sweet's actions in the conflict that follows. She is heroic'' (378). Taking his text from Genesis 2:21, the preacher concludes his Creation sermon by describing the equal creation of man and woman, thus recalling the theme of Mathilda Moseley's tale:

> Behold de rib!
> Brothers, if God
> Had taken dat bone out of man's head
> He would have meant for woman to rule, hah
> If he had taken a bone out of his foot,
> He would have meant for us to dominize and rule.
> He could have made her out of back-bone
> And then she would have been behind us.
> But, no, God Almighty, he took de bone out of his side
> So dat places de woman beside us;
> Hah! God knowed his own mind.
> Behold de rib!
>
> (*Mules and Men,* 151)

Following this pointed reminder of sexual equality, Big Sweet rises to heroic stature during various conflicts one evening at the "jook'' in the sawmill camp. From winning an "eye-balling'' match with Texas Red to "raking in the money at the Florida-flip game,'' Big Sweet competes with the men and beats them at their own games. Interspersed within the game playing is verbal banter between Big Sweet and the men, verbal games in which Big Sweet likewise competes and wins. But her grandest achievement occurs when the Quarters Boss comes into the jook and tries to break up the quarrel that is about to erupt among Ella Wall, Lucy, and Big Sweet. Big Sweet has been holding her own with her black brothers and sisters, but when she stands up to the white Quarters Boss, she defies the unspoken convention governing black/white interaction that "cussing Ole Massa" is never done to his face (83), and we realize the preceding events have been gradually building up to this chapter's grand finale—an interracial power struggle between Big Sweet and the Quarters Boss.

The Quarters Boss orders Big Sweet to give him her knife, but she surprises him and the community by defiantly standing up to him, saying "Naw suh! Nobody gits *mah* knife. Ah bought it for dat storm-buzzard over dere and Ah means tuh use it on her, too. As long as uh mule go bareheaded she better not part her lips tuh me. Do Ah'll kill her, law or no law. Don't you touch me, white folks!" (161). Following her tirade, the Quarters Boss immediately transfers his attempt to retain his role as the figure of authority from Big Sweet to Ella: He takes Ella's knife away instead and banishes her from the jook. The Quarters Boss then leaves the jook after having the last word, but his words merely mock his position of authority and implicitly acknowledge that Big Sweet has gotten the better of him. As if he were speaking to a sullen child, he cautiously chides her: "Now you behave yo'self, Big Sweet. Ah don't wanna hafta jail yuh" (162).

The reaction of the men at the jook validates Big Sweet's newly acquired authority and welcomes her as an (almost) equal into the privileged circle of language users; they recognize that she has outwitted the "white folks" with her words: " 'You wuz noble!' Joe Willard told her, 'You wuz uh whole woman and half uh man. You made dat cracker stand offa *you*' " (162). In the eyes of the community, Big Sweet has acquired discursive authority in a public, not a domestic, context. This entire chapter, beginning with the eye-balling contest and ending with the black-white, male-female standoff, dramatizes, through Big Sweet's interactions with the men, the way men (both black and white) attempt to control cultural rituals by controlling language and thus attempt to attain and retain power by denying women's voices and actions. Big Sweet, however, reverses this cultural convention.

Chapter 9 ends with a folktale that subtly parallels and reinforces the events that have just taken place in the jook. Cliffert tells a story about "Jack and de Devil buckin' 'ginst one 'nother to see which one was de strongest." As Big Sweet has just done, Jack wins the contest through his words, not his actions. He threatens to throw the Devil's hammer all the way to heaven, just as Big Sweet threatened the Quarters Boss.

Like Big Sweet, Jack never has to follow through. Jack's words and the Devil's fear of losing his hammer to heaven are enough to force the Devil to end the game, thus implicitly acknowledging that Jack is the stronger (164–65). In this tale, as in the portrayal of Big Sweet, Hurston redefines the meaning of "stronger." Power does not come from physical prowess, she suggests, but rather from discursive adeptness, the ability to outwit the "master" and thus to survive and prevail in an oppressive and potentially enslaving situation through verbal play.[2]

In chapter 9 Big Sweet gains a prominent place in the community's folk life and discourse through verbal threats, thus overturning the role of authority traditionally assumed throughout this work by men, both black and white. In chapter 10, the final chapter of part I of *Mules and Men* devoted to the Eatonville experience, we discover that Hurston, however, engaged in another reversal in the ongoing power struggle. While chapter 9 portrays Big Sweet's defining a positive role model as she breaks the silence surrounding women's voices, chapter 10 introduces, in both the tales and the narrative context, some of the most demeaning images of women found in the entire volume. Set against a backdrop of hostility, trivialization, and constant putdowns, Big Sweet's gestures and assertiveness take on even greater significance because in this chapter Hurston problematizes the role of the black woman folk teller. Now that Big Sweet has reached heroic and artistic stature in the insulated folk community of the Loughman sawmill camp, Hurston reveals some of the obstacles that the black woman storyteller must face as she moves away from a community rooted in oral tradition and lore into a community that a town like Pierce, Florida, represents, a town that is more in contact with the dominant culture and that has approximated what Toni Morrison identifies as the most "obvious" and the "worst" of white characteristics (140).[3]

In many ways chapter 10, which takes place in the more mainstream town of Pierce, Florida, can be read as an autobiographical account of Hurston's own artistic journey from the indigenous black community of Eatonville to the larger artistic community of the Harlem Renaissance. The treatment of women in this chapter parallels many details of Hurston's own treatment at the hands of such contemporaries as Langston Hughes (*The Big Sea*) and Wallace Thurman (*Infants of the Spring*). First of all, Hurston's message here is that women artists must confront a patriarchal notion of women's beauty: that is, that women are objects to be admired and that their appearance serves to please men. In both Hughes's and Thurman's recordings of the Harlem Renaissance, Hurston's artistic abilities are trivialized and her literary merits are often subordinated to discussions of her physical appearance and her behavior.

Likewise, in the narrative context of chapter 10, the storytelling of Good Bread, a large woman, is successfully stopped when Mack Ford insults her appearance and reinforces a conventional and male-defined notion of women's beauty. He tells Hurston that "li'l slim women" were put on earth to "beautify de world" while "big ones" are intended "to show dese slim girls how far they kin stretch without bustin' " (170).

In this verbal exchange, Good Bread tries but cannot defend her appearance against such ingrained social definitions of beauty. She says to the men, "You jus' leave me out yo' mouf. And furthermo' Ah don't crack" (170). But Christopher's response suggests she has overstepped the gender boundaries with her verbal retaliation. As a woman, she is not allowed to set her own standard of beauty: "She always tryin' tuh loud talk somebody. Ah hates women wid men's overalls on anyhow" (171). In other words, women who attempt to participate in the word games of the community, those who attempt to write their own texts, overstep cultural boundaries. They are trying to wear the overalls and emulate men, who, in this exchange, are the acknowledged cultural language users and namers. The resolution of this conflict scores a loss for women. Instead of holding her own with the men, Good Bread leaves, a leavetaking that is significant because it is first described in language pejorative to women ("Good Bread *flounced* on off" [171, emphasis added]), and next it suggests that once she is gone, the *male* storytellers can reclaim their rightful position in this lying session: "She so mad now she'll stay way and let Mack tell Zora some lies. Gwan, Mack, you got de business" (172). The "overalls" remain on Eatonville's idea of their rightful owner, the men, and Good Bread's ability as a folk teller has been judged according to patriarchal notions of gender and not literary merit.

The narrative context reveals other social prescriptions that become a barrier to the black woman folk artist, including Hurston herself, barriers that she must confront and overcome in order to earn the right to tell her own stories. For instance, women are shown to be frightened, timid, and needing the protection of men when Lessie Lee "snuggled up to Clarence with the eyes of Eve and said, 'He [A.D. and his scary tales] scares me too, Clarence. Less me and you hug up together" (183). And on another occasion, A.D. wants to tell a story about a "witch woman," but Baby-face Turl objects, saying "Naw, Ah don't wanta hear bout no witches ridin' nobody. . . . Ah been near rode tuh death in mah time. Can't bear tuh hear tell of it" (182).

In addition to the negative portrayals of women in the narrative context of chapter 10, portrayals that replicate many social barriers to the woman who would be an artist, images of woman in the formally structured tales suggest the socially sanctioned literary conventions that also serve as barriers to the emergence of a valid black women's literature. In "How a Loving Couple Was Parted," Hurston duplicates a stereotypical literary image of woman as a troublemaker and a conniver, out to disrupt the socially sanctioned institution of marriage and patriarchal social security. In this tale, the Devil entices a barefoot woman to break up a happily married couple by promising her a pair of shoes. The Devil himself is so outraged by the woman's evildoing that when she comes to collect her shoes, he ties them to the end of a long pole and hands them to her, saying "Anybody dat kin create mo' disturbance than me is too dangerous. Ah don't want 'em round me" (178). Another convention of patriarchal literature is the demeaning portrayal of the unmarried woman, the spinster. In "How the Squinch Owl Came to Be," Miss Pheenie, Ole Marster's "ole maid sister," is described as having a "stringy" neck because she'd never been married. Her jealousy of the young men courting her niece and her one desire to "git courted and married" motivate her to believe the promises of a "devilish young buck," and so she sits on the roof all night, freezes to death, and is turned into a squinch owl (181–82). The marriage and courting motif also characterizes the story about a young farmer who tricks his new bride into believing that he owns a lot of property in "All These Are Mine." These tales in chapter 10, combined with the actions in the narrative context, deliver a strong message from the men that women's rightful place is at the side of a man, not in overalls or the storytelling rituals.

Because of its conventional message regarding gender roles and how literature has served to reinforce social attitudes toward women, chapter 10 in may ways undermines Big Sweet's unconventional performance in chapter 9. At the end of chapter 10, Big Sweet even reinforces the message of some of the chapter's tales when she summons Hurston back to the Loughman sawmill camp to attend the wedding of Cliffert and Thelma. But in the last few pages of the folktales section of *Mules and Men*, the final actions show Big Sweet's saving Hurston from the threats of the knife-wielding Lucy.

The last two chapters following the Adam's Rib sermon on equality reveal a point-counterpoint volley. While many of the tales and even some of the narrative context reinforce fairly conventional and even demeaning stereotypes of women and suggest that the male storytellers are the rightful users of language to record and define their culture, the actions of Big Sweet and Hurston herself provide an alternative and, because of its somewhat buried nature, a subversive message. A proliferation of negative portrayals of women is juxtaposed with the growing physical and verbal strength of Big Sweet. Moreover, Hurston herself is the volume's ultimate storyteller. Together, these two women refute the socially expected and accepted roles of women. In *Dust Tracks on a Road,* Hurston explains how the alliance she and Big Sweet formed provided the occasion for the female storyteller to emerge. As Big Sweet says to Hurston, "You just keep on writing down them lies. I'll take care of all de fighting. Dat'll make it more better, since we done made friends" (189).

Susan Willis calls our attention to the last image of *Mules and Men,* arguing that "nowhere is Hurston's subversive intent and smug demeanor more evident than in the conclusion" (29). Hurston concludes her volume with a final folktale about Sis Cat, who is tricked into letting the rat go when he suggests she needs to mind her manners and wash her face and hands before eating. The second time the rat tries to trick Sis Cat, she gets the better of him by saying, "Oh, Ah got plenty manners. . . . But Ah eats mah dinner and washes my face and uses mah manners afterwards." Hurston then draws a parallel between herself and Sis Cat in a witty one-liner: "I'm sitting here like Sis Cat, washing my face and usin' my manners" (252). Susan Willis believes that the "gloating" Hurston likens herself to the smug Sis Cat because she has "just served up the body of black Southern folktales to the Northern white readership" and is now asking her readers, "Who's swallowed who?" (29). Willis correctly points to one important effect of Hurston's use of her Eatonville heritage: "turning the tables on the superior Northern establishment" (28). She neglects, however, to see that Hurston, writing with "confidence and satisfaction," is also turning the tables on her own culture's skewed gender prescriptions and values.[4]

Hurston, a black female writer, has encoded the evolution of a strong female discourse that arises out of the very culture that denies women access to its oral rituals and practices. The attempt to silence women's voices has, so Hurston reveals, caused the opposite. Both Big Sweet and Hurston herself earn respected positions in the predominantly male circle of storytellers. Theirs have been subversive activities as they have been engaged in the task of reshaping language so that it works for, not against, women. When Janie Crawford lashes out at the men on the porch in one of the most eloquent scenes in *Their Eyes Were Watching God,* she says, "You men don't know half as much 'bout us women as you think you do" (117). Janie could easily be speaking to Mack Ford, Gene Brazzle, Jim Mosely, Eugene Oliver, and all of the other male storytellers from Eatonville, who, as analogs to Hurston's male Harlem Renaissance contemporaries, represent patriarchal, social, and literary conventions that work to silence the voices of women writers. As they become speakers of their own texts, however, Janie and Big Sweet, like

Hurston herself, represent the indomitable spirit of black women inscribing their own voices and expressions, demanding respect and dignity, and struggling for and earning the right to tell their own stories.

Notes

1. In the narrative context of *Mules and Men,* Shug tells the same tale on p. 50. Another story recorded in the narrative context of *Mules and Men* about fast-growing corn is also found in *Florida* in the description of Belle Glade (474). An astute reader also suspects that the stories of Burwell Yates (130), Dr. Abraham (377), and Daddy Mention (379) are also written by Hurston, but to date I have found no way to document this observation. The descriptions of Maitland and Eatonville are taken directly from Hurston's *Their Eyes Were Watching God* (361–62).

2. See Robert Hemenway's discussion of "The First Colored Man in Massa's House" (*Mules and Men,* 85). In his introduction to *Mules and Men,* Hemenway claims this story, with its focus on vocabulary and language, "recreates the unsuccessful attempt at cultural genocide the slaves overcame" (1978, xxii).

3. I am grateful to Dana McKinnon Preu (Florida A&M University) for her observation that *Mules and Men,* Part I, takes place in three geographical locations: Eatonville, the Loughman sawmill camp, and Pierce. (See chapter 5 herein.) She believes that the events and folktales recorded in Loughman depict a more indigenous oral culture. Eatonville and Pierce, McKinnon claims, frame the Loughman sections and represent African-American culture that has had more contact with the dominant society and thus has assimilated more of its value systems, ideologies, and social practices.

4. In a recent article, "Speaking in Tongues," Mae Gwendolyn Henderson succinctly reminds us that black women's texts exemplify a "simultaneity of discourse." Believing that readers of black women's texts often decode a "gendered" text at the expense of a "racial" one or vice versa, she proposes a way of reading these texts that accounts for both their "gendered" and their "racial" encodings: "A mode of reading which examines the ways in which the perspectives of race and gender, and their interrelationships, structure the discourse of black women writers" (17). Henderson cautions us that to privilege "one category of analysis at the expense of others" risks "restrict[ing] or repress[ing] different or alternative readings" (17).

Works Cited

Abrahams, Roger D. "Negotiating Respect: Patterns of Presentation Among Black Women." *Journal of American Folklore* 88 (1975): 58–80.
Florida: A Guide to the Southernmost State. American Guide Series, Federal Writers' Project. New York: Oxford University Press, 1939.
Hemenway, Robert E. "That Which the Soul Lives By." Introduction to *Mules and Men,* by Zora Neale Hurston, xi–xxviii. Bloomington: University of Indiana Press, 1978.
———. *Zora Neale Hurston: A Literary Biography.* Urbana: University of Illinois Press, 1977.
Henderson, Mae Gwendolyn. "Speaking in Tongues: Dialogics, Dialectics, and the Black Women's Literary Tradition." In *Changing Our Own Words: Essays on*

Criticism, Theory, and Writings by Black Women, edited by Cheryl A. Wall, 16–37. New Brunswick: Rutgers University Press, 1989.

Hilliard, Asa. Keynote Address. Fourth Annual (McKnight) Fellows Meeting. Tampa, Florida, October 22, 1988.

Hughes, Langston. *The Big Sea.* 1940. Reprint, First American Century Series edition. New York: Hill and Wang, 1963.

Hurston, Zora Neale. *Dust Tracks on a Road.* 1942. 2d ed., edited and with introduction by Robert E. Hemenway. Urbana: University of Illinois Press, 1984.

———. *Mules and Men.* 1935. Reprinted, with introduction by Robert E. Hemenway. Bloomington: Indiana University Press, 1978.

———. *Their Eyes Were Watching God.* 1937. Reprinted, with foreword by Sherley Anne Williams. Urbana: University of Illinois Press, 1978.

Morrison, Toni. *The Bluest Eye.* New York: Washington Square Press, 1970.

Neal, Larry. "A Profile: Zora Neale Hurston." *Southern Exposure* 1 (1974): 160–68.

Spillers, Hortense. "A Hateful Passion, A Lost Love." *Feminist Studies* 9 (1983): 293–322.

Thurman, Wallace. *Infants of the Spring.* 1932. Reprinted, with afterword by John Williams. Carbondale: Southern Illinois Press, 1979.

Turner, Darwin. *In a Minor Chord: Three Afro-American Writers and Their Search for Identity.* Carbondale: Southern Illinois University Press, 1971.

Walker, Alice. *In Search of Our Mothers' Gardens: Womanist Prose.* New York: Harcourt, 1983.

Wall, Cheryl A. "Zora Neale Hurston: Changing Her Own Words." In *American Novelists Revisited: Essays in Feminist Criticism,* edited by Fritz Fleischman, 371–93. Boston: Hall, 1982.

Washington, Mary Helen. "Zora Neale Hurston: A Woman Half in Shadow." Introduction to *I Love Myself . . . A Zora Neale Hurston Reader,* edited by Alice Walker, 7–25. Old Westbury, NY: The Feminist Press, 1979.

Willis, Susan. *Specifying: Black Women Writing the American Experience.* Madison: University of Wisconsin Press, 1987.

CHAPTER SEVEN

"De Beast" Within: The Role of Nature in *Jonah's Gourd Vine*

ALAN BROWN

Life on the Florida frontier made an indelible impression on the mind and on the writing of Zora Neale Hurston. Eatonville, Florida, an all-black town located five miles from Orlando, had been incorporated for only fifteen years when she claimed to have been born there in 1901 (Washington, 125). In many ways the Eatonville that Hurston grew up in was still very much a part of the frontier that surrounded Orlando. In her collection of folktales, *Mules and Men* (1935), and in her autobiography, *Dust Tracks on a Road* (1942), Hurston explains how people living in Eatonville early in the twentieth century were molded by the harsh conditions that they encountered. In both books she makes the point that people living in rural Florida had to become tough—that is, more animalistic—in order to surmount the same obstacles that the creatures of the swamp had to cope with every day. On the other hand, Hurston also argues in her autobiography that the natural beauty that surrounded her brought out the poetic impulse that lay dormant within her and inspired her to be an artist. In her first novel, *Jonah's Gourd Vine* (1934), which was written after *Mules and Men* (though published before), Hurston does more than simply relate the tale of brave people trying to fashion a life for themselves out of the wilderness (Helmick, 1970). She draws from her own life experiences and from the folktales that she had collected to create the character of John Pearson, a product of his environment who is condemned by his community because of the animalistic and spiritual elements that coexist within him. In *Jonah's Gourd Vine,* therefore, John Pearson's external struggle with the forces of nature mirrors his internal struggle with "De Beast" that lives within him and ultimately defeats him.

The frontier setting of *Jonah's Gourd Vine* is a mental reconstruction of Eatonville as it existed in fact and in legend (Brawley, 11). In *Dust*

Tracks on a Road, Hurston portrays life in a frontier town in terms that are both idyllic and horrific. On the one hand, Eatonville around the turn of the century was a rustic paradise whose plenty was readily available to anyone: "There were plenty of oranges, grapefruit, tangerines, guavas and other fruits in our yard. We had a five-acre garden with things to eat growing in it, and we were never hungry" ([1942] 1984, 26). On the other hand, though, Eatonville during Hurston's childhood days was also an untamed wilderness, a neighborhood "where bears and alligators raided hog-pens, wildcats fought with dogs in people's yards, rattlesnakes as long as a man and as thick as a man's forearm were found around back doors..." (52). Even harmless plants posed a threat in Hurston's youthful imagination, which had been overly stimulated by the real terrors of the forest: "There was another tree that used to creep up close to the house around sundown and threaten me. It used to put on a skull-head with a crown on it every day at sundown and make motions at me when I had to go out on the back porch to wash my feet after supper before going to bed" (77).

While her body was being nourished on the tropical fruit that was readily available, her mind was nurtured on folktales, some of which appeared years later in *Mules and Men.* In this book, she recalled "lies" that her friends and relatives told of strange experiences that they had had while hunting the deer that abounded in the forest and gave them a year-round supply of meat. However, along with these tales of nature's bounty, Hurston also remembered the hostile side of nature. During her search for authentic black folktales in the 1920s, Hurston experienced firsthand the dangers that the swamp gang she was interviewing had to face every day: "My own particular crowd, Cliffert, James, Joe Willard, Jim Allen and Eugene Oliver, were to look out for me and see to it that I didn't get snake-bit nor 'gator-swallowed. The watchman ... had been killed by a panther two weeks before, but they assured me that nothing like that could happen to me; not with the help I had" (71). Presley, who has been listening to Jim and Cliff's stories about the snakes that proliferate in the area, pleads with them to change the subject: "Don't tell no mo' bout no snakes—specially when we walkin' in all dis tall grass.... Ah speck Ah'm gointer be seein' 'em in my sleep tonight. Lawd, Ah'm skeered of snakes" ([1935] 1978, 106). Even the plenty that the swamp provided posed a threat to the inhabitants of Eatonville, as is illustrated in *Mules and Men* by the tale of the man who is pulled in the water by a giant catfish on the Sabbath and who admonishes his wife to "fear God and catfish" (103).

Not only was the setting of Hurston's first novel shaped by her backwoods experience, but so were the characters, especially the male characters. In *Dust Tracks on a Road* Hurston demonstrates how people who live in a place where only the strongest survive eventually become as tough as the conditions that they cope with on a daily basis. She portrays her father as a man who "was struck by lightning and was not even knocked off his feet, but that lightning went off through the woods limping" (51). Growing up among men like her father, Hurston was impressed with their resourcefulness and, to a certain extent, their violent natures: "As in all frontiers, there was the feeling for direct action. Decency was plumb outraged at a man taking a beating and then swearing out a warrant about it" (52). In an area populated by impulsive men and dangerous beasts, violence was likely to erupt any minute; therefore, a high value was placed on physical prowess. In *Mules and Men,* Hurston recalls a story about two suitors who have to perform tremendous feats very quickly in order to win the hand of their beloved. After hiking in the woods seven or eight miles in search of a deer, one of the suitors "took aim and fired. Then he run home, run 'round behind de house an set his gun down and then run back out in de woods and caught de deer and held 'im till de bullet him 'im. So he won de girl" (43).

Ironically, the same environment that turned some people into fine physical specimens also inspired others to become poets. Stimulated by the tall tales that featured animals that could talk, Hurston's imagination conjured up other fanciful images: "Animals took on lives and characteristics which nobody knew anything about except myself. Little things that people did or said grew into fantastic stories. There was a man who turned into an alligator for my amusement. . . . In my imagination, his work-a-day hands and feet became the reptilian claws of an alligator" (*Dust Tracks,* 86). Even inanimate objects communicated with the little girl in ways that would eventually be transferred to her novels: "I picked up glints and gleams out of what I heard and stored it away to turn it to my own uses. The wind would sough through the tops of the tall, long-leaf pines and say things to me. I put in the words that the sounds put into me. Like 'Woo woo, you wooo!' The tree was talking to me, even when I did not catch it" (77).

While Hurston's natural surroundings acted as a catalyst for the development of her artistic sensibilities, the folklore to which she was exposed also influenced the creation of her most "poetic" character in *Jonah's Gourd Vine*: the preacher, John Pearson. According to tradition, preachers, who Hurston insists had to be poets as well to succeed in a black pulpit, were also products of their experiences with nature (Jones, 29). In *Mules and Men,* one of the storytellers declares that "hard work in de hot sun done called many a man to preach" (22). In the humorous tale that follows, a lazy field hand interprets God's unwillingness to knock him off a log as a sign that he is being called to preach.

Before Hurston's experiences found expression in *Dust Tracks on a Road* or *Mules and Men,* they were incorporated in her first novel, *Jonah's Gourd Vine.* In this autobiographical book, Hurston transforms the folk life of Eatonville into the essential experience of all southern blacks (see Washington, 130). The central male character of this novel, John Pearson, is a metaphor of all black men living in rural Florida in the early decades of the twentieth century. The adopted stepson of Ned Crittendon, John is a mulatto, the product of a union between the owner of a plantation, Massa Alf Pearson, and a slave, Amy. Ned is so jealous of John's light skin, which allowed many plantation blacks to have the privileged position of "house-nigger," that he "binds" John over to a cruel overseer to work his land. Amy, however, intervenes on her son's behalf and arranges for him to become a field hand on the plantation from which she had come.

Ironically, by forcing his stepson to work outdoors, Ned is providing him with the means by which black boys at this time became men in the accepted meaning of the word. In the time that he spends working in the lumber camp, John actually learns to like hard work: "All next day John wielded a broad axe, a maul and pestle with the rest. He found that he liked the rhythmic swing, the chant 'Cuttin' timber!' with the up stroke. Then the sure descent 'Hnh!'" ([1934] 1971, 104). Working in the lumber camp, John develops those physical traits that Hurston found so admirable in men who pitted their strength against the forces of nature: "He could chin the bar more times than anyone there. He soon was the best shot, the fastest runner and in wrestling no man could put his shoulders to the ground.... Coon could muscle out one axe, but John could balance two. He could stand like a cross, immobile for several seconds with an axe muscled out in each hand" (107). Working close to nature transforms John into a man who is proud of his body and who responds to its needs. Physical gratification, then, becomes a driving force in John's life.

Unlike his stepfather Ned, a former slave, John is set loose in a world that denies black men the avenues for the pursuit of manhood which are open to whites. Like many black males at this time, John is a tragic figure in the Greek sense of the term. As Hurston was trying to create a realistic portrait of the black males she was acquainted with in 1930s Florida, she realized that her tragic hero could not be afflicted with the normal tragic flaws of Greek tragedy—pride, arrogance, or excessive jealousy—because society would not permit these qualities to develop. Her personal observations led her to believe that the black man's route to manhood lay in the sexual conquest and exploitation of women (Gayle, 37). John's tragic flaw, therefore, lies not in some quirk of the mind, which was not allowed to develop to its full potential, but in one of the needs of his body, which, by contrast, was overly developed: John is sexually promiscuous.

Set against the primeval backdrop of the Florida frontier, John's outward struggle against the wilderness in his early years parallels his inner struggle with his own personal weakness after he is married. Hurston foreshadows John's later battles with his personal demons in the scene in which he impresses a girl he met in school, Lucy Potts, by killing a huge water moccasin that hides under a log bridge and terrifies everyone who walks by: "The snake went on guard, slowly, insolently. Lucy was terrified. Suddenly, he snatched the log from its place and, leaning far back to give it purchase, he rammed it home upon the big snake and held it there. The snake bit at the log again and again in its agony, but finally the biting and the thrashing ceased" (Jonah, 67). The snake, an "old devil...[that has] been right dere skeerin' de folks since befo' [Lucy] was borned" (67), is an outward manifestation of the evil side of man's nature that has tempted mankind since the Garden of Eden and becomes John's most powerful adversary after he and Lucy are married.

While working in the lumber camp, John confronts another denizen of the Florida swamps. Although "Coon" is actually a man, his brutelike nature allies him with his mammalian namesake. Like the bandit to which the "masked" animal is often compared, Coon steals a piece of John's bread and then taunts John into retrieving his property: "Don't you lak it, don't yuh take it, heah mah collar, come and shake it" (109). The violent streak that many frontiersmen are imbued with emerges in a bloody fight in which John demonstrates Hurston's belief that wild surroundings foster wild men: "John ran in and landed one smack in his enemy's mouth, and while Coon was spitting out his teeth, he ripped a mule-kicking right to the pit of Coon's stomach and the fight was over and done" (109). Invigorated by his defeat of the brutal camp bully, John is recognized by the rest of the camp and by himself as a man who enjoys the sting of battle: "John felt good. His first real fight. Something burned inside him" (109). Once again Hurston is providing the reader with a glimpse of the battler that John is to become years later when he contends with the most formidable opponent of all: himself.

Aside from serving as the catalyst for the development of the physical side of John's being, nature also brings out the poet in him. However, his relationship with nature is closer to that of the preacher in *Mules and Men* than to that of Hurston herself. Like the field hand who turns preacher in the folktale, John receives the call to preach because of nature's harshness. Not long after he marries Lucy, John visits a woman of easy virtue named "Big 'Oman." As he is riding home during a terrible storm, he has to cross a swollen river: "The river was full of water and red as judgment with chewed-up clay land. The horse snorted and went minging down to the bridge. Red water toting logs and talking about trouble, wrestling with timber, pig pens and chicken coops as the wind hauls up feathers, gouging out banks with timber and beating up bridges" (141). The personification Hurston employs in her description of the river appears once again in the prayer of thankfulness that John delivers in church:

> You are de same god, Ah
> Dat heard de sinner man cry
> Same God dat sent de zigzag lightning tuh
> Join de mutterin' thunder
> Same God dat holds de elements
> In uh unbroken chain of controllment. . . .
> We thank Thee that our sleeping couch
> Was not our cooling board,
> Our cover was not our winding sheet.
> Please tuh give us uh restin' place
> Where we can praise Thy name forever. (145)

The imagery contained in the prayer illustrates John's belief that nature has conspired with God to punish him for his sinfulness.

John's war with himself begins immediately after he confesses his adultery to Lucy. In the metaphors that Hurston employs, it becomes clear that John has turned into one of the "beasts" that he had previously contended with in the forest: "Dat's de brute-beast in me, but Ah sho aim tuh live clean from dis on if you 'low me one mo' chance" (144). Because he is a creature of appetite as well as a man of the spirit, John is able to remain faithful only as long as Lucy is able to satisfy him sexually (Gayle, 39). When Lucy becomes pregnant, he has another affair with a woman named Daphne, repents, steals a hog, and flees to Eatonville in a futile attempt to run away from his past and himself.

The beast imagery that John applies to himself continues to reflect his primal drives through the remainder of his marriage to Lucy. When Alf Pearson learns of John's affair with Daphne, he suggests that Lucy "take a green club and frail John good" (Jonah, 146), just as one would do to a disobedient dog or mule. Even though John finds a prestigious job as preacher of a large church, he continues to have affairs. It is his affair with the town vamp, Hattie Tyson, though, that literally kills Lucy, causing her to declare on her deathbed, "Big talk ain't changin' whut you doin'. You can't clean yo' self wid yo' tongue lak uh cat'' (204). One suspects that the parallel that Lucy makes between her husband and an animal notorious for its aggressively sexual nature—the tomcat—is deliberate.

The two impulses within John that have been cultivated through his contacts with nature—the carnal and the spiritual—also produce friction within the community after Lucy dies. With no one around to redirect his energies, the countdown begins for John immediately upon her death. After losing his position in the church as a result of character assassination, he takes up carpentry but discovers that no one will hire him. Shabby and rejected, John has a dream that serves as a sort of epiphany and leads to action. His dream of rescuing Lucy from the snake that hid under the footlog is a subconscious expression of his desire to overcome the snake that he could not kill: the one that nestled in his heart. Finally he leaves town altogether as a broken man, defeated by his sexual license. Clearly society, even on the edge of the frontier, cannot tolerate a person who is truly a natural man, both as a lover and a poet.

John's dilemma is more than an isolated case of a preacher who is condemned by his peers for being a man's man as well as a man of God. In *Jonah's Gourd Vine,* Hurston dramatized a basic tension that has characterized American civilization since at least as early as the mid-eighteenth century. The tension is not that which springs from the conflict of Man with Nature; rather, it is the product of a conflict that has informed and continues to inform American life: the desire to be the unfettered master of one's life as well as a participant in a strong, well-ordered society. As John Pearson discovers, these two states are mutually exclusive.

John is a prime example of Crevecoeur's hunter, who was instrumental in opening up the wilderness to society. In *Letters from an American Farmer,* Crevecoeur recognized that as society developed and the frontier declined, the hunter figure became an irritating anachronism. Once established, society could no longer tolerate the hunter, nor could the hunter put up with the restraints of society: "What are we in the great scale of events, we poor frontier inhabitants? What is it to the gazing world, whether we breathe or whether we die? Whatever virtue, whatever merit and disinterestedness we may exhibit in our secluded retreats, of what avail? We are like the pismires destroyed by the plough, whose destruction prevents not the future crop'' (209). Crevecoeur's fear of being assimilated into society is based on his observation of the futile attempts that were made to civilize the American Indian: "For, take a young lad, give him the best education you possibly can, load him with your bounty, with presents, nay riches ... and on the first opportunity he can possibly find, you will see him voluntarily leave behind him all you have given him, and return with inexpressible joy to lie on the mats of his fathers'' (220). Crevecoeur's sympathies clearly lie with the man of the wilderness, the "noble saveage," whom he believed was a superior being because of his fiercely independent spirit: "They live without care, sleep without inquietude, take life as it comes, bearing all its asperities with unparalleled patience, and die without any kind of apprehension for that they have done, or for what they expect to meet with hereafter" (220).

John Pearson, while not a hunter in the strictest sense of the word, is, like Crevecoeur's hunter, a threat to the stability of civilization. He is continually "on the prowl," looking for more additions to his long list of sexual conquests. In an egalitarian society, a person who takes more liberties than other people is not only a misfit but a bad influence on others, especially if he happens to hold a position that requires him to be a role model, as John does. Before he moves to Eatonville, John also exerts his free will by breaking civil law, an act that turns the black community against him, as Judge Perkins tells Lucy: "Listen, Lucy, this is serious. Your family is well-thought of roundere and lots of folks think John needs a good whipping before he goes to the gang" (*Jonah,* 192). Being a rugged individualist, John also violates the moral codes of the community, a fact that Lucy learns of through the "grapevine": "You either got tuh stop lovin' Hattie Tyson uh you got tuh stop preachin'. Dat's whut de people say" (192). Although gossip is not an official instrument of church and society, it serves the same purpose in that it condemns the actions of an individual who puts himself above moral and civil law. Therefore, when John rails from the pulpit against the innuendo that has found him guilty without trial, his heroic stature is increased all the more. By deploring gossip, he is also rejecting those social forces that promote equality but foster mediocrity: "But some yuh y'all dat got remembrance wid 'im, but some yuh y'all day got remembrance tuh wid sich long tongues dat it kin talk tuh yuh at a distance, when y'all is settin' down and passin' nations thew yo' mouf, look close and see if in all mah doin's if dere wuz anything good mingled uhmoungst de harm Ah done yuh. Ah ain't got no mind. Y'all is de one dat is so much-knowin' dat you kin set in judgment" (197). As Crevecoeur observes, the natural man cannot be true to himself without unintentionally infringing on the rights of others, and therein lies the tragedy of Hurston's novel.

Appropriately enough, John's final confrontation with the forces of conformity occurs in Eatonville, a place where civilization has a much stronger foothold. His larger-than-life status as a preacher is enhanced by the freedoms he enjoys until he assumes, like Crevecoeur's noble savage, almost mythic proportions. Pointing to his seven children during his last sermon at the Eatonville pulpit, he renounces this superhuman role that has been thrust upon him by society: "Ahm uh natchel man but look lak some uh y'all is dumb tuh de fack" (197). Like Crevecoeur's savage, John never really leaves his "wild side" in the wilderness. After Lucy dies, he takes a step that marks him as both a strong-willed individual and as a man who cannot abide by laws that were designed to ensure equal freedom to all by limiting the freedom of the "wild men": John marries a woman whose animal nature is as prominent as his. Scandalized by Hattie Tyson's reputation as a "loose woman" and by John's audacity in choosing her as Lucy's replacement only three months after her death, the deacons marshal their forces against him in an effort to preserve the status quo. The deacons who have been delegated to complain to Pearson about his marriage to the town slut make note of the fact that John and his wife do not live in a way that is socially acceptable, especially in the area of child-raising: "Well, de somebody you got sho ain't seein' after 'em. They's round de streets heah jes' ez raggedy ez jay-birds in whistlin' time. Dey sho ain't gittin' uh damn bit uh 'tention" (217). Deacon Hambo is especially incensed because the parson's wife is a brazen hussy instead of the model of decorum that he expects a preacher's wife to be: "Dat strumpet ain't never done nothin' but run up and down de road from one sawmill camp tuh de other and from de looks of her, times was hard. She ain't never had nothin'— not eben doodly-squat, and when she gits uh chance tuh git holt uh sumpin, de ole buzzard is gone on uh rampage" (217). John's harassment by the pillars of the community continues, even after he is removed from the pulpit years later: "Lucy had counseled well, but there were those who exulted in John's ignominious fall from the Moderatorship after nine years tenure, and milled about him like a wolf pack about a tired old bull—looking for a throathold, but he had still enough of the former John to be formidable as an animal and enough of his Pagan poesy to thrill" (221). By the end of the novel, Hurston makes it clear that the contempt that was shown John Pearson—the sexually potent bull—by the upright members of the community—the ravenous, cowardly wolves—was fueled by a lethal combination of fear and jealousy.

Although Hurston's sympathies certainly lie with Lucy Pearson, whose loyalty, perseverance, and love border on the messianic, her novel is not a total indictment of Lucy's husband. In fact, she seems to have a grudging admiration for a man who will not allow himself to be the paragon of virtue that the community requires him to be. The Christianity that is practiced by this formerly enslaved communal society cannot tolerate a preacher who, ironically, is saintlike in that his Christian will toward agape is constantly being challenged by Eros, the carnal impulse (Neal, 26). Obviously thinking of her own father, a preacher who married a predatory woman after his wife died, Hurston implicitly condemns the community in *Jonah's Gourd Vine* because it cannot tolerate his "natchel" side. Two years after the publication of *Jonah's Gourd Vine,* Hurston explicitly voiced her objection to this narrow-minded way of thinking in a letter that she wrote to Carl Van Vechten: "Just a word about my novel... I have tried to represent a Negro preacher who is neither funny nor an imitation Puritan ram-rod in pants.... I see a preacher as a man outside of his pulpit and so far as I am concerned should be free to follow his bent as other men" (Jones, 29). In the character of John Pearson, Hurston unearthed a tragic element that no previous black writer had found in that most prestigious of black institutions, the preacher.

Like any good writer, Zora Neale Hurston filed everything away for future reference. In *Jonah's Gourd Vine,* the frontier as she imagined it and as she experienced it served as the setting for one man's attempt to come to terms with the nature that dwells on the inside and on the outside of us all. Thus, *Jonah's Gourd Vine* is more than just a regional or an ethnic novel. John Pearson's inability to resolve the conflict that exists between the physical and spiritual forces is also society's and, ultimately, mankind's tragedy as well.

Works Cited

Brawley, Benjamin. "One of the New Realists." In *Zora Neale Hurston,* edited by Harold Bloom, 1–14. New York: Chelsea House, 1986.

Crevecoeur, J. Hector St. John. *Letters from an American Farmer.* Garden City, NY: Dolphin Books, 1971.

Gayle, Addison. "The Outsider." *Zora Neale Hurston,* edited by Harold Bloom, 35–42. New York: Chelsea House, 1986.

Helmick, Evelyn Thomas. "Zora Neale Hurston." *The Carrel* (June-December 1970): 1–19.

Hurston, Zora Neale. *Dust Tracks on a Road.* 1942. Reprint. New York: Arno Press, 1984.

———. *Jonah's Gourd Vine.* 1934. Reprint. Philadelphia: Lippincott, 1971.

———. *Mules and Men.* 1935. Reprinted, with introduction by Robert Hemenway. Bloomington: Indiana University Press, 1978.

Jones, Kirkland C. "Folk Humor as Comic Relief in Hurston's *Jonah's Gourd Vine.*" *Zora Neale Hurston Forum* (Fall 1986): 26–31.

Neal, Larry. "The Spirituality of *Jonah's Gourd Vine.*" In *Zora Neale Hurston,* edited by Harold Bloom, 25–27. New York: Chelsea House, 1986.

Washington, Mary Helen. "A Woman Half in Shadow." In *Zora Neale Hurston,* edited by Harold Bloom, 129–35. New York: Chelsea House, 1986.

CHAPTER EIGHT

Voodoo as Symbol in *Jonah's Gourd Vine*

BARBARA SPEISMAN

In April 1985, Wade Davis, a young ethnobotanist from Harvard University, traveled to Haiti to research voodoo, a word that comes from the Fon language of Dahomey and means simply "god" or "spirit." Davis believed that the rich religion of the Haitian traditional society deserved to be recognized as a religion that had its roots in African heritage. One of the main reasons, as well as an inspiration, for his journey was that he had carefully read Zora Neale Hurston's account of voodoo in her 1938 publication of *Tell My Horse.* Hurston had gone to Haiti because she was no newcomer to the belief that voodoo was definitely a religion and an inherent part of Afro-American folklore. At this time when racism was fashionable, she had boldly written in her essay "The Sanctified Church" that the "Hoodoo doctors of the American South practice a religion every bit as strict and formal as that of the Catholic church" (1983, 83).

Davis's research resulted in his solving the secret of the formation of the poison that produces a zombie, a person who may be considered "the living dead." Hurston, however, had detected the ingredients of this poison years before after she had spent a day with a zombie victim and had observed her and discussed her symptoms with a doctor. Yet at the time, no one would believe her. Finally, in his popular *The Serpent and the Rainbow* (1987), Davis gives Zora Neale Hurston credit for being an extraordinary anthropologist who understood the logic of the voodoo culture not only in Haiti but in her American South (256).

Reared at the turn of the century in a small all-black village in Florida, Hurston sensed at an early age the African roots of her people. She had listened to her father's preaching in the Macedonian Baptist Church in Eatonville and she recognized, in the frenzy of his service and the wailing gospel hymns, the influence of the African voodoo ceremony. In her

essay about the influences of voodoo on Hurston's fiction, Elaine Southerland says: "If one were to branch the religious thing in her fiction,
there would be a new dimension of religious thought where concepts are
made visible through the use of symbols traceable to Voodoo ceremony"
(136). As a child Hurston recognized the powers of voodoo in her own
community; as a young woman she traveled to New Orleans to study it
formally. In *Mules and Men* (1935) and scholarly articles, she publicly
expressed her belief that voodoo is a religious force. I agree with Southerland that close study of much of Hurston's fiction also reveals symbols
and concepts inherent in the voodoo faith. In particular, one finds symbols related to voodoo in her first novel, *Jonah's Gourd Vine* (1934).

Hurston wrote *Jonah's Gourd Vine* in two short months during the
summer of 1933. No novice to creative writing, she had previously written not only prize-winning short stories but also plays. However, this
was her first attempt to write a novel. With only a few dollars to survive
upon, she returned to Sanford, Florida, where she had previously written
Mules and Men, and the one-room shack where she could close the door
and escape into a solitary, creative world. There she recalled her vivid
memories of growing up as the daughter of John Hurston, a Baptist
preacher. All her love and hate for her father consumed her as she
wrestled with her private ghosts of memory. She says in her autobiography, *Dust Tracks on a Road,* that all the Hurston children once admired
their father and called him "Big Nigger" (1942 [1984], 91) because he
wore store-bought shoes and was a figure of respect. It is interesting that
Hurston first considered entitling her novel *Big Nigger.* However, Zora's
mother, Lucy Hurston, died when Zora was still a young girl. Her father
turned immediately to another woman who hated the children (98).
Hurston's affection toward her father gradually turned to dislike. She
never was to have an abiding love affair or marriage; perhaps her disil-
lusionment with her father influenced her relationships with other men..

The one relationship that eventually became a form of personal myth
was her attachment to her mother. All readers who love Hurston's
autobiography and *Jonah's Gourd Vine* feel the presence of small, ener-
getic, intellectual Lucy who fights her husband, as well as her supersti-
tious neighbors, in order that her daughter might get a chance to "jump
at de sun" and be somebody. The conflict between the parents is obvious.
John, who realizes that Lucy is above him, dares to win and marry her
even though he had been born across the creek. Lucy, who even on her
deathbed opposes the primitive beliefs that surround her, begs her daughter not to let them practice their voodoo upon her. Her wish, however,
is not heeded, and John turns the mirror to the wall so that it will not

reflect the face of the dead for eternity. The neighbors move the deathbed to the east, the direction in which the square-toed god of death waits for the dying woman. And all the while the child struggles and screams until she is thrust out of the house and her mother dies in the house of voodoo and superstition (1934, 89).

According to Robert Hemenway in *Zora Neale Hurston: A Literary Biography, Jonah's Gourd Vine* lacks structural and character development, which weakens the novel. Hemenway states that the scene in which John slaps Lucy is not convincing because Hurston has not presented him previously as a man capable of physically abusing his wife (912). On the other hand, we gain a clearer understanding of the underlying structure of the novel if we interpret John's character as that of a minister who has renounced the tenets of Christianity and embraced the concepts and basic symbols of voodoo. Hurston, in a letter to James Weldon Johnson, stated that she wished to create in John a preacher who has not been "tampered with and consequently becomes Presbyterian or Episcopal," but rather one "who has the power to bring barbaric splendor of word and song which relates to the influences of the elements which were brought over from Africa and grafted in to Christianity" (Hemenway, 193). Thus, John may be conceived of as a voodoo doctor who turns away from God and uses voodoo to gain his power over his family and congregation.

That *Jonah's Gourd Vine* is autobiographical has been widely admitted. However, other influences in the novel have not been examined so fully. Hurston, during the summer of 1933, had been working diligently for several years on a book of folklore and voodoo that would later be titled *Mules and Men.*

At the time, however, the manuscript was buried in the vault of Mrs. Mason, the rich patron who had given Hurston the funds to research and write it. Hurston had promised Mrs. Mason that she could decide on the date when the book would be published (Hemenway, 30). However, she had not promised not to take much of the book's subject matter and transform it into a work of fiction.

The folklore of Eatonville and her parents' lives influenced the novel. Also, Hurston had recently studied voodoo with Luke Turner, the nephew of the famous two-headed doctor, Marie Leveau, in order to become a practitioner of the voodoo religion. Turner had made her lie face down and naked in a coffin for three days, "crowned with a consecrated snake skin" (1935 [1978], 208). He told her of the power that the snake has in voodoo; it represents Damballah, or the unknown spirit who creates everything. Moses's rod, in voodoo belief, turned into a snake, which meant that Moses was the greatest hoodoo man of all time.

According to legend, when Moses built the first Hebrew temple in Jerusalem, he planted his staff in the place where the centerpost of a holy voodoo temple still exists. Marie Leveau had been visited by a snake when she was ready to become a two-headed doctor, and "The snake stayed with her always" (290).

Another symbol of voodoo adapted by southern blacks is the drum, for "the drums used for the Voodoo ceremonies have come to symbolize Voodoo itself" (*Sanctified Church*, 103). Early in *Jonah's Gourd Vine* this relationship of the drums to the mysteries of Africa is mentioned:

> So they danced. They called for the instrument that they had brought to America in their skin-the-drum and they played upon it. With their hands they played upon the little dance of drums of Africa. The drums of kid skin. With their feet they stomped it, and the voice of Kata-kumba, the great drum, lifted itself within them and they heard it. The drum with the man-skin that is dressed with human blood, that is beaten with a human shinbone and speaks to gods as a man and to man as a God. (59)

However, the main symbol of voodoo adapted by southern blacks is the power of the preacher himself, who "chanting his barbaric thunder-poem recalls the African past when the priest of Hounigan used Voodoo customs and symbols to inspire his worshippers" ("Sanctified Church," 109). In her original dedication (never published) to *Jonah's Gourd Vine*, Hurston says: "To the first and only real Negro poets in America—the preachers who bring barbaric splendor of word and song into the very camp of the mockers" (Hemenway, 195).

Thus, Hurston's experiences as the daughter of the preacher of the Macedonian Baptist Church in Eatonville, Florida, as well as her more recent experiences studying voodoo in New Orleans, made the three symbols of voodoo, the snake, the drum, and the sermon, foremost in her mind as she conceived and rapidly wrote her first novel.

In *Dust Tracks on a Road* Hurston admits her fascination with snakes. "In contrast to everybody about me, I was not afraid of snakes. They fascinated me in a way which I still cannot explain. I got no pleasure from their death" (38). The snake as a symbol can be related to the title of the novel. *Jonah* is one of the shortest books of the Old Testament and deals with the two times when Jonah's pride makes him deny God. He is punished both times for his transgressions, once by being cast into the flood and swallowed by a giant fish; the other when a worm eats away at the vine that God has created to protect him from being exposed to the sun's hot rays. In many religions the worm is considered a representation of the snake.

In *Jonah's Gourd Vine,* shortly after John Pearson meets Lucy and is taking her home, they encounter a snake that lives in the creek. Lucy tells John to leave the snake alone, but John decides to kill the snake. He says, "Turn me go, Lucy. If you didn't want yo' ole snake kilt yuh oughta not showed 'im tuh me" (67). John snatches up a log and uses it as a weapon to destroy the big snake. "The snake bit at the log again and again in its agony but finally the biting and the thrashing ceased." John has killed the snake. The death of this snake is recalled throughout the novel, and after Lucy dies tragically and John has lost his position as a preacher and is abandoned by all, he has a dream in which he remembers when he destroyed the snake. In the dream, Lucy sits beside a stream and cries because she is afraid of a snake. He kills it and carries her across in his arms. He sees a white shell road; he and Lucy race down it together. However, Lucy suddenly disappears and he is alone but happy because the "Dead snake was behind him" (287).

The train, which appears throughout the novel, provides another symbolic representation of the snake. Immediately after his first meeting with Lucy, John sees a train for the first time. "John stared at the panting monster for a terrified moment, then prepared to bolt ... that great eye beneath the cold-breathing smokestack glared and threatened. The engine's very sides seemed to expand and contract like a fiery monster." He watches the train "until it had lost itself down its shiny road and the noise of its going was dead" (37). Both the death of the snake at the creek and the first appearance of the train seem to be forewarning of the disasters that later occur.

John marries Lucy, and they are happy for a while. However, he becomes infatuated with other women and betrays his wife. Shortly after Lucy has given birth to another of his children, he beats up her brother who has stolen the very bed upon which she lay. John is forced by the law to leave and decides that he will travel to Florida in search of a new home. For the first time he actually gets on a train, which takes him away from Lucy. "He marveled that just anybody could come along and be allowed to get on such a glorified thing. ... The greatest accumulation of power that he had ever seen" (169). The train takes him to Florida and eventually Eatonville, an all-black town. Lucy joins him and he achieves great success through his oratorical talent, which allows him to become the town's preacher.

Happiness once again recedes, however, as he, like Jonah, is cursed by the sin of pride. The women of the congregation fawn over him, and he betrays his wife by falling in love with a woman who practices voodoo and places both him and Lucy under a spell. The spell causes Lucy to sicken and die, but John, still under the spell, curses and strikes her in her last moments. John's pride has caused him to sell his soul to the powers of evil. The death of Lucy, his good angel, results in his final fall from grace. Near the end of the novel, after his dream of the snake, he has a final rendezvous with a woman. Knowing his guilt, he drives away, not seeing an oncoming train. "The ground-mist lifted on a Florida sunrise as John fled. He had prayed for Lucy's return and God had answered. . . . He drove on but half-seeing the railroad. . . . The engine struck the car squarely and hurled it about like a toy. John was thrown out and lay perfectly still" (309). Before writing the novel, Hurston learned that her own father had been killed when his car was struck by a train.

After John's death the minister preaches a "barbaric requiem poem" (311). As drums were played at the beginning of the novel when John was a boy of fifteen, so they are played at the occasion of his funeral. They are the ancient voodoo drums of O-go-doe: "Not the little drum of kid skin, for that is to dance with joy and to call to mind birth and creation, but O-go-doe, the voice of death that promised nothing, that speaks with tears only, and of the past" (311).

Did Hurston conceive of her father not as a man of the Christian faith but as a practitioner of voodoo? It must be remembered that at the turn of the century, Eatonville was completely separated from Orlando, Maitland, and other white communities surrounding it. It was an all-black town still rooted in the days of slavery and African tradition. Its inhabitants remembered a time when communication took place by drums so that white slave owners would be ignorant of the slaves' messages. It was a town in which the preacher had the same power to persuade and influence as the two-headed doctor in Africa. The southern black preacher's gift of words caused his "congregation to be restored to its primitive altars under the new name of Christ." As Hurston states in "The Sanctified Church," "there is a continuation of the African possession by the gods. The gods possess the body of the worshippers" (213). "It must be noted that the sermon in these churches is not the set thing. . . . It is loose and formless and is in reality merely a frame upon which to hang songs. Every opportunity to introduce a new rhythm is eagerly seized upon. The whole move of the Sanctified Church is a rebirth of song-making! It is putting back into Negro religion those elements which were brought over from Africa and drafted into Christianity as soon as the Negro came in contact with it, but which are being rooted out as the Negro approaches white concepts" (104).

Certainly, the climax of the novel is when John preaches his final sermon to his congregation. This sermon was based on one that Hurston heard the Reverend Lovelace present in 1929 in Eau Gallie, Florida. The sermon itself is remarkably similar to James Weldon Johnson's poem "The Creation"; both present a "folksy" God who creates man out of his own likeness.

> He dipped some water out of de might deep
> He got him a handful of dirt
> From de foundation sills of de earth
> He seized a thimble full of breath
> From de drums of de wind, ha!
> God, my master!
> Now I'm ready to make man!   (*Jonah*, 272)

It also is interesting that, as in so many black sermons, the image of God appears driving a train going to hell or paradise.

> I can see him step out upon the rim bones of nothing
> Crying I am de way
> De truth and de light
> I can see Him grab de throttle
> Of de well ordered train of mercy
> I see kingdoms crush and crumble . . .
> He died for our sin.
> Wounded in the house of his friends.
> That's where I got off de damnation train.   (280)

One of John's officers in his church makes the statement that the Bible is "de best conjure book in de world." He compares John to Jonah, for John's pride, like Jonah's, will cause him to be cut down, and states that he would like to "cut down dat Jonah's Gourd vine in uh minute" (156). Eve in the Old Testament listened to the snake and fell from grace. John, like Eve, cursed with the sin of pride, kills the snake and, in turn, is destroyed.

By writing *Jonah's Gourd Vine*, Hurston made a final peace with the memory of her parents and their deaths. Both deaths were tragic, but perhaps by writing the novel she was better able to forgive herself for not answering her dying mother's silent plea to "not let them practice their Voodoo upon her." And perhaps as she imagined her father's death, she could begin to think of him once again as "Big Nigger" and forgive the pain he had caused her. The minister who preaches John's funeral finally says: "He wuz a man and nobody knowed it but God!" (236). Hurston, however, certainly knew more about her father and mother as she wrote those words, and she knew that in the creation of *Jonah's Gourd Vine* much of her pain was ended. The ghosts of memory were exorcised.

Works Cited

Davis, Wade. *The Serpent and the Rainbow.* New York: Warner Books, 1987.

Hemenway, Robert. *Zora Neale Hurston: A Literary Biography.* Urbana: University of Illinois Press, 1978.

Hurston, Zora Neale. *Jonah's Gourd Vine.* Philadelphia: Lippincott, 1934.

———. *Dust Tracks on a Road.* 1942. Reprint. Urbana: University of Illinois Press, 1984.

———. *Mules and Men.* 1935. Reprint. Bloomington: Indiana University Press, 1978.

———. "The Sanctified Church." Berkeley: Turtle Island, 1983.

Southerland, Elaine. "The Influences of Voodoo on the Fiction of Zora Neale Hurston." In *Sturdy Black Bridges,* edited by Roseann P. Bell, Bettye J. Parker, and Beverly Guy-Sheftall. Garden City, NY: Anchor Books, 1979.

CHAPTER NINE

The Shape of Hurston's Fiction

 ROSALIE MURPHY BAUM

> We, the critics of black literary traditions, owe it to those traditions
> to bring to bear upon their readings any "tool" which helps us to
> elucidate, which enables us to see more clearly, the complexities of fig-
> uration peculiar to our literary traditions. —Henry Louis Gates, Jr. (4)

Despite Virginia Woolf's warning to women that the great female writer
must not write as a woman but as a human being and must transcend
the sociopolitical issues of gender, many readers and critics have asked that
black authors write as blacks and address themselves primarily to critical
sociopolitical issues of race. Keith E. Byerman notes that, in a literary
scene that emphasized "revolutionary usefulness as a principal measure of
artistic merit" until the later 1960s, Zora Neale Hurston (with Ralph
Ellison and Jean Toomer) was one of the black "writers sometimes attacked for being insufficiently 'black'" (1). The very act of authorship
itself, and black authorship in particular, was not considered a strong (or
helpful) enough political act.

Only recently have critics begun to recognize the "revolutionary cultural nationalism and feminism" of Hurston (Pullen, 172) and to realize
the degree to which Hurston's work reveals "the multiplicity of life issues
that converge with black American women's historic and coeval experience" and thus shares "a broadly thematic synonymity" (Spillers, 250)
with that of other black women writers from Nella Larsen, Jessie Fauset,
and Ann Petry to Alice Walker, Toni Morrison, and Paule Marshall. As
Barbara Johnson suggests in her recent analysis of *Their Eyes Were Watching God*, "Hurston's work is often called non-political simply because
readers of Afro-American literature tend to look for confrontational *racial*
politics, not sexual politics" (371). Clearly, as Barbara Christian notes,

Hurston anticipated "future black women writers who would attempt to define themselves as persons within a specific culture rather than primarily through their relationships with whites" (60).

The impatience of many of Hurston's fellow artists (both contemporaneous and contemporary) who have sought more explicit sociopolitical treatment of racial issues actually stems largely from what Alice Walker admires most in Hurston's work: "racial health; a sense of black people as complete, complex, *undiminished* human beings, a sense that is lacking in so much black writing and literature" (85). Hurston herself, in the 1930s, realized the anger many blacks would feel against her work in a time of great ideological need, but refused, as she put it in an interview with Nick Aaron Ford, to "lecture on the race problem," to write "a treatise on sociology" rather than art (quoted in Bloom, 8). In *Dust Tracks on a Road* she explains, "Negroes were supposed to write about the Race Problem. I was and am thoroughly sick of the subject. My interest lies in what makes a man or a woman do such-and-so, regardless of his color. It seemed to me that the human beings I met reacted pretty much the same to the same stimuli. Different ideas, yes. Circumstances and conditions having power to influence, yes. Inherent difference, no" ([1942] 1969, 214).

Until recently, the ideological need of both the black and white communities—striving to understand, define, and (re-)form—has overshadowed much of the aesthetic accomplishment of black literature. As Henry Louis Gates, Jr., has observed, "the structure of the black text has been *repressed* and treated as if it were *transparent*" (5). This treatment has been especially true of Hurston's early short fiction, which has been largely ignored. With "storytelling . . . an integral part of life in Hurston's Eatonville" (Howard, 56), "the roosting place of Hurston's imagination" (Bone, 144), there is an apparent, misleading simplicity and naturalness in stories like "Isis" (first published as "Drenched in Light," 1924), "Sweat" (1926), and "The Gilded Six-Bits" (1933), which make them appear techniqueless.

These three stories are clearly in the tradition of the folktale, even though they use little identifiable folklore other than variations of the trickster figure[1] (Isis in "Isis," Sykes in "Sweat," and Slemmons in "The Gilded Six-Bits"), the snake as devil, Joe Clarke as village philosopher, the insult of comparing Sykes to a "suck-egg dog" in "Sweat" ([1926] 1985, 48), and perhaps Isis's singing and dancing in "Isis." But Hurston's stories do represent "the processes of folkloric transmission," primarily by "emphasizing the ways of thinking and speaking which grew from the folk environment" (Hemenway, 242) and by re-creating the folktale's "easy narrative element, its story-telling, yarn-spinning quality" (Cartey, 13).

Unrecognized thus far stylistically is the degree to which the simple, even episodic, plots, relaxed chronological development, and realistic situations and actions remain in the reader's imagination as a series of framed moments, or "condensations of action and vision" (Caws, 3),[2] arrested by reductively portrayed characters who are often silent or operate within limited roles, an omniscient narrative voice, and, especially, symbolic structure.

Hortense J. Spillers comments, in her afterword to Conjuring, that there are two kinds of fiction: popular fiction and the "fiction of the classroom," which teachers privilege "because it supports and reenforces the myth of 'complexity,' the figures of irony, and our virtually religious predisposition to 'ambiguity' as the law of the new world." Fiction written by women, especially black women, she continues, has tended to maintain "as a general rule, not only an allegiance to 'power to the people,' but also 'talking' to 'the people' in the now-familiar accents of representation and mimesis" (259). In characterizing the ethos of this mimesis, Spillers also notes that "the influence of naturalism, or an ideology of the environment, was not pronounced among black American women writers" until Ann Petry's The Street in 1946 (254).

In this chapter, focusing on three of Hurston's apparently simple (and hence neglected) early stories, I will examine a few of the ways in which Hurston tantalizes the reader with a realism highlighted by framed moments but skirts the naturalistic potential of her characters' situations and thereby asserts the possibilities (the meaningfulness) of human life while quietly (and disturbingly) leaving the suspicion that trouble is just around the corner. Certainly, Marjorie Pryse is correct in asserting that "black women novelists challenge the authenticity and accuracy of an American history that failed to record their voices and a literary history . . . that has compounded the error of that neglect" (4), and Spillers rightly describes the black women's writing community as "a matrix of discontinuities" (251) and writers "passing" each other as if they had never heard of each other, much less read each other (252). However, I wish to press further and suggest that Zora Neale Hurston—perhaps challengingly (to blacks and whites, males and females), perhaps ironically or playfully, perhaps unconsciously—most asserts her zest for life, a black life, by creating short stories with all the potential for reducing her characters to mere "ciphers in either a cosmic storm or a chemical process" (Pizer, 1976, 46) while refusing, at least at the time of her early storytelling, to allow the naturalistic strategies she flirts with to render her characters' lives insignificant or contemptible.

In examining the realistic elements of Hurston's stories, I will rely primarily upon Donald Pizer's definition that realistic fiction (broadly speaking) posits a "progressive view of time," a belief that man can "interact meaningfully with his world and . . . benefit from this interaction," that "experience . . . can guide, instruct, or judge human nature." Naturalistic fiction, on the other hand, tends "to reverse or heavily qualify this expectation," questioning if "experience has any meaning aside from the existential value of a collision with phenomena," while often continuing to affirm "the significance and worth of the skeptical or seeking temperament, of the character who continues to look for meaning in experience even though there probably is no meaning" (Pizer, 1982, 9). As Pizer urges, however, the argument will rely less upon an "ideal construct of the naturalistic ethos" (1976, 44), and more upon devices and techniques that Pizer identifies with the naturalistic ethos.

Hurston's early short stories appear to be simple, realistic portrayals of fairly simple situations. In "Isis," an eleven-year-old girl of irrepressible imagination and vitality excitedly pursues the joys of the world around her. In "Sweat," a husband and wife struggle in the last days of their failed marriage. In "The Gilded Six-Bits," a happy marriage is threatened when the wife has an affair in order to obtain some gold money for her husband.

All three stories suggest that the protagonists are capable of highly meaningful actions, partially because of their "perpetual sense of the possibilities of another day." Hurston's art, in the words of Harold Bloom, "exalts an exuberance that is beauty, a difficult beauty because it participates in reality-testing" (3). Equally significant is the fact that this "reality-testing" usually occurs within an "insular folk community," which offers "a world view that can sustain" Hurston's characters and the community itself (Christian, 60). Pursuing survival outside a dominant culture that at worst victimized them and at best condescended to them, blacks developed a complex folkloric system of signs, superstitions, and remedies in which they had more potential (the remedy might not be found in time) control over injustice, evil, dangers, and death than the dominant culture with its educational, legal, and medical systems.[3] In this world of continual possibilities, where man is certainly not "a diminished thing" (Frost, 150), Hurston's work confirms C. W. E. Bigsby's statement that the apparently implacable forces of history that offer "the face of determinism" to the southern white writer stand as a "symbol of myths and realities which are to be acknowledged only as a necessary prelude to transcendence" for the black writer (5).

All three of the stories also offer successful resolution to conflicts which suggest that their characters are significant. "Isis" can be described as a closed story[4] in that the reader, who has delighted in the black child's simple pleasures during the day, catches a last glimpse of Isis as she rides off in a "large, powerful" Packard, one of the "heavenly chariots"([1924] 1985, 17), to spend the evening singing and dancing at the Park Hotel in Maitland for Helen, a white woman. The spirited Isis feels that she is moving from a world in which she has depended largely on daydreams to the reality she has imagined. The story can also be considered closed in the sense that the conflict between Isis, who pursues life's joys, and her grandmother, who tries to curb her granddaughter's impulses, has been resolved by Isis's escape from her grandmother's supervision for at least an evening. Clearly, "the passage of time profits the bold and good hearted" (Pizer, 1976, 44) Isis.

Both "Sweat" and "The Gilded Six-Bits" can be seen as having closed endings, with the conflicts around which the stories are constructed being resolved and the imperfect protagonists having overcome the difficulties of previous days. In fact, the closings are consistent with what Frank Kermode has termed apocalyptic endings, in which truth "imposes causality and concordance, development, character, a past which *matters* and a future within certain broad limits determined by the project of the author rather than that of the characters" (17, italics added).

In "Sweat," Delia's husband, Sykes, increases his mistreatment of her, first by flaunting his affair with the fat Bertha and second by trying to frighten and then kill Delia with a rattlesnake. In the ironic conclusion, Sykes himself is killed by the rattlesnake, while Delia is freed first of the psychological bondage that has caused her to tolerate his abuse and then of the marriage itself. In "The Gilded Six-Bits," Missie May and Joe, their relationship painfully damaged by her infidelity, slowly work to rebuild their marriage. The birth of their son—"de spittin' image" ([1933] 1985, 67) of Joe—and Joe's efforts to sort and control his overwhelming feelings create a new basis for a less innocent but perhaps deeper relationship. In both stories, life has direction—the long-suffering Delia is saved from her husband by his own treachery; the repentant Missie's efforts to save her marriage are successful. In both stories, the worth of the imperfect characters (except for the dead Sykes) is clear. Experience does "guide, instruct . . . judge human nature" (Pizer, 1982, 9).

Supporting the sense that the emotional and spiritual movement of the characters is progressive and that this progression indicates a meaningful interaction between man and his world are the series of frames that structure each story. These frames are defined by Mary Ann Caws as "condensations of action and vision" (3), scenes "heavily bordered" with "their importance . . . heightened" (1), scenes complete within themselves but "conveyors of revelation and insight" (8), scenes clearly metonymic in their significance.

In "Isis," the most obviously framed scene, one architecturally outlined, is that of Isis under the "center table with its red plush cover with little round balls for fringe." Here Isis crawls to lie on her back and imagine herself as "various personages": "She wore trailing robes, golden slippers with blue bottoms. She rode white horses with flaring pink nostrils to the horizon . . . She . . . pictured herself gazing over the edge of the world into the abyss" (12). This scene, one-third of the way into the story, parallels the closing scene, in which Isis is framed in the Packard, "on the rear seat between the sweet-smiling lady and the rather aloof man in gray" (18). In the first, she loses herself in a world of the imagination; in the second, she actually enters a part of the world of her imagination. Isis "had often dreamed of riding in one of these heavenly chariots but never thought she would, actually" (16).

These two framed scenes, in which Isis is physically enclosed but quite free imaginatively, contrast with the second kind of frame Hurston employs in the story, that of Isis on stage.[5] The story is actually a sequence of scenes, with the action of the scenes privileged and the active Isis spotlighted: Isis on the gate post waving at "passing vehicles on their way South to Orlando, or North to Sanford" (9); Isis "snuggled down . . . in the saddle" (10) behind the white cattleman, Jim Robinson; Isis romping with the dogs; Isis giving the dog Jake "a swim in the dishpan" (11); Isis doing "a fair imitation" (14) of a Spanish dance at a barbecue and log-rolling; and Isis splashing and singing with "a tiny 'gator and a huge bullfrog" (16) in the creek. These flashing portraits of Isis *alive*—interrupted only by the longer scenes in which she and her brother Joel plan to shave Grandma—are like animated sequence photographs or frames. Their stylistic effect is both to spotlight Isis and to convey something of the breathless, active quality of her physical life and thus suggest her vitality. With such structuring, the reader accepts quite readily the "sweet-smiling" white lady's identification of Isis with sunshine (18), the many spotlighted frames merging into a single source of light, "Isis the Joyful" (10).

"Sweat" is formed around two kinds of framed espisodes, some occurring eight or more weeks apart, the other forming two doorway scenes at the end of the story. The scene of Delia, the laundry, and the snake appears twice, once at the beginning of the story, once near the end; but it is implied at least eight other times. This scene defines Delia's life: work and mistreatment by the husband she struggles to support. The scene also clearly establishes two of the main symbols of the story, the white folks' laundry, which causes the sweat of the title, and the snake, which personifies Sykes's hatred of Delia, especially since he knows that her fear of snakes is so great that she has "a fit over a earthworm or a string" (39).

The differences between the two dramatized scenes of Delia, the laundry, and the snake—as well as the weekly laundry scenes that are not portrayed—also indicate the eventual progression of Delia's life: from "Sweat, sweat, sweat! Work and sweat, cry and sweat, pray and sweat!" (40) to freedom. In the first scene, Delia takes the white folks' laundry out of the hamper in the bedroom and is sorting it in the kitchen when "something long, round, limp and black . . . falls upon her shoulders" (38). Her husband has used his long bullwhip to frighten her. This scene concludes with Sykes's kicking the sorted clothes "helter-skelter" (40) and the usually meek Delia's standing up to him, apparently for the first time in fifteen years. As the next eight or so weeks pass, the reader is aware that Delia continues to do her weekly laundry, that Sykes wants to displace her in the house with his mistress and has placed a rattlesnake in a box outside the kitchen door to frighten his wife away, that Delia has moved her church membership to Woodbridge so she will no longer have to take the sacrament with Sykes, and that she has told her husband she hates him. Thus, the conflict between the two is clearly escalating to a dangerous level; but Delia is never actually portrayed again doing the white folks' weekly laundry; this lack creates what Caws describes as "a noticeable delay in time . . . [which] serves to stress the episode it precedes or follows, or both" (24).

In the second laundry scene, toward the end of the story, Delia opens the hamper to remove the white folks' laundry and discovers a rattlesnake at the bottom. Thus, although the two points of reference in the scene remain the same, Delia and the laundry, the bullwhip has become a dangerous snake: no longer a snake in a box outside the kitchen door, now a snake in her house, in her hamper. This scene, superimposed on the earlier laundry scene, prepares the reader for the final change in Delia's attitude toward Sykes. Terrified of the snake, Delia flees "to the darkness of the yard, slamming the door after her." First she is a "gibbering wreck" (50); then she experiences "a cold, bloody rage"; and finally she settles into "an awful calm" (51). Thus, the reader is not surprised when Delia, lying in the hay barn, does not warn the approaching Sykes that the snake is now loose in the house. She knows that in this marriage she has "done de bes' . . . [she] could" (51).

The final two scenes of the story are architecturally framed, with Sykes standing outside the kitchen door in the first, Delia in the second. When Sykes hangs outside the door "some minutes" before entering and then stands "some minutes more inside" (51) before walking to the stove, he, of course, assumes that Delia has been bitten and is probably dead. In fact, when he realizes the snake is after him, he mutters, "Ah thought he'd be too sick" (52). The reader has hardly adjusted to the horror of Sykes's expectation and the snake's attack on him before a second doorway scene is superimposed. Now it is Delia, sick with horror, who stands outside the door looking in. There is little morning light, but she is able to see the "despairing" (52) Sykes, creeping "an inch or two toward her—all that he was able . . . his horribly swollen neck and his one open eye shining with hope" (52–53).[6] The man who has loomed above her through the years now crawls toward her, his fallen state emphasized by the frame of the door and Delia's standing figure; the man who has treated her with continuous contempt and cruelty now hopes for help from her. It is too late for Sykes to receive any help: "Orlando with its doctors was too far" (53). But Delia squelches her "surge of pity" (53); hardened and resolved, she flees rather than stoop to the crawling figure to offer him any comfort in his dying moments. Sykes dies, with eyes that cannot "fail to see the wash tubs" outside the door and with eyes that must have seen Delia at the door, "must know by now that she knew" (53). In turning her back on Sykes, Delia denies the folk belief that one must alleviate the suffering of those who die hard or be haunted by the person's spirit and denies the Christian belief in mercy. Metonymically, she stands as she has never stood before.

The two primary framed scenes in "The Gilded Six-Bits" operate in a very different fashion. The single scene in which Joe finds his wife in bed with Slemmons is doubly framed, architecturally by the doorway and perceptually by Joe's gradual, sensual awareness. When Joe makes his surprise visit home and steps over the doorsill of his bedroom, he slowly realizes what is happening and, framed by the doorway, feels "eternity" stand "still" (62). The changes in lighting within the bedroom then shift the focus to Joe's perceptions. At first Joe can see nothing because "The light went out." Then, by the light of the match he strikes, he can see only "the man's legs fighting with his breeches in his frantic desire to get them on." Finally, after he lights the lamp, Joe does not see at all; he hears, hears "his wife sobbing and Slemmons pleading for his life" (62). Such a scene may be a cliché in literature, but not as Hurston portrays it, focused by a man who "stood and felt without thinking and without seeing with his natural eyes . . . [who] kept on feeling so much and not knowing what to do with all his feelings" (63).

The central scene around which the story is structured, a scene that recurs twice, is equally poignant. The first scene of interaction for the protagonists in the story, the scene that defines their marital happiness, is one of "joyful mischief," with Joe throwing silver dollars at the door for

Missie May "to pick up and pile beside her plate at dinner," Missie coming to the door to scold anyone who would "be chunkin' money" at her, and the two entwining in "a furious mass of male and female energy" (55) until Missie has emptied Joe's pockets of the candy kisses, chewing gum, and other sweets he brings her every Saturday. It is the "play-fight" (56) of an innocent young man and innocent young woman who love each other deeply and take great joy in both life and their relationship, which they hope will soon include a child.

After Joe's discovery of Missie's affair, however, their relationship becomes stiff and formal. Joe is "polite, even kind at times, but aloof." There is "no laughter, no banter" (64); there are "no more Saturday romps" (65). Hurston is clearly using "the noticeable delay in time," the emptiness of the protagonists' lives, and the sense of their waiting and healing to prepare for the brilliantly rendered final scene, in which Joe once again throws coins at the door. This time, however, Missie May cannot run to the door; she has just delivered a baby and can now only creep "there as quickly as she could" (68). She cannot now wrestle with the man who has dared to chunk money at her door in that way; she can only promise, "You wait till Ah got mah strength back and Ah'm gointer fix you for dat" (68). The closing scene, similar to yet strikingly different from the earlier one, clearly offers a metonymic indication of the current relationship between the two.[7] There probably can never again be innocent romps. But Missie *can* move from creeping to walking to running; gradually her physical strength will return, as will the strength of their love. Someday there can again be laughter, bantering, and, at least, bittersweet romps.

"The Gilded Six-Bits" offers one additional frame, its remarkable one-sentence opening paragraph: "It was a Negro yard around a Negro house in a Negro settlement that looked to the payroll of the G and G Fertilizer works for its support" (54). Here Hurston plays with the physical borders of a yard, the economic borders of a laborer's payroll, and the conceptual borders of a limited way of life. The passage frames in, but also frames out, frames out a huge amount of human experience. The opening with the neuter (nonhuman) word "it," the generative rhetoric of the predicate nominative, and the repetition of the word "Negro" surely makes a political statement. Lest, however, a reader attempt to cry "naturalism," the life of man circumscribed, Hurston opens the second paragraphs with a clear objection: "But there was something happy about the place" (54). The description of yard and house that follows attests to order, beauty, and care by both husband and wife. Thus, the opening frame of "The Gilded Six-Bits" complements the framed "joyful mischief" of this young couple, emphasizing the richness of their lives before Missie May's fall.

The heightened perception and focus of Hurston's framed passages in these stories is made possible not simply by the "internal organization" (Genette, 255) of her stories but also by the almost minimalist portrayal of her characters and the nature of the undramatized narrator.[8] Hurston's scenes in these stories lack depth; they are not pictorial. Rather, they focus on flattened characters, characters presented, in the terms of photography, as high-contrast images or line images. Such presentation does not necessarily mean that Isis, Delia, Sykes, Missie May, and Joe are not potentially round characters. (A few brief flashbacks and the conversation of the village men in "Sweat," for example, indicate Delia's potential as a round character.) The stories simply focus on one significant day or period in the characters' lives and let almost silhouetted (focused) characters pulsate with the human emotions and capacities most engaged by the particular situation in which the reader finds them.

The role of the undramatized narrator, who is clearly sympathetic to all of the characters except Sykes, contributes to the focused effect of the stories. The narrator's voice blends with the characters' comments in "Isis," supplements the characters' statements in "Sweat," and interprets for the largely inarticulate Joe and Missie May in "The Gilded Six-Bits." Thus, both standard usage and black dialect merge for one impression, with, appropriately, the striking images, the world of metaphor, more characteristic of the black dialect.

In addition, the undramatized narrator represents the outside world in each story, thereby offering a different perspective that either validates the actions of the characters or ironically (politically?) comments on those actions. For example, in "Sweat," the conversation of the village men and their refusal to share their watermelon with Sykes clearly indicate their judgment of the relationship between Sykes and Delia. The frequent emphasis that the laundry Delia does belongs to the "white folks" could create some ambiguity in the reader's mind toward Sykes's attitude (not toward his cruel behavior). But the narrator also tells us that the village men clearly state that Delia does the work because her husband does not work and that for fifteen years he has beaten Delia " 'nough tuh kill three women" (43). These men also philosophize about the kind of man who treats his wife "lak de do a joint uh sugar-cane. It's round, juicy an' sweet when dey gits it. But dey squeeze an' grind, squeeze an' grind an' wring tell dey wring every drop uh pleasure dat's in 'em out. When dey's satisfied dat dey is wrung dry, dey treats 'em jes' lak dey do a cane-chew. Dey throws 'em away" (43–44). In "Isis," the narrator places the young girl's joy in the context of the more usual world, of her grandmother, who is protective of Isis and concerned about proper behavior, and of the sophisticated, jaded world of the "sweet-smiling" (18) but despondent

Helen and "indifferent" (17), "aloof" white men with "short, harsh" (18) laughs. And in "The Gilded Six-Bits," the narrator makes a very strong political statement when he recounts the comment of the unthinking and unknowing clerk in the candy store about the anguished Joe: "Wisht I could be like these darkies. Laughin' all the time. Nothin' worries 'em" (68).

The final technique that contributes to the framed moments of Hurston's stories—symbolic structure—also clarifies her relationship to realistic and naturalistic art. For example, one of the familiar strategies of the naturalist is the creation of a "paradise," the dazzling world of the "others," that is, the trains and ships of Gabrielle Roy, the hotels and big cities of Theodore Dreiser. It is these "far horizons dormant in the depths of every man's being" (Roy, 250) that prevent the visual or conceptual delimiting of the protagonists' lives but that also, of course, heighten their dissatisfaction with the narrow confines of their own existence. For Hurston's adults, however, except for Sykes, the dazzling world of the "others" is rejected—after much pain—for the richness and comfort of home in the insular black community.

In "Sweat," any dreams that Delia may ever have had of a happy marriage are "debris" (41); and part of her grief has been caused by the "ovahbearin" Sykes's attraction to "far horizons": the many trips he took to Orlando to spend all his wages; his arrogance after learning to drive from "dat white 'oman from up north" (44). Delia's happiness now centers upon her church (the sacrament, the "love feast") and "her little home. She had built it for her old days, and planted one by one the trees and flowers there. . . . It was lovely to her, lovely" (41). In "The Gilded Six-Bits," the only taste of the "far horizons" that Joe and especially Missie May experience leads to Missie's affair and the couple's unhappiness. Missie—happy in the "Negro yard around a Negro house in a Negro settlement" (54)—nevertheless goes to bed with "Mister Otis D. Slemmons, of spots and places—Memphis, Chicago, Jacksonsville, Philadelphia and so on" (58) (that is, "far horizons") only because she hopes to obtain some of Slemmons's gold money for her husband, who, despite his satisfaction with his own life, does express some envy of Slemmons.[9] Hurston's statement about that gold and "far horizons" recalls Stephen Crane's "A man saw a ball of gold in the sky" (1976, 37). Missie May discovers that Slemmons's gold dollar is in fact "no gold piece" but "a gilded half-dollar" (65). She and Joe realize that Slemmons has no riches; they do.

Only "Isis"—the story of an eleven-year-old, still then largely unformed—offers a good example of the outward look's being sustained and remaining hopeful and thus comes closest to a naturalistic perspective. Isis shrugs off raking the yard and washing the dishes, the realities of her day-by-day life. Her eyes are fixed "yearningly" on "the gleaming shell road that leads to Orlando" (9); and at the end of the story she is on her way to Maitland, at least for the evening. In addition, Isis's imaginative life does suggest—again, at least in childhood—a strong yearning for romance, glitter, excitement, plentitude. Her view is certainly that of the Carries (*Sister Carrie*) and Robertas (*An American Tragedy*) of the world.

A second familiar naturalistic strategy is the creation of "a pervasive and striking symbol which, in a sense, accompanies the protagonist on his adventures" (Pizer, 1976, 44). Laundry and the wash tubs clearly accompany Delia; the snake, Sykes; the marital games, and then gold, Missie May and Joe; their lovely homes, both Delia and Missie May and Joe. No symbol accompanies Isis, but perhaps that is because Isis herself (the fertility goddess) has symbolic power in the story. Always in motion, always joyful, she becomes a symbol of life, of vitality, of sunshine, not only for the white woman who craves "a little light today . . . a little of her sunshine to soak into my soul" (18) but also for the reader.

Pizer argues that in a naturalistic work, such symbols often function ironically "in that they structure and inform our sense not only that human beings are flawed and ineffectual but also that experience itself does not guide, instruct, or judge human nature." This occurs because the characters remain "motionless in time": "they have moved through experience but still only dimly comprehend it and themselves, and thus their journeys through time are essentially circular journeys which return them to where they began" (1976, 45). However, only in the case of Sykes can Hurston's symbols be said to be ironic in this way. Sykes is both flawed and ineffectual; he does not learn from experience, not from Delia's goodness for fifteen years or her anger for several months or from the reactions of the black community. He progresses from frightening his wife with a whip to frightening her with a caged snake and finally attempting to kill her with the snake. Thus, if the snake is viewed as evil or the devil (a usual folkloric identification), Sykes immerses himself so much in evil that it, ironically, destroys him rather than his wife. But Delia learns and changes; her life will be different in the future. Missie May and Joe learn and change; their happiness may have a bittersweet edge in the future, but it will be less innocent and thus safer. Isis, being only eleven, of course, remains an unknown.

This reading offers a clear picture of Hurston's undramatized narrators' creation of an affective, moral, intellectual, and ideological (Genette, 255–56) whole that posits a "progressive view of time" and a belief that man can "interact meaningfully with his world and . . . benefit from this interaction" (Pizer, 1982, 9). Despite this clear evidence of a realistic outlook, however, there is no question that Hurston is flirting with naturalistic tendencies at the same time that she is, ultimately, rejecting them. The sun of "The Gilded Six-Bits"—that *"impersonal* old man that beams as brightly on death as on birth" (64, italics added)[10]—makes that very clear. The oppressive world of the white man exists in these stories—in Delia's white folks' laundry, in Sykes's white woman from the north who teaches him to drive, in "de white womens in Chicago" (59) that Slemmons says gave him his gold, in the white clerk at the candy store who knows that "darkies" (68) laugh all the time and have no worries, in the grandmother's "Oh, yessum, yessum" (18) to Helen as she lets Isis go to Maitland, and in the men and women in the Packard who take Isis off to her imaginary world. That world exists, but it is not decisive in these early stories of Hurston. The world of the American Dream—with its signs of plentitude—surrounds these blacks in their modest homes. But that world also is not decisive.

The naturalistic tendencies exist even more strongly if we open up the endings of each of the stories. What is going to happen to Isis? Is she going to enjoy pleasures in the white world of Maitland that will feed her imaginative tendencies and make her more dissatisfied with her life, with her own family? Is she ultimately going to leap over the gate post and join the ranks of girls who are ruined in the city? How significant is Isis's imaginative gaze "over the edge of the world into the abyss" (12) just before her grandmother's spool of cotton falls? What is going to happen to Delia? Is she going to be haunted by Sykes? Is she, an unusually good woman, going to be tortured by the fact that she did not warn him and that she did not comfort him? Has Delia (Delilah) emasculated her Samson by taking in white folks' laundry, even by threatening to go "tuh de white folks 'bout *you*, may young man, de very nex' time you lay you' han's on me" (49)? If the snake is seen as a phallic symbol, an indication of Delia's impotence, will her neurotic behavior take other forms? What is going to happen to Missie May and Joe? Is the baby clearly Joe's? (How can anyone say that a newborn is the spitting image of anyone?) Will the child be a continual reminder of Missie May's affair with Slemmons? Missie May has succumbed to worldly temptation once. Will she succumb again? Her "ma used tuh fan her foot 'round right smart" (67). Can Missie May escape that environmental influence? Is her name actually a declaration that Missie (noun) may (verb)?

These early stories by Hurston are clearly assertions of meaning in a world that carries the threat of nonmeaning—Hurston's careful inclusion of such threats, explicit and implicit, makes that clear—*and*, perhaps even more significantly, of meaning in a literary world that has largely adopted the naturalistic view that man is fatally circumscribed and knowledge is elusive. A real tension exists between the capacity of the characters in her insular black community to live a good (if flawed) and meaningful life and the "outside world" of the dominant culture, which tends to question such a possibility. Educated readers, black and white, coming from this "outside world" may impose their expectations of chaos and unfulfillment on these early stories and read them as naturalistic works or dismiss them as naive, sentimental, simplistic. Hurston's assertion, however, is of a promising world outside the dominant culture, a world created by human beings as a stay against confusion, as a potent denial of sacrifice and suffering. This world's existence is a tribute to the human being, however flawed he or she may be.

Notes

1. Including the trickster as the vanquished stronger figure.
2. The discussion of framing in the stories is based largely on Mary Ann Caws's study *Reading Frames in Modern Fiction*.
3. Keith E. Byerman argues that folklore is "the antithesis of closed, oppressive systems. Closed systems . . . seek to suppress individuality, community, imagination, voice, freedom, or even life itself by imposing a homogeneous order on a heterogeneous reality" (3).
4. David H. Richter explains that "some of the works most commonly termed open-ended . . . seem complete to me, not only in the trivial sense of having a final page with 'The End' obligingly inscribed upon it, but in the sense of recounting a completed process of change, either in external circumstances or in internal consciousness, taking place in the protagonists." His study of closure, *Fable's End*, is concerned with novels in which closure is based less on plot than on "doctrines, themes, attitudes, or theses" (vii).
5. The grandmother's scolding in "Isis" is a form of verbal repetition that can be considered a form of framing. See Caws, 25.
6. Sykes crawls because he has been bitten by the snake—which he had intended to kill Delia—and is dying. Shortly before, Delia had crawled over to the four-o'clocks "and stretched herself on the cool earth to recover" (52) from hearing and seeing Sykes killing the snake with a window stick after the snake has bitten him. Part of her horror is no doubt a sense of complicity because she did not let her husband know that the snake was loose in the house.
7. For an extended study of this concept, see Barbara Johnson's "Metaphor, Metonymy, and Voice in Zora Neale Hurston's *Their Eyes Were Watching God.*"
8. See Karla F. C. Holloway's *The Character of the Word* for a study of the narrator's role in Hurston.
9. Joe says "wistfully" that he wishes he had a build like Slemmons, a build that comes with being rich. He tells Missie May that he knows he "can't hold no light to Otis D. Slemmons. Ah ain't never been nowhere and Ah ain't got nothin' but you" (58).
10. This passage recalls the "high cold star" in Stephen Crane's "The Open Boat" (1960, 300).

Works Cited

Bigsby, C. W. E. *The Second Black Renaissance*. Westport, CT: Greenwood Press, 1980.

Bloom, Harold. Introduction. In *Zora Neale Hurston*, edited by Harold Bloom, 1–4. New York: Chelsea House, 1986.

Bone, Robert. *Down Home: A History of Afro-American Short Fiction from Its Beginnings to the End of the Harlem Renaissance*. New York: G. P. Putnam's Sons, 1975.

Byerman, Keith E. *Fingering the Jagged Grain: Tradition and Form in Recent Black Fiction*. Athens: University of Georgia Press, 1985.

Cartey, Wilfred G. O. "Africa of My Grandmother's Singing: Curving Rhythms." In *Black African Voices*, edited by James E. Miller et al., 9–19. Glenview, IL: Scott Foresman, 1970.

Caws, Mary Ann. *Reading Frames in Modern Fiction*. Princeton, NJ: Princeton University Press, 1985.

Christian, Barbara. *Black Women Novelists*. Westport, CT: Greenwood Press, 1980.

Crane, Stephen. "The Open Boat." In *The Red Badge of Courage and Other Writings*, edited by Richard Chase, 290–313. New York: Houghton Mifflin, 1960.

———."A man saw a ball of gold in the sky." In *The Poems of Stephen Crane*, 37. New York: Cooper Square Publishers, 1976.

Frost, Robert. "The Oven Bird." *Complete Poems*, 150. New York: Holt, Rinehart and Winston, 1964.

Gates, Henry Louis, Jr. *Black Literature and Literary Theory*. New York: Methuen, 1984.

Genette, Gerard. *Narrative Discourse: An Essay in Method*. Translated by Jane E. Lewin. Ithaca, NY: Cornell University Press, 1980.

Hemenway, Robert E. *Zora Neale Hurston: A Literary Biography*. Urbana: University of Illinois Press, 1977.

Holloway, Karla F. C. *The Character of the Word: The Texts of Zora Neale Hurston*. Westport, CT: Greenwood Press, 1987.

Howard, Lillie P. *Zora Neale Hurston*. Boston: G. K. Hall, 1980.

Hurston, Zora Neale. *Dust Tracks on a Road*. Philadelphia: Lippincott, 1942. Reprint. New York: Arno Press, 1969.

———. "The Gilded Six-Bits" (1933). Reprinted in *Spunk*. Berkeley, CA: Turtle Island Foundation, 1985.

———. "Isis" (1924). Reprinted in *Spunk*. Berkeley, CA: Turtle Island Foundation, 1985.

———. "Sweat" (1926). Reprinted in *Spunk*. Berkeley, CA: Turtle Island Foundation, 1985.

Johnson, Barbara. "Metaphor, Metonymy, and Vocie in Zora Neale Hurston's *Their Eyes Were Watching God*." In *American Fiction 1914 to 1945*, edited by Harold Bloom, 361–74. New York: Chelsea House, 1986.

Kermode, Frank. *The Sense of an Ending: Studies in the Theory of Fiction*. New York: Oxford University Press, 1967.

Pizer, Donald. "Nineteenth-Century American Naturalism: An Approach Through Form." *Forum* 13 (1976):43–46.

———. *Twentieth-Century American Literary Naturalism: An Interpretation*. Carbondale: Southern Illinois University Press, 1982.

Pryse, Marjorie. "Introduction: Zora Neale Hurston, Alice Walker, and the 'Ancient Power' of Black Women." In *Conjuring: Black Women, Fiction, and Literary Tradition*, 1–24. Bloomington: Indiana University Press, 1985.

Pullen, Faith. "Landscapes of Reality: The Fiction of Contemporary Afro-American Women." In *Black Fiction*, edited by A. Robert Lee, 173–203. New York: Barnes and Noble, 1980.

Richter, David H. *Fable's End*. Chicago: University of Chicago Press, 1974.

Roy, Gabrielle. *The Tin Flute*. Translated by Alan Brown. Toronto: McClelland and Stewart, 1980.

Spillers, Hortense J. "Afterword: Cross-Currents, Discontinuities: Black Women's Fiction." In *Conjuring: Black Women, Fiction, and Liteary Tradition*, 249–61. Bloomington: Indiana University Press, 1985.

Walker, Alice. "Zora Neale Hurston: A Cautionary Tale and a Partisan View." In *In Search of Our Mothers' Gardens*, 83–92. New York: Harcourt Brace Jovanovich, 1983.

CHAPTER TEN

The Artist in the Kitchen: The Economics of Creativity in Hurston's "Sweat"

 KATHRYN LEE SEIDEL

Zora Neal Hurston's short story "Sweat" (1926) presents a radical transformation of an oppressed black domestic worker who attempts to envision her work as a work of art. The story is remarkable in Hurston's body of work for its harsh, unrelenting indictment of the economic and personal degradation of marriage in a racist and sexist society.

To accomplish this, "Sweat" functions at one level as a documentary of the economic situation of Eatonville in the early decades of the twentieth century. Hurston uses a naturalistic narrator to comment on the roles of Delia and Sykes Jones as workers as well as marriage partners, but ultimately the story veers away from naturalistic fiction and becomes a modernist rumination on Delia as an artist figure. The story's coherence of theme and structure makes it one of Hurston's most powerful pieces of fiction.

Preserved not only as a place but as an idea of a place, Eatonville, Florida, retains the atmosphere of which Hurston wrote. As putatively the oldest town in the United States incorporated by blacks, Eatonville possesses understandable pride in its unique history. When Hurston writes of Eatonville in "How It Feels To Be Colored Me," she implies that her childhood place was idyllic because "it is exclusively a colored town" ([1928] 1979, 152), one in which the young Zora was happily unaware of the restrictions that race conferred elsewhere. However, this gloss of nostalgia can be read simultaneously with "Sweat," published only two years earlier. Although Hurston's biographer, Robert Hemenway, writes perceptively that "Sweat" is a personal story without identifiable local folklore (73), in the story Hurston reveals the somber and multifaced variations of life in Eatonville in the first part of this century.

Economically Eatonville in "Sweat" exists as a twin, a double with its neighbor, the town of Winter Park. Far from being identical, the twin towns are configured like Siamese twins, joined as they are by economic necessity. Winter Park is an all-white, wealthy town that caters to rich northerners from New England who journey south each fall to "winter" in Florida—"snowbirds," as the natives call them. Winter Park then as now boasts brick streets, huge oaks, landscaped lakes, and large, spacious houses. To clean these houses, tend these gardens, cook the meals, and watch the children of Winter Park, residents of Eatonville made a daily exodus across the railroad tracks on which Amtrak now runs to work as domestics. This pattern has been described in detail by sociologist John Dollard whose study *Caste and Class in a Southern Town* (1937) remains the classic contemporaneous account of a small segregated town in the 1920s and 1930s, approximately the time in which the action of "Sweat" occurs. What is unique about Eatonville and Winter Park is that they are not one town divided in two but two towns. Eatonville's self-governance, its pride in its historic traditions, and its social mores were thus able to develop far more autonomously than those in the many towns of which Dollard wrote where the black community had to struggle to develop a sense of independent identity.

In "Sweat" we see the results of this economic situation. On Saturdays the men of the town congregate on the porch of the general store chewing sugarcane and discussing the lamentable marriage of Delia and Sykes Jones. Although these men may be employed during the week, Sykes is not. Some working people mentioned besides Joe Clarke, the store owner, are the woman who runs a rooming house where Bertha, Sykes's mistress, stays, the minister of the church Delia attends, and the people who organize dances that Sykes frequents. Work as farm laborers on land owned by whites is probably available, but it pays very little and is seasonal. Jacqueline Jones points out that in 1900, not long before the time of the story, 50 to 70 percent of adult black women were employed full time as compared to only 20 percent of men (113). A black man might be unemployed 50 percent of the time (124). One reason that unemployed men congregated at the local general store was not merely out of idleness, as whites alleged, nor out of a desire to create oral narratives, as we Hurston critics would like to imagine, but there they could be "visible to potential employers," as Jones asserts (125).

There is not enough work for the men as it is, but the townspeople discuss Sykes's particular aversion to what work is available. Old man Anderson reports that Sykes was always "ovahbearin' . . . but since dat white w'eman from up north done teached 'im how to run a automobile, he done got too biggety to live-an' we oughter kill 'im" ("Sweat," [1926] 1979, 201). The identity of this woman and her exact role in Sykes's life is not referred to again, but if she was a Winter Park woman, then perhaps Sykes worked for a time as a driver for residents there. All the more ironic, then, his comment to Delia in which he berates her for doing white people's laundry: "ah done tole you time and again to keep them white folks' clothes outa this house" (198). The comment suggests that Sykes does not work out of protest against the economic system of Eatonville in which blacks are dependent on whites for their livelihood. Has he chosen to be unemployed to resist the system? Within the story, this reading is fragile at best. The townspeople point out that Sykes has used and abused Delia; he has "squeezed" her dry, like a piece of sugarcane. They report that she was in her youth a pert, lively, and pretty girl, but that marriage to a man like Sykes has worn her out.

In fact, Delia's work is their only source of income. In the early days of their marriage Sykes was employed, but he "took his wages to Orlando," the large city about ten miles from Eatonville, where he spent every penny. At some point Sykes stopped working and began to rely entirely on Delia for income. As she says, "Mah tub full of suds is filled yo belly with vittles more times than yo hands is filled it. Mah sweat is done paid for this house" (198). Delia's sense of ownership is that of the traditional work ethic; if one works hard, one can buy a house and support a family. That Delia is the breadwinner, however, is a role reversal but not ostensibly a liberation; her sweat has brought her some meager material rewards but has enraged her husband. Although she may at one time have considered stopping work so that Sykes might be impelled to "feel like man again" and become a worker once more, at the time of the story that possibility is long past. Sykes wants her to stop working so she can be dainty, not sweaty, fat, not thin. Moreover, he wants to oust her from the house so that he and his girlfriend can live there. Robert Hemenway perceptively notes that Sykes's exaggerated reliance on phallic objects—bullwhips and snakes in particular—is an overcompensation for his "emasculated" condition as a dependent of his wife (71). Sykes's brutality is a chosen compensation because he does not participate in the work of the community. He chooses instead to become the town's womanizer and bully who spends his earnings when he has them; he lives for the moment and for himself.

Houston A. Baker's ideological analysis of *Their Eyes Were Watching God* emphasizes what he calls the "economics of slavery" in Hurston's works (57). This term refers to the historical use of human beings for profit, a potent theme he identifies in African-American authors from Linda Brent and Frederick Douglass to Hurston. In this context, one can point out that Delia's work, difficult as it is, is productive; it allows her to sustain herself (and Sykes) and to become a landowner, a rare situation for blacks, as John Dollard points out. With her house she possesses not only a piece of property, but she also gains the right to declare herself as a person, not a piece of property. Because Sykes has not shared in the labor that results in the purchase of this property, he remains in a dependent state. He is rebellious against Delia whom he feels controls him by denying him the house he feels ought to be his; his only reason for this assertion is that he is a man and Delia is his wife.

Thus, the economics of slavery in "Sweat" becomes a meditation on marriage as an institution that perpetuates the possession of women for profit. Indeed, Sykes is the slaveholder here; he does not work, he is sustained by the harsh physical labor of a black woman, he relies on the work of another person to obtain his own pleasure (in this case buying presents for his mistress Bertha). He regards Delia's property and her body as his possessions to be disposed of as he pleases. Sykes's brutal beatings of Delia and his insulting remarks about her appearance are the tools with which he perpetuates her subordination to him for the sixteen years of their marriage.

Sykes has been transformed during his marriage, or perhaps because of it, from contributor to the family economy to the chief recipient of its benefits. Delia is a producer of goods (she grows food) and a provider of services (cooks, cleans); she also works at a service activity that brings in cash. Sykes responds by becoming a consumer. He uses her to buy the goods and services he desires (Bertha's favors, liquor, dances, etc.) rather than using this income to contribute to the family. Because he is a consumer only, he cannot become an owner of real estate, for he has a cash-flow problem. As a result, to use Walter Benn Michaels's terminology, Sykes determines to possess the owner, to regard her body and her property as his possessions (56–57). Like the Simon Legrees of abolitionist fiction, Sykes proves his ownership by the brutality he shows toward Delia. His hatred of her rests not on a feeling of inferiority because she owns the house; rather, he hates her because as one of his consumable goods, she ought to be desirable, not sweaty; compliant, not resisting. He prefers Bertha because her fatness suggests an overly fed commodity; like a cow, she has been opulently and extravagantly fed beyond her needs. Sykes desires the large and the luxurious commodity; he does not want what he needs.

Given this hopeless set of economic forces, the story does not sink into a trough of despair, largely because of Hurston's choice of its narrative point of view. While generally Hurston is associated with the lyrical, oral structure of *Their Eyes Were Watching God* (1937), the narrative strategy of "Sweat" is a sophisticated amalgam of the naturalistic narrator and narrative voice that Henry Louis Gates identifies in *Their Eyes Were Watching God* as that of "speakerly text." Gates defines such a text as incorporating oral tradition, indirect discourse, and a transcendent, lyrical voice that is "primarily ... oriented toward imitating one of the numerous forms of oral narration to be found in classical Afro-American vernacular literature" (181). Gates points out further that in oral tradition the speaker tells the story to a listener who is part of the teller's group; thus, in *Their Eyes Were Watching God*, Janie tells her tale to her friend, Phoeby, with the result that the first-person narrative is subtly shaped by the implied and the explicit dialogue. This type of novel is sharply defined in Alice Walker's *The Color Purple* (1982), in which the epistolary frame embodies the dialogic, oral tradition to which Gates refers. Gates contrasts this narrative mode with that of Richard Wright's *Native Son* (1940). In that work the third-person narrator is a removed authoritative, third commentator who possesses the knowledge of the larger context but does not permit characters to develop self-knowledge. Hurston's speakerly text exists to permit the main character, Janie, to search for self-knowledge, indeed for self, in a way that focuses on central themes but does not rely on the architectural plot scaffolding that characterizes Wright's fiction.

It is important to recognize that the narrative mode of "Sweat" is more similar to that of *Native Son* than *Their Eyes Were Watching God*. In "Sweat" the third-person narrator speaks in past tense about the events in the lives of Delia and Sykes. The narrator's voice is one of an educated observer who has complete knowledge of the sociology of the town of Eatonville, its place as a poor, all-black town in central Florida, and the litany of troubles in Delia's fifteen-year-long marriage. This narrator is, in short, the narrator of naturalism, who sees Delia's life as a short, brutish thing because of the nature of marriage within an economic miasma of poverty and powerlessness. At first glance, the story conforms to Donald Pizer's definition of naturalistic fiction as that which "unites detailed documentation of the more sensationalistic aspects of experience with heavily ideological [often allegorical] themes, the burden of these themes being the demonstration that man is circumscribed" (xi). Not only has Delia's life been a stream of "her tears, her sweat, her blood" ("Sweat," 199), as the narrator despairingly reports, but her marriage to a womanizer and wife-beater becomes worse when he also adds attempted murder to the list of forces that literally threaten her. This narrative mode allows Hurston a wider context for Delia's misery, the context of the economics of a central Florida community composed of black women who work as domestics in elite, white Winter Park. Hurston's narrator is especially effective when speaking of the setting itself, the long, hot central Florida August that both parallels and contributes to the climax of the story. The narrator gives shape to the natural cycles that influence Delia and Sykes, as in this passage that forms a transition to the story's climax: "The heat streamed down like a million hot arrows . . . grass withered, leaves browned, snakes went blind . . . and man and dogs went mad" (202). But the perils of choosing an omniscient naturalistic narrator sometimes results in heavy-handed didacticism: "Delia's workworn knees crawled over the earth in Gethsemane and up the rocks of Calvary many, many times" (202).

Because Hurston's narrator in "Sweat" has many features of the naturalistic narrator, the question arises as to whether this story itself is naturalistic. Donald Pizer points out that the 1930s was a time when naturalistic fiction such as *The Grapes of Wrath* offered at least partial solutions to the problems besetting the protagonist. One of the remarkable aspects of "Sweat" is Hurston's variation and escape from the naturalistic narrator. In the classic rhetoric of naturalism, characters are often curiously untouched by self-insight, as Pizer points out (6–7). In Theodore Dreiser's *Sister Carrie* (1900), for example, Carrie's victimization is unchallenged by anything more than a vague film of discontent that she feels now and then. Delia does fall from a state of relative success only to become brutalized, but she then begins the treacherous journey to self-knowledge and then self-esteem, the very journey that Janie makes in *Their Eyes Were Watching God*. Delia's marriage is far worse than any of Janie's; her economic situation is more impoverished. She does not have a friend like Phoeby or a grandmother to provide support, information, sympathy, and love. Yet Delia does change and grow in spite of her circumstances and her narrator. How does Delia (and Hurston) escape the narrator?

Hurston moves beyond the naturalistic narrator by employing a Henry Louis Gatesian dual focus; she uses the townspeople as a chorus who comment orally on the characters of Delia and Sykes. From them we learn of Delia's former beauty, of Sykes's early infatuation with her, of his difficult and brutal personality. We also learn that the town does not condone this behavior at all, but considers it an anomoly at best that their town should have produced a Sykes. Hurston sets up a dialogue between the narrator and the townspeople, the result of which is a double focus upon central characters. Unlike a Greek chorus, the townspeople are not omniscient; they are, on the contrary, interested in maintaining peace and harmony. They praise Delia's work, regarding her weekly delivery schedule with respect: "hot or col', rain or shine, jes ez reg'lar ez de weeks roll roun' Delia carries em an' fetches 'em on Sat'day" (199). Delia's work has become a predictable ritual for the town. Their reaction clarifies the attitude toward work: Work is admirable; the fact that Delia works on a Saturday and is as predictable as the seasons establishes her as worthy of their respect.

It is her work and her own attitude toward it that ultimately allow

Delia to become a person who possesses self-esteem, pride, and the ability to create an ordered and harmonious existence. Delia has created her small world; she has lovingly planted trees and flowers in the garden around her house; her home and garden are "lovely, lovely" to her, as the narrator explains. For all her woes, Delia takes joy in her tidy house, her garden, and her work. These images establish the archetypal undertone of the story, that of the Edenic place. Hurston presents Delia's portion of Eden/ Eatonville as a female-created place, ordered and beautiful because of the efforts of a woman.

Among Delia's efforts, and the central focus of the story, is her work. Although the stereotype of the mammy is all too pervasive as a symbol of black women's work, Jacqueline Jones points out that the most frequent job for black women in the early twentieth century was not as a full-time domestic in the household of whites. For over 50 percent of working black women, "washing and ironing clothes provided an opportunity to work without the interference of whites, and with the help of their own children, at home" (125). Mothers generally were reluctant to leave their own young children and to tolerate the all too frequent humiliation by their white women employers. Being a "washerwoman" was as arduous a task as being a field hand, and thus was of lower status and lower pay than that of a maid or cook within a household—but it did offer a measure of independence.

Jones found that the typical laundry woman collected clothes on Monday, boiled them in a large pot, scrubbed them, "rinsed, starched, wrung out, hung up, and ironed" often in the hot days of summer. Starch and soap she paid out of the one or two dollars a week she received. She delivered the clothes on Saturday and collected the next week's if she was lucky; otherwise she had to return on Monday (125–26). This pattern matches Delia's, but her work assumes an importance beyond sociological accuracy.

Delia's work acts as a metaphor for the work of the human creator, that is, the artist. Susan Gubar describes metaphors for the female artist in her essay "'The Blank Page' and the Issues of Female Creativity." She comments that "many women experience their own bodies as the only available medium for their art. . . . Within the life of domesticity, the body is the only accessible medium for self expression" (296). When we apply these statements to Delia, the sweat of her body, which has laundered, cooked, and scrubbed, is the corporal medium of her art. Her basket of pristine laundry stands as the artistic object created by her body. Her creation exists surrounded by home and garden, a miniature Eden made by a woman.

The laundry is a brilliant and evocative symbol in the story. It is, of course, white, pure white, the narrator reports; its whiteness and purity connote Delia's innate goodness as opposed to the evil darkness of Sykes's snake. The whiteness also indicates that her created object is indeed a blank page waiting for inscription; however, the appropriate inscriber, Delia, must of necessity keep her canvas blank; only Sykes writes upon it with the dirt of his boots and eventually the male object, the snake/penis, that symbolizes his desire to be the controller of the objects Delia's body has created.

The laundry has been created by the sweat and blood of her body; it rests quiet and serene like a tabula rasa, awaiting purposeful fulfillment. Nestled snugly in a basket, the laundry is an object Delia protects and to which she devotes her time, her attention, and her body. The laundry thus functions as a cherished child, the child of their own that Sykes and Delia do not have. One can only speculate that Delia's hard-muscled thinness coupled with the stress of the work itself and the cruelty of her husband have rendered her physically infertile. How much more pregnant, then, the potential fruitfulness of the laundry, the object of Delia's devotion, the object of Sykes's hatred. Had the laundry been literally a child, the story would devolve into a naturalistic tale on child abuse. But Hurston establishes herself as a writer, *the* Afro-American writer of her time and among the greatest in our century, by transcending such a cul-de-sac.

In *Invisible Man,* written twenty-four years after "Sweat," Ralph Ellison's nameless narrator, himself a blank page, ruminates on the qualities of whiteness and blackness in the brilliant section in the paint factory. The whiteness of the paint, considered so desirable, so good, so pure by white customers, results from the minute drops of blackness carefully, artistically added by the black paint makers. Ellison's scene is prefigured in "Sweat." Hurston takes the discourse on whiteness suggested by the laundry far beyond the stereotype that white is right and black is invisible. One could line up the side of the good in the story with Delia, the laundry, and whiteness opposed to Sykes, the snake, and blackness, but this easy dichotomy would overlook Hurston's ultimate accomplishment. The laundry created by Delia does not belong to her. The laundry, her creation, belongs to the white people of Winter Park, her patrons, who will be the ultimate inscribers of it; they will turn the laundry into clothes. Delia has prepared the perfect canvas for her patrons, but she is not able to participate in the use, evaluation, or assignment of worth to the creation. Like Hurston as an artist, Delia depends ultimately on the white patron for recognition. As Hurston was in the late 1920s the companion of Fannie Hurst, a white patron indeed, the story shades into a troubling comment on Hurston's relationship with her employer as a restriction on her art. Delia does not own her art. If the laundry represents a baby, then the baby is not Delia's; it is a white person's baby whom Delia tends so carefully. She is its mammy, creating the child but not owning it. But again, Hurston avoids the simple sociological statement of making the object of Delia's sweat an actual child.

In keeping with the Edenic imagery is the serpent in Delia's house, her husband. Sykes is not an Adam at all; his potential as a mate has been supplanted by the bullwhip he carries, which is the satanic object associated with a snake as it "slithers to the floor" when he threatens to strike Delia with it, as Robert Hemenway has noted (71). Sykes attempts to destroy everything Delia has created. He begins by complaining that she should "keep them white folks' clothes outa dis house" (198), and purposely kicks the neatly folded stack of white laundry into a dirty, disordered heap. His demand is irrational on a literal level because these clothes are their only source of money. In an ironic way, however, Sykes is reflecting a lingering Adamic need to establish his home as terrain in which he too has power. He owns nothing of his own; the house legally belongs to Delia. His protest against a white-controlled labor system embodies a somber problem for black men, but Sykes's anger and frustration cannot be directed toward the white perpetrators of his situation because he lacks the power to change the status quo. Instead he passes his days with careless pursuits and becomes increasingly violent with Delia. Her response to his violence has been excruciatingly passive, but when Sykes criticizes her work, he is not only protesting against his own economic condition. He has intuitively violated the one object, the laundry, that Delia values about all others.

Sykes's attack on the laundry brings about Delia's first assertion against him in fifteen years of marriage. When she grabs a heavy iron skillet from the stove, she is threatening her husband with a female object used for creation, in this case a cooking pot. Sykes responds by threatening her with the object of male creativity and violence with which he is most familiar, the bullwhip. The choices of these objects reveal that to Hurston, male creativity (the whip) exists only to injure and destroy; female creativity (the pot) *can* be used destructively but is intended primarily to be positive, that is, to cook and create a meal. Thus, women can use their creative power to defend themselves against the destruction that is the only intended use of male power.

The scene acts as a foreshadowing of the couple's climactic confrontation when Sykes brings home in a crate the satanic object of destruction, a snake. He leaves the snake in the kitchen for several days; Delia is terrified and terrorized by the snake, but she repeats her assertive stance by ordering her husband to remove it. Sykes responds by criticizing Delia's appearance. This apparent non sequitur reveals Sykes's attempt to control Delia by reminding her of the role he expects her to play, that of wife/sex object, prettied up and passive for the husband's use. Sykes criticizes her thin, hard-muscled body; he prefers fat women with flaccid bodies. Delia is strong because she works hard, another Sojourner Truth in her ability to work like a man. But as a representative of patriarchal masculinity, Sykes cannot prize Delia for what she is; he expects her to make herself, her body, into the image he prefers.

In the climax of the story Delia picks up the basket of white laundry and sees the snake in it. She drops the basket, runs outside in terror, and huddles in a gully beside a creek; Sykes returns home to the darkened house, picks up the snake's cage, and discards it. In this way the reader realizes that Sykes knew the snake was no longer in the cage; thus, it was Sykes who had placed it in the basket in order to murder Delia. When he goes inside to verify her death, he cannot see the snake in the dark house. Delia must decide whether to call out to warn her husband. If she does, he will live another day to take her life. She can save his life or she can save her own. In placing the snake in the laundry, Sykes has violated Delia's creation; he has disordered her house and finally actually intends to take her life. Delia chooses not to call out; the snake strikes, and Delia is permitted the gruesome revenge of seeing Sykes die before her eyes.

Delia's decision involves not only saving her life but preserving her vision of reality; her alternative choice would be to save her oppressor and thereby perpetuate not only her bondage to him but also to the corrupt, diseased vision of life he represents. As a female artist figure, Delia represents the power of the female artist who must adopt strategies that directly and violently bring change and allow her art to thrive. The debased condition of Sykes and of their marriage, even though it is in part a product of the economic disenfranchisement of black men, is not salvageable in this desperate story. Delia's choice implies that the oppressors of the woman worker/artist must be eliminated because they are evil, that the oppressors will bring about their own destruction. The tension for the black woman of creating art in a milieu controlled absolutely by whites remains unresolved. Hurston's story suggests that women artists must be free to create art and to contribute to a harmonious, ordered world. The issue of the need for a world that suits both men and women remains to be addressed, a task Hurston takes up in her later writing, especially in *Their Eyes Were Watching God* (1937). The issue of the situation of the black female artist remained her lifelong subject.

Works Cited

Baker, Houston A., Jr. *Blues, Ideology, and Afro-American Literature.* Chicago: University of Chicago Press, 1984.

Dollard, John. *Caste and Class in a Southern Town*. 1937. Reprint. New York: Doubleday, 1957.

Dreiser, Theodore. *Sister Carrie*. New York: Doubleday, Page, 1900.

Ellison, Ralph. *Invisible Man*. New York: Random House, 1952.

Gates, Henry Louis. *The Signifying Monkey: A Theory of Afro-American Literary Criticism*. New York: Oxford University Press, 1988.

Gubar, Susan. "'The Blank Page' and Issues of Female Creativity." In *The New Feminist Criticism: Essays on Women, Literature, and Theory*, edited by Elaine Showalter. New York: Pantheon, 1985.

Hemenway, Robert E. *Zora Neale Hurston: A Literary Biography*. Urbana: University of Illinois Press, 1977.

Hurston, Zora Neale. "How It Feels To Be Colored Me". (1928). Reprinted in *I Love Myself...*, 152–55. Old Westbury, NY: The Feminist Press, 1979.

———. "Sweat." 1926. Reprinted in *I Love Myself When I Am Laughing...* Old Westbury, NY: The Feminist Press, 1979.

———*Their Eyes Were Watching God*. Philadelphia: J.B. Lippincott, 1937. Reprint. Urbana: University of Illinois Press, 1978.

Jones, Jacqueline. *Labor of Love, Labor of Sorrow: Black Women, Work, and the Family from Slavery to the Present*. New York: Basic Books, 1985.

Michaels, Walter Benn. *The Gold Standard and the Logic of Naturalism: American Literature at the Turn of the Century*. Berkeley: University of California Press, 1987.

Pizer, Donald. *Twentieth Century American Literary Naturalism*. Carbondale: Southern Illinois University Press, 1982.

Walker, Alice. *The Color Purple*. New York: Washington Square Press, 1982.

Wright, Richard. *Native Son*. New York: Harper, 1940.

CHAPTER ELEVEN

Hurston as Dramatist: The Florida Connection

❦ WARREN J. CARSON ❦

While a considerable amount of scholarly work exists on the writing career of Zora Neale Hurston, the bulk of it concerns her novels, in particular *Their Eyes Were Watching God* (1937), which is considered by most to be her finest literary achievement. Her other works, including short stories, folklore studies, and the autobiography, *Dust Tracks on a Road* (1942), occasionally attract some critical attention, especially in the last decade. Other dimensions of Hurston's long career, which spanned nearly forty years, have largely been ignored altogether or at best afforded only a passing mention. This is true of her several early poems, her journalistic work, and especially her plays. That Hurston's plays have not triggered any critical interest to speak of is interesting enough in itself, particularly when we consider that it was a play that brought her to the attention of Harlem Renaissance circles, and when we consider her life-long interest in drama and the stage. The purpose of this chapter, then, is twofold: to examine, briefly, Hurston's career as a dramatist, and to point out the Florida aspects of her few plays.

Hurston's entry into the Harlem Renaissance circle was marked by the publication of several short stories and the 1925 prize-winning play *Color Struck*. The play marked the beginning of a strong interest in writing and producing dramatic art that was to stay with Hurston throughout the remainder of her career. Shortly after *Color Struck* won second prize in the drama division of the 1925 literary contest sponsored by *Opportunity*, the official magazine of the National Urban League, a second play, *The First One*, was entered in the 1926 *Opportunity* contest and "later printed in Charles S. Johnson's collectanea of Renaissance writing, *Ebony and Topaz* (1927)" (Hemenway, 68). Actually, Hurston had submitted another play in 1925 along with *Color Struck*. Nothing is known about it except its title—*Spears*—because, according to Robert Hemenway, it was lost (74).

In subsequent years Hurston—in addition to writing novels and compiling folklore collections—produced shows that included drama, native dance, and music gathered during her folklore expeditions. More important, Hurston was involved in several collaborative efforts: Her 1930 collaboration with Langston Hughes produced the play *Mule Bone* and resulted in a major dispute between the two collaborators. In 1939–40, Hurston worked with noted North Carolina playwright Paul Green. And in 1944 Hurston's collaboration with Dorothy Waring produced *Polk County: A Comedy of Negro Life in a Sawmill Camp, with Authentic Negro Music.* Sadly enough, neither of the plays written with Hughes or Waring has been published or widely produced, and the intended collaboration with Green never came to fruition, although Hemenway reports that "she and Green toyed with the idea of collaborating on a play called 'John de Conquerer'" (255).

The account of *Mule Bone* is certainly an interesting one, not so much from the standpoint of the play itself as from the controversy that it sparked between Hurston and Hughes. According to Hemenway, "Hughes claimed that he was to do the construction, plot, characterization and some dialogue, and that Hurston was to provide the authentic Florida color, give the dialogue a true southern flavor, and insert turns of phrase and 'highly amusing details' from her collecting trips" (137). However, exactly who did just what is not known. What is known is that Hughes and Hurston each claimed that he or she did the greater portion of the work on the play and went about claiming it as his or her own. There were numerous disputes over a proposed production, and the whole episode eventually ended with Hurston and Hughes actively avoiding each other for the rest of their lives. The play itself remains in manuscript form, although "[a]fter Hurston's death he [Hughes] permitted the third act to be published in *Drama Critique*" (145).

A study of this act will certainly verify Hurston's obvious presence at work in *Mule Bone*, whatever the nature of her role. The Florida setting— this time "near a Negro village in the Florida backwoods" (Hughes and Hurston, [1930] 1964, 103)—is just as colorfully drawn and as intricately detailed as the Florida settings of Hurston's major works. Furthermore, the scene, which takes place on "a high stretch of railroad track through a luxurious Florida forest" (103), is drawn with the care, fondness, and empathy that only one familiar with it could recount. Most important, however, is the language, the dialogue with "true southern flavor," which Hurston adds with her firsthand knowledge of its flair and cadences. This colorful language abounds in *Mule Bone*, suggesting a plethora of amusing images, from "box-ankled" and "ugly-rump" Negroes to "half-pint Baptists" and "gator-faced jigs." Moreover, the very importance of oral skills in the black community is addressed when a verbal contest ensues between Jim and Dave as they try to convince Daisy of the superiority of their individual affections. For example, when Jim assures Daisy that "I love you like God loves Gabriel—an' dat's His best angel," Dave counters with "Daisy, I love you harder than de thunder can bump a stump—if I don't, God's a gopher" (104). This generally good-natured bantering between friends (although they have had a fight over Daisy and Jim has attacked Dave with the bone of a dead mule) can be recognized as yet another aspect of the rich oral tradition that includes the dozens (a verbal contest that often consists of trading insults), the work song, the blues, the Negro spiritual, and rap, to mention a few of its popular manifestations.

The other interesting point about *Mule Bone* is that its subject matter did not die for Hurston. Parts of the original story continued to show up in subsequent works, particularly in *Their Eyes Were Watching God* and *Polk County.* It is also interesting to note that portions of her proposed collaboration with Paul Green also showed up in *Polk County.*

Rather than being a fully developed drama, *Polk County,* set in a sawmill camp in central Florida some fifty miles from Hurston's hometown of Eatonville, is more akin to the "revues" for which she became a popular producer in the late 1920s and early 1930s. These revues, which included "The Great Day" (1932) and "From Sun to Sun" (1933), both depicting life at Florida railroad camps, combined dialogue with native music and dance and were designed, from Hurston's point of view, to advance her philosophy of a *real* Negro American drama. In a letter to Langston Hughes dated April 12, 1928, Hurston wrote, "The Negro's outstanding characteristic is drama. That is why he appears so imitative. Drama is mimicry . . . " (quoted in Hemenway, 114). Hurston was primarily concerned with authenticity in drama, a concern no doubt made more urgent by her training as an anthropologist. She felt, according to Hemenway, that while white playwrights like Eugene O'Neill, Paul Green, and Dubose Heyward were well meaning, their re-creations of black life were not as realistic or as actual as they ought to be (115). In the letter quoted above, Hurston writes, "Did I tell you before I left about the new, the *real* Negro art theater I plan? Well, I shall, or rather we shall act out the folk tales, however short, with the abrupt angularity and naivete of the primitive 'bama Nigger. Quote that with naive [*sic*] settings" (115). It is clear, then, as we shall see, that Hurston indeed tried wherever possible to present the real, the pure essence of black life in her work.

Hurston's first play, *Color Struck,* is subtitled "A Play in Four Scenes." Actually, it consists of four sketches strung together in a rather loose fashion, and certainly it does not show Hurston at her best. Indeed, it is the work of a young and immature writer, for the scenes are not sufficiently developed and the characters, for the most part, are not convincingly delineated. Furthermore, from a technical standpoint, the play is probably too brief to justify the difficulty that would be incurred in staging it.

The story line is a simple one. Aboard a train, a group of blacks are bound for central Florida to participate in the statewide cakewalk (a dance contest with cakes as prizes for the most accomplished walking steps), which is probably an annual event. Among the group are the principal characters, John Turner and Emma Beazeby, an attractive couple from Jacksonville who are expected to win the cakewalk. During the trip and all during the festivities, Emma hounds John about looking at the light-skinned ladies; in fact, she becomes so upset by her obsessive jealousy that she cannot participate in the grand finale, even though she and John have been named the winners of the semifinal round. The final scene takes place twenty years later when John returns from the North to seek Emma's hand in marriage, but finds that Emma, who during the course of those years has given birth to an extremely light-complexioned child, is just as obsessed with color as ever. Emma, having misinterpreted John's attempt to comfort her sick daughter, accuses him of still being "color struck." Stung by the unfair accusation, John leaves; Emma is left alone with her daughter.

John, the protagonist, is by far the most fully developed of the characters in *Color Struck*. Hurston portrays him as fun-loving, but not to the point of being unfaithful or dishonorable; sensitive, but not to the point of being indecisive. John loves Emma: that much is clear; and that he occasionally looks at another woman in no way detracts from his feelings for her. When Emma refuses to "walk the cake" with him—for which he has practiced almost a year—John promptly, though reluctantly, seeks out another partner, who just happens to be the mulatto Effie Jones, so as not to have spent his time practicing in vain and to relish his status as the most popular cakewalker in the state. When we see John some twenty years later, he is still loving and compassionate, yet he knows when he has been beaten. He leaves Emma as he finds her—still obsessively jealous over what she perceives as John's obsession with light skin. John finally realizes that Emma will never change: "So this is the woman I've been wearing over my heart like a rose for twenty years! She so despises her own skin that she can't believe any one else could love it" ([1925], 1926, 14).

On the other hand, Hurston portrays Emma as an unsympathetic character. She is flat and shallow. Her major trait is jealousy, which leads to self-pity, something that Hurston obviously cannot abide. Emma is described in the *dramatis personae* as "a black woman." When we first see Emma she is berating John for daring to look at a light-skinned woman: "You wuz grinning at her and she wuz grinning back jes lake a ole chessy cat!" (8); and several lines later: "Jes the same every time you sees a yaller face, you *takes* a chance" (8). In the last scene, twenty years later, Emma is more obsessed than ever and continues to hurl the same accusations at John: "I knowed it! A half white skin" (14). Emma indulges in self-pity to the point that she can neither enjoy the pleasantries of life nor accept any love from John. The extent of her self-pity is characterized by such statements as "Oh—them yaller wenches! How I hates 'em! They gets everything, they gets everything everybody else wants! The men, the jobs—everything! The whole world is got a sign on it. Wanted: Light colored. Us blacks was made for cobblestones" (11). Hurston clearly objects to such self-indulgence by showing the debilitating power that such jealousy and self-pity have on an individual, for even after twenty years, Emma is still "unable to accept the love of a good man" (Hemenway, 47). Moreover, she continues to wallow in jealousy and self-pity. Ironically, Emma has fallen prey to the very thing she has continued to accuse John of: she has given birth out of wedlock, fathered by a near-white man (or perhaps white), which makes all the more poignant and pathetic her earlier lamentation, "Oh, them half whites, they gets everything, they gets everything everybody else wants!"

As mentioned previously, none of the four scenes are well developed. Hemenway concludes, and rightly so, that the play's "only memorable scene is the cakewalk" (47). The cakewalk is indeed a colorful, rather elegant affair. The participants have come from points all across Florida for fellowship and to compete. The ladies and gentlemen are resplendent in their finery, including "plug" hats for the men. The air is one of joviality; the Jacksonville delegation certainly has a good time en route to the cakewalk, and, except for Emma, all appear to enjoy themselves while there, and we may assume they will on the return trip home, especially since John and Effie won the cake in a unanimous decision. The only other scene that bears some mention is the opening scene aboard the train. While it does not generate any excitement, it can be juxtaposed against another train scene that Hurston was to use more than twenty years later in her autobiography. In *Color Struck,* ladies and gentlemen of a rather bourgeois background occupy the coach. While there are baskets of food, they are neatly deposited in the overhead compartments; and while "There is a little friendly pushing and shoving" (7), the riders are mostly orderly and well behaved. This contrasts directly with the picture drawn in "My People! My People!" from *Dust Tracks on a Road,* where some of the coach occupants are characterized as coarse, loud, boisterous, rude, uncouth, and certainly not the kinds of persons that the more refined blacks would want to sit down with. This is but one example of Hurston's tendency to use and reuse material until all its dimensions have been examined and exhausted, or at least until she has discovered the dimension she was looking for.

Finally, scene 3 must be mentioned as the most technically problematic of all the scenes. One supposes, of course, that it is designed as an interlude. While this is certainly acceptable in drama, it is seldom done with so little dialogue—there are two announcements by the master of ceremonies, nothing else—or with a curtain in the middle of a single scene. In today's technologically advanced theater, what Hurston intended could certainly be achieved by lighting. As this was not the case in 1925, however, it seems that she might have adopted a smoother, less obtrusive technique for marking the change of the moment; perhaps it would have been easiest to rewrite the scene, for its action could have been incorporated in scene 2 without great difficulty. Whatever the remedy, something should have been done to eliminate, or at least minimize, the structural fragmentation the scene poses.

One very wonderful feature of the play is the language. Hurston demonstrates very early in her career her knack for capturing the vernacular of southern speech, especially that of black Floridians. Her use of language also shows her fondness for folk speech. *Color Struck* is rich not only in dialect, but more important, in cleverly disguised insults such as "mullet-head Jacksonville Coon" (9), referring to the scavenger fish with the large, ugly, monstrous, protruding forehead; and "She calls herself a big cigar, but *I* kin smoke her" (10), meaning that if all else fails, one can assert a superior physical prowess over another. Hurston continued using dialect and other folk elements of speech throughout her career. Sometimes it is used to evoke humor or sympathy, or to command respect; but as with its use in *Color Struck,* it is never used condescendingly. Rather, Hurston recognizes dialect's worth and employs it to its fullest in presenting reality as she saw it. Her ability with regard to language is certainly a mark of her genius.

By far the most outstanding feature of the play is its theme—color struck. As used in black communities, "color struck" is an ambiguous term, although Hemenway sees it only as "the intraracial color consciousness addressed by the bourgeoisie . . . [which] addresses those who envy whites biologically and intellectually" (47). This assessment identifies only one aspect of being "color struck." Lighter-hued blacks can be color struck by thinking they are superior to darker-skinned blacks because their skin color more closely approximates that of whites; dark-complexioned blacks can be color struck by thinking likewise, that lighter skin and straighter hair would somehow make them better and more acceptable. This dimension can manifest itself in three ways: (1) dark-skinned persons may abuse blacks with light skin; (2) they may try to make themselves lighter through the use of chemical skin lighteners and hair straighteners; or (3) they may resign themselves to an obsessive self-indulgence and self-pity. Emma certainly embodies each of these manifestations.

An old maxim that used to be popular in certain black circles, and that still surfaces occasionally today, states:

If you're light, you're all right;
If you're brown, stick around;
If you're black, get back!

This is obviously how Emma Beazeby perceives her own situation vis-à-vis Effie Jones. Her obsession with color is clear from the beginning, as she accuses John of gawking at and ogling every light-skinned woman he sees. Emma then resorts to pouting, verbal abuse of Effie, threats of physical violence, and finally, self-pity. Emma's jealous love for John is compounded by her inferiority complex regarding her own dark skin. She ruins her chances for any happiness by alienating John; even when asked to marry him twenty years later, Emma is still not able to forget her obsession with color. Once again she alienates John, and in the end is left alone. Moreover, as mentioned, Emma has conceived a near-white child out of wedlock, which adds an ironic twist to her constant accusations of John. In Emma, we find Hurston challenging not only the ridiculous uselessness of the notion of color but of obsession of any kind. It is John, the protagonist, who speaks Hurston's philosophy of affirmation when he says "Dancing is dancing no matter who is doing it" (*Color Struck*, 8). In other words, life is for the full enjoyment of everyone.

It is interesting, and, I think, important, to note the timing of the play. In the Harlem of the mid 1920s, Marcus Garvey's Universal Negro Improvement Association was in its heyday, with its motto "Africa for Africans at Home and Abroad." Garvey believed in the purity of the black race and overtly attacked products of miscegenated bloodlines as being "devils" like their pure-white ancestors. Knowing Hurston's disdain of race prejudice and her impatience with extremity of any sort, we may conjecture that this is her answer to what she considered the incredible foolishness of intraracial prejudice. Whatever the motivation, *Color Struck* does, for all its faults, show that Hurston is not afraid to meet challenges head on, even when they involve the touchy, almost taboo, subject of being color struck; furthermore, the play is indeed a sensitive and realistic portrayal of an important social event in the black communities of the South.

Color is also the central theme of Hurston's second play, *The First One* (1927), which won first place in the drama division of the 1927 *Opportunity* contest and was published that same year in Charles S. Johnson's collection of Harlem Renaissance writing, *Ebony and Topaz*. This short one-act play is actually a dramatization of the biblical story of Noah's curse on his youngest son, Ham, which resulted in Ham and his descendants being accursed with black skin and destined to be servants of mankind forever. The brief account is found in Genesis 10: 21–27. Hurston expands this account in an effort to explore the age-old preoccupation with skin color, and she goes even further to establish the negative emotions that continue to be associated with the color black. For example, after Noah, who is still in a drunken stupor, utters his curse, the others shrink back in horror, and one character exclaims, "Black! He could not mean *black*" (*The First One* [1927], 1971, 56). Later, when Ham becomes aware of the curse and examines himself, he "gaz[es] horrified at his hands" and exclaims, "Black! . . . Why Noah, my father and lord of the Earth, why?" (57). As the other family members withdraw from Ham, as if his diabolical color will perhaps contaminate them, Noah seals Ham's banishment with the following pronouncement: "Thou are black. Arise and go out from among us that we may see thy face no more" (57), which serves, in Hurston's estimation, as a precursor to "If you're black, get back."

While *The First One* offers nothing by way of a Florida connection as such, the play itself is far more skillfully wrought than its predecessor, *Color Struck*. For example, because *The First One* is limited to only one scene within the one act—unlike *Color Struck*—Hurston achieves far more unity; in other words, *The First One* does not suffer from an overpowering sense of fragmentation as does the earlier play. In addition to her technical improvement as a playwright, Hurston evinces in *The First One* her early interest in African-American folklore, which, of course, becomes more pronounced in *Mules and Men* (1935) and *Tell My Horse* (1938), and her interest in an Afrocentric interpretation of the Bible, which receives wider attention in *Moses, Man of the Mountain* (1939) and the novel about Herod Hurston was writing just prior to her death.

Hurston's *The Fiery Chariot*, another one-act play based on "Ole Massa and John Who Wanted To Go to Heaven" from *Mules and Men*, also has a Florida setting. The play version survives only in typescript, but its story is essentially the same as the folktale, give or take a few details. *The Fiery Chariot* is set on a plantation in Florida prior to the end of the Civil War. The central characters are Ike, his wife, Dinah, and the white "Massa" of the plantation, and the story is a humorous portrayal of "getting what you pray for." Ike prays insistently for Jesus to come and rescue him from the evils of plantation life and take him to heaven aboard a fiery chariot. Dinah has warned Ike repeatedly that one day he might just get what he asks for. One day the "Ole Massa" overhears Ike's lamentations and his pleading for comfort, and decides to "spook" Ike; thus, "Ole Massa" dons a white sheet and informs Ike that he has heard his pleas and has come to take him to heaven. What follows is a hilariously funny account of Ike's continued stalling and excuse making, even his trying to get Dinah to go in his place, and finally his asking this would-be God to step back: "Yessuh, Jesus. Oh Lawd, the radiance of yo' countenance is so bright, Ah can't come out by yuh. Stand back jes' a lil' bit please" (6). After repeating this request several times and finally being accommodated, "Ike leaps past him out of the door" (6). In her study of *The Fiery Chariot*, Adele Newson observes that this play "supports both the well known motif of John the trickster and the stereotypical image of black men possessing superior physical speed" (36). The humor of the play, however, remains its most salient and important feature, deeply rooted as it is in African-American folklore. Furthermore, Dinah wryly notes that "God ain't got no time wid yo' pappy and him barefooted too" (7), which Newson rightly observes as adding "humor both to the motif and the stereotype"(36).

Clearly, the study of Hurston's few plays reinforces her insistence that black drama should be a sincere, realistic reflection of black life. The strong sense of place, the powerful imagery, the incorporation of music, dance, and spectacle, and the dramatic use of language are tributes not only to Hurston's immense and versatile talent, but underscore her philosophy regarding the ingenuity of black culture.

Works Cited

Hemenway, Robert. *Zora Neale Hurston: A Literary Biography.* Urbana: University of Illinois Press, 1977.

Hughes, Langston, and Hurston, Zora Neale (1930). *"Mule Bone: A Comedy of Negro Life,* Act III." *Drama Critique* (Spring 1964): 103–7.

Hurston, Zora Neale. *Color Struck* (1925). In *Fire* 1 (1926). Facsimile reprint by the Negro Universities Press, 1970, 7–14.

———. *Dust Tracks on a Road.* 1942. Reprint, with introduction by Robert Hemenway. Urbana: University of Illinois Press, 1984.

———. *The Fiery Chariot* (1935). Typescript. James Weldon Johnson Collection, Yale University Library, New Haven, CT.

———. *The First One* (1927). In *Ebony and Topaz,* edited by Charles S. Johnson, 53–57. Facsimile reprint by Books for Libraries Press, 1971.

———. *Polk County: A Comedy of Negro Life in a Sawmill Camp, with Authentic Negro Music* (1944). James Weldon Johnson Collection, Yale University, New Haven, CT.

———. *Their Eyes Were Watching God.* Philadelphia: Lippincott, 1937.

Newson, Adele S. "The Fiery Chariot." *Zora Neale Hurston Forum* 1, no. 1 (Fall 1986): 32–37.

CHAPTER TWELVE

Zora Neale Hurston at Rollins College

ᴍᴀᴜʀɪᴄᴇ J. O'Sᴜʟʟɪᴠᴀɴ, Jʀ., ᴀɴᴅ Jᴀᴄᴋ C. Lᴀɴᴇ

In the spring of 1932 Zora Neale Hurston, recently returned from New York City to Eatonville—"my native village" (*Dust Tracks on a Road,* 1942, 208)—to shape her folklore notes into what would become *Mules and Men* (1935), stopped in The Bookery, a bookstore in neighboring Winter Park, to ask for advice about publishing her manuscript. The owner, H. S. Thompson, suggested she contact Edwin Osgood Grover, who held the curious title Professor of Books at Rollins College in Winter Park and who had spent thirty years in the publishing industry in Boston, New York, and Chicago. Her letter to Grover would not only begin a long friendship with him and the college, but it also would help resurrect her flagging literary career.

Hurston's return to Eatonville had been a strategic retreat in the face of personal, economic, and professional crises. A number of her friendships, most notably with Langston Hughes, had proved unable to bear the weight of her strong personality. Even before the Great Depression dispersed the community of writers, artists, and intellectuals who gathered in New York during the Harlem Renaissance, Hurston had found a patron in Charlotte Osgood Mason, a wealthy white woman who supported her field research in the South and the Bahamas. But that relationship was now coming to an end. Hurston's work in developing a black folk theater had not found financial support. And, according to a brief, unpublished memoir by Grover, the manuscript of *Mules and Men,* which she had just finished, "was in the hands of a typist in Philadelphia, but Zora didn't have money to pay for getting it out of hock" (1).[1]

In a letter to Grover on June 15, 1932, Hurston wrote, "I feel that the real Negro theatre is yet to be born and I don't see why it should not first see the light of day in Eatonville. I have lots of material prepared to this end and would love to work it out with the help of some one who

knows a lot that I don't" (Hurston Papers). Her interests in folklore and
theater had begun to come together in 1926 when she discussed with
Langston Hughes the possibility of an opera about black folk life. She and
Hughes worked on the project which became *Mule Bone,* a work never
produced or published in its entirety. Her belief that theater was the
perfect medium for expressing black culture led to frustrating experiences
working on black revues like *Fast and Furious* (1931) and the unfortunately
titled *Jungle Scandals* (1931). An attempt to transcend such exploitative
work, *The Great Day,* a folk opera based on her research and performed
in New York at the John Golden Theater on January 10, 1932, had met
significant critical but little economic success.

Grover, accepting the role of academic patron—Hurston's life at times
seems to involve a succession of patrons—introduced her to Robert
Wunsch, a young theater director at Rollins who had been developing
parallel ideas. Bob Wunsch had come to the college from the University
of North Carolina where he had roomed briefly with Thomas Wolfe. He
was one of many young artists attracted to the Winter Park campus
because of its reputation for innovative arts programs. Sinclair Lewis, in
fact, had praised Rollins in his acceptance speech for the 1930 Nobel Prize
for the college's "interest in contemporary creative writing."

Because Wunsch had been searching for ways to develop among his
students "a genuine interest in American folk material" (Wunsch to Holt,
October 29, 1932), the possibility of working with Hurston offered both
a source of material and a contact with the community. His excitement is
apparent in a letter he wrote to Hamilton Holt, president of Rollins:

> I have set as my objective for the year the breaking of the ground,
> as it were: to make the students sensitive to the lyric beauty of
> swamp and citrus grove, sense the pageantry of the Ponce de Leon
> explorations, find the drama in the life of fisherfolk and sponge divers
> and cowboys, sense the tragedy and comedy of the boom days,
> revivify the old days of the missions and fortresses—in a word, to
> get the students to "dip their nets where they are."
>
> I can think of no better way to introduce the students to the
> honest-to-the-soil material at their own doorsteps than to present to
> them in a program of folk songs and dancers a group of Eatonville
> negroes, headed by Zora Hurston. Zora, a national authority on
> negro ways, has won an enviable place for herself in American dra-
> matics. (October 29, 1932)

Wunsch's proposal came at a difficult time for both Rollins and its
president. For the past ten years the college had been undergoing a transformation that would turn a small failing conservative institution into a

nationally recognized progressive college. The impetus for this change was the ascendancy of Hamilton Holt to the presidency. A former editor of the *Independent,* a prominent and influential liberal magazine, Holt became an active participant in the national Progressive Movement, particularly in its internationalist wing. Thus, he brought with him to Rollins not only a national reputation but also a liberal outlook. A college ripe for change had found itself a reformist president.

As with many progressives who thought about education, Holt rejected the prevailing college educational pedagogy of lecture/recitation. Instead, he proposed a student-centered rather than a subject-centered approach to learning. Basing his educational ideas on his experience in the *Independent* editorial rooms, Holt proposed that classrooms should resemble workrooms where apprentice students worked closely and cooperatively with master teachers. The essence of this relationship, Holt argued, was in the condition of association, based on the idea that learning was a cooperative effort. The solution to the college malaise lay in transferring the associational experiences of the newsroom into the classroom.

With the help of his faculty, Holt immediately instituted a classroom reform he called the Conference Plan. According to the plan, classes would be arranged in two-hour blocks on a workshop model with professors designing courses that would allow students, with all required books, sources, and references available in the classroom, to work and study under the teacher's supervision. The teacher functioned as a resource person rather than as a lecturer.

Within a few years, with the Conference Plan well established, Holt turned his attention to progressive curriculum reform to match the classroom transformations. Aware of how closely the new Rollins program had drawn on the principles of the progressive education movement, Holt decided to call upon the leading theoretician of that movement, John Dewey, to head a curriculum conference at Rollins. Bringing together the leading theoreticians and practitioners of progressive education in January 1931 at Winter Park, the conference successfully established a coherent set of principles for college curricula.

By the following year, however, Rollins was facing a more practical crisis that would have equally important effects on higher education in the United States. As the depression cut deeply into the college's resources, Holt asked his faculty to take a 30 percent cut in salaries. A faculty committee questioned the need for the cut and, by implication, Holt's stewardship. At the same time, the financial crisis was exacerbated by an ideological conflict between Holt and a group of faculty led by John Andrew Rice, professor of classics. Among their many differences of opinion with the president, this faction had begun challenging the efficacy of the Conference Plan.

For years Holt had seen himself as a progressive in a southern community, Winter Park, full of New Englanders and harboring a profound conservatism about change. He saw himself waging daily fights to protect controversial faculty members. When Royal France, professor of economics, became president of the state's Socialist Party or when France invited Hurston to stay at his home in Winter Park as a guest or when the Rollins faculty lobbied the state legislature in Tallahassee to prevent the passage of a bill prohibiting the teaching of evolution, it became Holt's responsibility to deal with the wrath of the college's neighbors.

John Andrew Rice, however, proved too much for him. A popular teacher and leader of the college's dissidents, Rice represented a confrontational style that Holt abhorred. Implicit in much of Rice's opposition was an objection to the administration's paternalistic style. Holt fired Rice at the end of the 1932–33 academic year. The variety of charges Holt leveled against Rice—charges ranging from insubordination to wearing a jockstrap at the college beach house—indicate the depth of Holt's anger. When a committee from the American Association of University Professors (AAUP), led by the distinguished philosopher Arthur O. Lovejoy, investigated the firing, it concluded, in the slightly stilted language of official reports, that Holt's charges "would in most American institutions of higher education not be regarded as grounds" for dismissal (Duberman, 26).[2]

Despite his vindication in the AAUP report, Rice and a group of supporters fired after publicly defending him left Rollins with the idea of starting an experimental college. One of Rice's supporters who was not fired but resigned in protest was Bob Wunsch, who not only suggested Black Mountain, North Carolina, as the site of the new college but joined the academic expatriates. Black Mountain College opened in 1933 with Rice as rector. When he stepped down in 1939, Wunsch replaced him until 1945 when he was forced to resign after a scandal.

But in the fall of 1932 the actions that would lead to Holt's purge were several months in the future. Then he was still hoping to find some ground for compromise with Rice and his supporters. Wunsch, anxious to promote folk theater, had sought the president's permission to produce Hurston's play at Rollins. Holt replied with a prudently worded letter reflecting not only his personal style and his awareness of the economic and personnel crises he was facing, but also his sensitivity to the Winter Park community's conservatism. His solution was to suggest—Holt rarely commanded—a set of guidelines that recognized the surrounding community's sensibilities:

I see no reason why you should not put on in recreation hall the
negro folk evening under the inspiration of Zora Hurston, but I
assume you will go over the thing enough to know that there will
be nothing vulgar in it. Of course we cannot have negroes in the
audience unless there is a separate place segregated for them and I
think that would be unwise.

I do not think I would advertise it very much outside our own
faculty and students but I may be wrong about this. (Holt to
Wunsch, November 1, 1932)[3]

With this cautious support, Wunsch could begin his collaboration with
Hurston. In the middle of November he brought one of his English classes
to hear her talk about her life and research. After discussing her background, she explained to the students her dissatisfaction with John Golden's production of *The Great Day.* According to an account in the college
newpaper, the *Sandspur,* she told the students that she wanted to work
"with a cast of the true negro type rather than that of the New York-
ized negro [to develop] a production of enduring value" (November 16,
1932, 1).

Hurston ended the class with stories, songs, and a sermon from her
research. Clearly overwhelmed by both the material and the lecturer—
"pure poetry, full of poetic figures, utterly lovely" (November 16, 1932,
1), the class won from her a promise to take it soon to a black church
service in Orlando. The students' rapture may account for the identification of Hurston's home town as "Edenville."

For the rest of the year Hurston and Wunsch worked on her "negro
folk evening." The production, called *From Sun to Sun* (see program,
appendix 1), was essentially the same as *The Golden Day,* her New York
performance at the John Golden Theater. Wunsch, clearly recognizing
the qualifications in Holt's letter, decided to hold the show's premier on
January 20, 1933, as the first production for a new experimental community theater, The Museum, in Fern Park.[4] It was so successful that the
play was repeated the following week and eventually brought on campus
for a performance on February 11 in a major theater, Recreation Hall.
Although the reviews reflected the values of their day, they recognized
the power of Hurston's work. A brief note in the *Orlando Morning Sentinel*
concluded with a comment about the audience's appreciation: "An audience of invited guests showed its unmistakable approval by calling the
performers back repeatedly for encores" (January 25, 1933, 5). The *Winter
Park Herald*'s cultural column, "The Listening Post," praised not only
the achievement of the premier, but the idea behind it:

This negro folk-lore as presented in the Museum was perhaps the most dramatic entertainment . . . that has been given in Winter Park. It gripped the audience with a sense of native rhythm and harmony which is hard to fully comprehend unless seen and felt. . . . What the negro has brought to America is too vital to be allowed to vanish from the earth. His barbaric color adds pattern to the Nordic restraint about him. America needs this because its civilization, like Minerva, sprung full grown from the head of Europe, and so there is not the wealth of native folk-lore as in Europe, Asia, Africa, and other continents where civilization had to grow through long ages. (January 26, 1933, 5)

The *Sandspur* offered a similar rave for the January 27 performance, "one of the most effective productions given at the college this year." After praising the work's "unselfconscious spontaneity," the review attempted to capture the spirit of the evening in describing the show's climax: "The dancers, at first wary, as if feeling their ground, gradually became more and more heated, until one expected and hoped for an orgy. The rhythm pressing harder and harder into one's very being, the seductive movements of the gayly-clad bodies, the shining eyes in their dark faces, brought thunderous applause and continuous demands for more" (February 8, 1933, 3). Like most appreciation of black art in the thirties, the reviews emphasized the primitivism and rhythm of Hurston's songs and stories.

The only discordant note during the performances came from a *Winter Park Herald* columnist, Will M. Traer, on February 2. In his column, "Some Observations," he responded to the *Herald*'s review with the kind of comments Holt and his faculty regarded as too typical of their neighbors:

I note mention in The Listening Post of Zora Hurston's effort to advance negro music and dramatic art. Something very wonderful along the line can no doubt be accomplished by those who know what they are doing. Without knowing anything about Zora Hurston's work along this line, I want to express an opinion that to me the grand kind of negro music is coming from a simple soul, both words and music. . . . The most true to life negro song that I have heard during late years is the "Blue Yodd" by Jimmy Rogers. This song might not interest some but it draws a wonderful picture for me of a lazy, indolent negro telling his troubles to the world. (February 2, 1933, 6)[5]

But Traer's disapproval, grounded in self-confessed ignorance, was a clear exception to the praise Hurston's *From Sun to Sun* gathered. The college community was so pleased with her work that in March, when the noted dancer Ruth St. Denis visited campus, Zora Hurston "and her company of negroes" were invited to offer a special half hour performance. Apparently the administration was still sensitive to the local community, because "[t]he audience included only the directors of the Museum and several invited students and townspeople" (*Sandspur,* March 8, 1933, 3).

Hurston's involvement with the college also had a significant effect on her professional life outside central Florida. Soon after working on *From Sun to Sun* with her, Bob Wunsch read one of Hurston's short stories, "The Gilded Six-Bits," to a creative writing class and sent it to *Story* magazine, which published it in August 1933. After reading the story, Bertram Lippincott wrote on behalf of his publishing company to ask if she was working on a novel. Never one to lose an opportunity, Hurston told Lippincott that she was and then immediately began writing *Jonah's Gourd Vine* (1934). Her appreciation to Wunsch is apparent in the book's curiously worded and spelled dedication, a dedication that seems to recognize his courage in a number of difficult environments:

> To Bob Wunsch
> Who is one of those long-wingded angels
> Right round the throne
> Go gator and muddy the water.

By the time the book appeared in 1934, Wunsch had spread his wings and soared to Black Mountain.

Hurston remained fond of Rollins, and especially Edwin Osgood Grover, even after Wunsch's departure and Holt's purge of the Rice faction. In November 1933 Grover wrote her to pass on a request: "President Holt has asked me what has become of you, and whether you had more things to put on at Rollins this winter" (November 15, 1933, Hurston Papers). Never short of inspiration or material, she presented *All De Live Long Day* (see program, appendix 2) on January 5, 1934, in Recreation Hall.[6] Like *From Sun to Sun,* the play followed a group of black workers through the day. It was not, however, quite as well received in the college paper as her earlier work. Even the praise seems qualified by a reviewer who clearly misses some of the earlier material:

> It is felt that no criticism should be attempted. Presented humbly, as it was, with all the spontaneous enthusiasm and brilliance of natural artists, this play can arouse only appreciation and a curious exuberance in those who see it.
>
> To those who are familiar with the work of Zora Hurston, there was something disappointing in that all of the features so popular in last year's production *From Sun to Sun* could not be included in this

program. However, more indigenous material and new talent made of *All De Live Long Day* the best thing of its kind—a most enlightening and worthwhile entertainment. (*Sandspur,* January 10, 1934, 1)

Hurston's success at Rollins, together with the college's imprimatur, led to more productions of her work around the state, an invitation by Mary McLeod Bethune, a good friend of Holt's, to teach at Bethune-Cookman College in Daytona Beach, Florida, and eventually an offer to produce a revision, which she titled *Singing Steel,* in Chicago.

She returned to Rollins only once more to bring a group of local singers to perform in April for the women's club before taking them to the Fifth National Folk Festival in St. Louis. But she never forgot the college and its faculty's role in her career. When she published *Moses, Man of the Mountain* in 1939, she dedicated it to Grover, who supported her work throughout her life. He followed her career, despaired at her setbacks in later years, and when he heard that she had died, attempted to discover her burial place. As a memorial, he encouraged the University of Florida Library to develop a Hurston collection by donating to it his correspondence with her.

Hurston herself offered a fitting epilogue for her relationship with Rollins shortly after *Dust Tracks on a Road* was published in 1942. In the book she mentioned the college and the faculty she remembered from the time they had helped resurrect her career. But she recognized that her book had not quite done justice to the time she spent there. She wrote to Hamilton Holt to acknowledge her debt to the college more fully: "You know, I had a lot more about Rollins College and Winter Park in the original script, but my publishers did not like it. I wanted to show more awareness of what had happened to me at Winter Park, and my gratitude toward several people there, as well as some in New York. But it was cut out. Now, I look like a hog under an acorn tree guggling without ever looking up to see where the acorns came from" (February 11, 1943, Hurston Papers).

From Sun to Sun
(a day in a railroad camp)

A program of original Negro folk-lore

1. The Arousal:
   Place: In the Quarters
   Time: Before Day
   a. The Shack-Rouser wakes the camp (John Hamm); male chorus then sings
   b. "Joe Brown" is sung as they leave the Quarters.
2. Whipping Steel:
   Place: Down the Railroad Track a Piece
   Time: Broad Daylight
   a. "Jonah Head"—lining rhythm led by Lawrence Williams.
   b. "Oh, Lulu"—spiking rhythm led by William Brown.
   c. "Can't You Line It"—lining again led by Lawrence Williams.
   d. A woman walks down the track counting railroad ties and sings her blues: "East Coast Blues"—sung by Zora Hurston.
   e. "Mule on de Mount"—spiking more steel led by Lawrence Williams.
   f. "John Henry"—led by Lawrence Williams.
3. Back in the Quarters:
   Place: In and Around the Jook
   Time: Dusk-dark
   a. Children's games.
   b. "Mister Frog"—lullaby sung by Florence Moseley.
4. In the Quarters:
   Place: In and Around the Jook
   Time: Dusk-dark
   a. A walking preacher wanders in. He is given momentary notice.
   b. "You Can't Hide, Sinner"—led by James Tobbs.

c. Sermon.

d. "Sid Down, Angel."

INTERMISSION: TEN MINUTES

5. Black Dark in the Night:
   Place: In the Jook
   a. "Cold Rainy Day."
   b. Piano Solo played by Evelyn Moseley.
   c. "Let the Deal Go Down" (with Georgia Skin).
   d. "Alabama Bound"—led by James Tobbs.
   e. Guitar Solo played by David Calhoun.
   f. "If You Ever Been Down"—led by Lawrence Williams.
6. "The Fiery Chariot": An original Negro folk-play (a folktale dramatized by Zora Hurston).
7. Way in the Midnight:
   Place: In the Palm Wood
   a. Bahaman fire dance.
   b. "Bellamina"—led by Lawrence Williams.
   c. "Mama Don't Want No Peas"—led by James Tobbs.
   d. "Evalina"—led by Zora Hurston.
   e. "Ring Play."
   f. Crow Dance led by Zora Hurston.
   g. "Good Evening."

CURTAIN

The Actors:

Water Boy	John Hamm
Shack-Rouser	John Hamm
The Preacher	Reverend Isiah Hurston

In the One-Act Play:

Dinah	Zora Hurston
Ike	James Tobbs
De Lawd	Oscar Anderson
The Child	Nelson

The Singers:

Oscar Anderson   David Calhoun
James Tobbs   Evelyn Moseley
John Hamm   Reverend Isiah Hurston
William Curtis   Rosa Lee Taylor
William J. Brown   Ruth Marshall
Lawrence Williams   Florence Moseley
Maxie Day   Zora Hurston
Leonard Horton

The Children:

Laura Crooms   Willie Dukes   Laura Alexander
Hoyt Crooms   Malinda Crooms   Nelson

THE SONGS

"Shack Rouser":

It is customary on the railroad, and in the lumber and turpentine camps to have the workers aroused. The man whose duty it is to make a round of the shacks, knocking on the walls, doors, or porches with a stick, is called the shack rouser. Being a Negro, however, he never contents himself with the mere knocking and calling. He chants rhymes. Some of the rhymes are traditional, others are improvised at the moment.

"Joe Brown":

This song attaches itself to the one-time sheriff at Titusville. Since there are no coal mines in Florida, the setting must have come from somewhere outside the State. The song, however, has not been found outside of Florida.

"Jonah Head":

A rhythm song fitted to the business of laying the steel rails before they are spiked down. This is called "lining track." The rhythm is constant, but the lyric treats of a variety of things.

"Oh, Lulu":

A rhythm song suited to the spiking routine. It is heard only in the railroad camps. It comes from around Miami.

"Can't You Line It?":

A lining song found in Orange County particularly and in spots all over Central Florida.

"East Coast Blues":

A genuine folk-song of the social type popularly known as blues. This song follows the true Negro poetry form: that is, a sentence repeated two times without necessary rhyme. The variation is in the tune, the first two lines being almost identical, the contrast or climax coming on the third line. This song is from Polk County, the most fertile field for Negro folk-song in America.

"Mule on de Mount":

The most widely distributed Negro folk-song extant. It is built to the spiking rhythm.

"John Henry":

This song is not so widely distributed as the preceding song or "Uncle Bud": it stands possibly third: but there are more variants of "John Henry" despite its evident recent origin than there are of any other known folk-song.

"Cold Rainy Day":

This is a blues song also from Polk County. It is sung in the Jook. The Jook is a pleasure house in the Quarters where the Negroes dance, game, love, and create songs.

Piano Solo:

This style of piano playing is peculiar to the Negroes. It is called "jooking," that is, playing in the manner used in the Jooks or pleasure houses.

"Let the Deal Go Down":

This is a gaming song suited to "George Skin," the most popular game of chance among Negroes in the South, not excepting dice. It came from the Bostwick turpentine still near Palatka.

"Alabama Bound":

A folk song of wide distribution; it has, like the "St. Louis Blues," been commercialized.

"Even Been Down?":

This is a blues from the East Coast area. It was discovered at Palm Beach; it has been found also up as high as Fernandina.

"Mama Don't Want No Peas":
A husband's complaint against the marital attitude of his wife.

"Evalina":
The girl thinks there should be a marriage, the boy thinks not.

"Good Evening":
A very emaciated horse gets into a neighbor's corn field in Baintown, a suburb of Nassau City, and destroys the crop. What he didn't eat he wallowed upon. The farmer explains it to a neighbor.

The spirituals are self-explanatory.

—ZORA HURSTON

Source: Program, *From Sun to Sun.* 1933. Rollins College Archives.

All De Live Long Day

1. Making This Time—Daybreak
   a. "Baby Chile"
      Pauline Foster and Female Ensemble
   b. "I'm Goin' to Make a Graveyard of My Own"
      Gabriel Brown, guitarist, and Male Chorus
2. Working on the Road
   a. "Cuttin' Timber"
   b. "You Won't Do"
      Buddy Brown and Ensemble
   c. "John Henry"
      A. B. Hicks, tenor-baritone
   d. "Please Don't Drive Me"
      Buddy Brown and Ensemble
   e. "Halimuhfack"
      Bernice Knight, soprano
   f. "Fat Gal"
      Mellard Strickland, A. B. Hicks, and Oscar Anderson
   g. "Water Boy"
      A. B. Hicks, tenor-baritone
3. "De Possum's Tail Hairs"—A One-Act Folk Play
   De Possum   Maggie Mae Fredericks
   Brer Noah   Lewey Wright
   Ham   Gabriel Brown
4. Spirituals
   a. "O Lord"
   b. "I'm Going Home"
      Ensemble

   c. "Sit Down"
     Buddy Brown and Ensemble
   d. "Swing Low"
     A. B. Hicks, tenor-baritone
   e. "All My Sins"
     Ensemble
   f. "Go Down Moses"
     A. B. Hicks, tenor-baritone
   g. "I'm Your Child"
     Ensemble

INTERMISSION

5. "Funnin' Around"
   a. "Ever Been Down?"
     Female Quartet—Bernice Knight, Willaouise Dorsey, Maggie Mae
     Fredericks, Billy Hurston
   b. Harmonica Solo
   c. "Let the Deal Go Down"
   d. Guitar Solo
     Gabriel Brown
   e. Buck and Wing Specialties
     Curtis Bacott, Willie Matthews, Alphonso Johnson
   f. "St. Louis Blues"
     Bernice Knight, soprano
   g. Piano Solo
     Curtis Bacott
   h. "Break Away"—Folk Dancing
     Ensemble. John Love, fiddler
6. String Band in the Negro Manner

          Banjo   S. E. Boyd
          Fiddle   John Love
          Guitar   Bubble Mimms

7. On the Niger
   a. Ahaco
   b. Bellamina
   c. Mama Don't Want No Peas
   d. Courtship—"Jumping Dance"
     George Nichols, Maggie Mae Fredericks, Lewey Wright
   e. Crow Dance   ZORA HURSTON

f. Fire Dance

Ensemble. George Nichols, African drummer, and Oscar Anderson, "Kuta-Mah-Kah" (beating the off rhythm on the rear end of the drum).

Source: Program, *All De Live Long Day.* 1934. Rollins College Archives.

Notes

1. About *Mules and Men* Grover noted, "Someone asked her, 'Why drag in the men?' Her quick answer was, 'That's what the mules wanted to know.'" (1).

2. The Rice Affair is reconstructed from material in Duberman's study and the Rollins College Archives.

3. As Robert Hemenway points out, Hurston was unhappy with Holt's guidelines: "She wrote to Mrs. Mason, 'Tickets to the general public—except Negroes. I tried to have the space set aside, but find that there I come up against solid rock'" (185).

4. The description of the theater in the *Winter Park Herald* (January 26, 1933) suggests that it must have been a curious environment for Hurston's work: "the interior is painted blue, the stage curtain is bright pink and is decorated with lambs, rabbits, ducks [and] modern flowers."

5. Royal France's memoirs offer a similar instance of one faculty member's ironic description of the disapproval of his neighbors when France and his family socialized with Zora Hurston (1957, 75–76).

6. Hemenway's excellent biography does not mention either *All De Live Long Day* or the second museum performance of *From Sun to Sun*.

Works Cited

Duberman, Martin. *Black Mountain: An Exploration in Community.* New York: Dutton, 1972.

France, Royal. *My Native Grounds.* New York: Cameron Associates, 1957.

Grover, Edwin Osgood. "The Story of Zora Neale Hurston, Author." Typescript (n.d.). Rollins College Archives, Winter Park, FL.

Hemenway, Robert. *Zora Neale Hurston: A Literary Biography.* Urbana: University of Illinois, 1977.

Holt, Hamilton. Correspondence. Rollins College Archives, Winter Park, Florida.

Hurston, Zora Neale. Correspondence. Zora Neale Hurston Papers. University of Florida Library, Gainesville.

———. *Dust Tracks on a Road.* Philadelphia: Lippincott, 1942.

———. *Jonah's Gourd Vine.* Philadelphia: Lippincott, 1934.

———. *Moses, Man of the Mountain.* Philadelphia: Lippincott, 1939.

———. *Mules and Men.* Philadelphia: Lippincott, 1935.

"The Listening Post," *Winter Park Herald,* January 26, 1933, 5.

Orlando Morning Sentinel, January 25, 1933, 5.

Rollins College *Sandspur.* November 16, 1932, 1; February 8, 1933, 3; March 8, 1933, 3; January 10, 1934, 1.

Traer, Will M. "Some Observations," *Winter Park Herald,* February 2, 1933, 6.

Wunsch, Robert. Correspondence. Rollins College Archives. Winter Park, Florida.

CHAPTER THIRTEEN

"Adaptation of the Source": Ethnocentricity and "The Florida Negro"

 CHRISTOPHER D. FELKER

In his essay "The Work of Art in the Age of Mechanical Reproduction," Walter Benjamin argues that when an artistic piece is freed from its "aura" of tradition and authenticity, it automatically enters the domain of politics. American literary critics are now used to considering writers as more than mere recorders of the dominant characteristics of their times and places. The recent poststructuralist scholarship in American studies understands culture to consist of "interworked systems of construable signs." Culture is not an entity, "something to which social behaviors, institutions can be causally attributed; it is a context, something within which they can be intelligibly described," as Clifford Geertz remarks (14). This chapter looks at Zora Neale Hurston's participation on the Florida Federal Writers' Project (FWP) in an effort to render a textured and flexible portrait of an African-American artist exercising her craft for the purpose of generating mass culture. In particular, Hurston's career with the Florida FWP reflects the experiences of all participants in that project as they navigated the special problems the Works Progress Administration (WPA) experience brought to the surface: the imprisonment and anxiety of celebrity (both in terms of authorship and black culture more generally) and the distortion of potentially democratic causes. I recognize that Hurston's involvement with the WPA is clearly a contribution to an "extrinsic history" of African-American letters, but as I hope to show, her experience can also be read as an "intrinsic history" that explains her following a path that challenged and resisted the cultural mainstream though she was complicit in its workings.[1]

Evidence that professional American writers were cultural mediators exists from the very origins of the nation, but the idea of literary artists actively promoting culture through their works peaked in the Progressive Era when, as Christopher Wilson notes, "The American marketplace of words finally achieved a full national reach and modern structure" (2). During the depression, the integration and coordination of professional writers and the government through the Federal Writers' Project created the nation's first vast and cohesive "culture industry." The program began in 1935 and ended in 1943. In those nine years the program provided jobs for 3,500 to 6,700 writers, editors, researchers, and clerical workers (2 percent of the total WPA workforce): spent $27 million and produced 276 books, 701 pamphlets, and 340 articles, leaflets, radio scripts (Stott, 2). The FWP, one of four WPA "arts" projects, created work for people who had no employment. The Theater, Music, and Art programs were responsible for producing plays, concerts, murals for public buildings, paintings, and graphics. FWP writers collected interviews, life histories, folklore, historical records: These things were presented to audiences of the day through the volumes of the American Guide series.

Writers who participated in the program were given an unparalleled opportunity to generate mass culture through the production of state guides that examined the local history and characteristics of each state and its people for the benefit of automobile travelers. The existence of the automobile along with newspapers, the radio, and movies served to distribute the products of a mass culture generated primarily in metropolitan areas deep into the nation's more rural areas. The 1930s was the first decade to experience fully the impact of the communications and managerial revolutions of the Progressive Era. The literary market was a potent and vital link for the dissemination of cultural messages. We now understand the history of the period covered by the America Guides to have been primarily a cultural product: That is, the image Americans received in the guides reflected the understandings in the minds of the American people. As Bill Stott records, "The 'people's' America presented in the Guides was a good deal more hopeful and resilient than many Americans then felt their nation to be. Some critics criticized this and talked about the FWP's 'romantic nationalism' and "fictitious Americanism" (4).

On April 25, 1938, Zora Neale Hurston joined the editorial staff of the Florida Federal Writers' Project. Her supervisor in the Negro section, Nancy Weiss, claims that Hurston's involvement with the project provided "means, psychological support, and creative strength to develop her art" (Hemenway, 271 n. 10). Among other things, Hurston's tenure on the project severed her from a purely independent practice of literature and anthropology. Under the aegis of the Florida FWP, Hurston practiced her craft in an environment of professional expertise and democratic activism. Writers on the project were not free to follow the capricious trails of the "inner muse"; instead, the work ethic on the project stressed ritualized routines, hard field work, and a responsibility to the market/audience of the American people. The ideological assumptions underlying employment in the WPA served to enlarge a writer's social scope and provided writers with new agendas that supplemented, superceded, and sometimes conflicted with their own interests.

Hurston's primary role on the editorial staff involved collecting and editing material for a book to be entitled *The Florida Negro*. The book was to be patterned after an earlier volume published about blacks in Virginia. Robert Hemenway, Hurston's biographer, notes: "By June of 1938 Zora was acting as supervisor of the Negro unit of the Florida Federal Writers Project, traveling to Washington to charm Henry Alsberg, the FWP director, into supporting the effort. She wrangled a salary increase for the supervisor and more travel money for the folklore collecting, and by July she was visiting black communities in the Everglades with a recording machine liberated from Washington despite a mountain of red tape" (252). Because the eventual product lacked a unifying structure and was overly burdened by sociological prose, it has remained in manuscript form.

Hurston labored on the project for a year and a half. Her efforts gave her insight into how a native aesthetic might be developed for the appreciation and consumption of blacks, yet as a writer on a "committed" project she understood the American market with its economic advantages and broad-based appeal to be more than a commerical outlet for artistic works. Hurston's involvement with the project showed that the work of art is itself the product of a negotiation between a creator or a class of creators (equipped with a complex, communally shared repertoire of conventions) and the institutions and practices of society. Of course, in the negotiation process the society's dominant currencies, money and prestige, are invariably involved. The market for *The WPA Guide to Florida* was a "crucible of a new cultural style"; the status afforded the "professional writer" in the FWP encouraged the writers to see themselves as symbols and repositories "of new national values: strenuousity, political activism, the outdoor life" (Wilson, 2).

Huston's work on the Florida FWP was punctuated by a concentration on native black aesthetics. She came away from her Harlem encounters earlier in the decade with a sense of purposeful commitment to the vernacular traditions of rural blacks. It would be wrong to assume, however, that she completely sublimated her tempestuous character to assume the mantle of efficient bureaucrat. Indeed as Hemenway notes: "Operating out of the main office in Jacksonville, she would frequently leave for a week or more at a time, telling no one where she was going. It was assumed she was collecting folklore for the Florida Guide, but one was never sure. (It is clear now that she had also begun working hard on her next book, *Moses, Man of the Mountain.*) Admonished by the administrators for her truancy, she would reingratiate herself, pick up her weekly paycheck, and then sometimes disappear again" (252). Nevertheless, Hurston was a profoundly professional writer in that she came to see her craft predominantly as a product of technical expertise rather than inspiration, viewed the market as the primary arbiter of literary value, and was guided by an internal sense of responsibility to their public (Wilson, 204n). The fact that the project isolated the local, specific, and ethnic detail within a text marketed and designed with the widely conceived American public in mind suggested to Hurston that the materials of a vibrant black culture apprehended at the source might also be interesting to a larger multiethnic audience.[2]

In the manuscript "The Florida Negro" and in the published text of the Florida guide, Hurston's primary areas of inquiry were mythical places rendered in folktales and black music. In the area of folklore, she submitted a section to the manuscript of "The Florida Negro" titled "Negro mythical places." One such place was Diddy-Wah-Diddy, where everything is so grand that "dogs can stand flat-footed and lick the crumbs off of heaven's tables." In the Florida guide, Hurston's own hometown of Eatonville is surrounded by a "mythic territory" that embraces the legends of Florida and draws them within the limits of a single town: "The world's largest alligator, it is said, is no other than a slave who escaped from a Georgia plantation and joined the Indians during the Seminole War. When the Indians retreated, he did not follow but instead made 'big medicine' on the lake shore, for he had been a celebrated conjuring man in Africa. He transformed himself into an alligator, the god of his tribe, and slipped into the water. Now and then he resumes human form, so people say, and roams the country about Eatonville" (Federal Writers' Project, 362).

Folklore and music held ethnocentric messages that Hurston sought to apprehend and then inscribe within the cultural patternings of the state as a whole. The "distinctiveness" of black contributions to American life is frequently attributed to vernacular sources in folklore, architecture, music, or literature. The Florida guide emphatically grounds the state's musical traditions within an African-American source:

Negro spirituals and secular tunes have been given their present character by improvisors, work gang choruses, religious groups, dance bands, and music clubs. Perhaps the most vital aspect of music in Florida today, this growing Negro art reaches back to African and Indian music and out toward the Cuban: it influences—and is influenced by—contemporary musical composition. Music always has been an emotional outlet for the Florida Negro, and his songs have multiplied and shaped themselves to his tasks, his tribulations, and his irrepressible spirits. (149)

Houston Baker, using the rhetoric of poststructuralism, locates the nexus of African-American culture within the complex, reflexive matrix constituted by the blues tradition:

A matrix is a womb, a network, a rock bearing embedded fossils, a rocky trace of a gemstone's removal, a principle metal in an alloy, a mat or plate for reproducing print or phonograph records respectively. The matrix is a point of ceaseless input and output, a web of intersecting, crisscrossing impulses always in productive transit. Afro American Blues constitute such a vibrant network. They are what the French philosopher Jacques Derrida might describe as the "always already" of Afro American culture. They are the multiplex, enabling script in which Afro American discourse is inscribed. (1988, 13)

Less urbane and more rural in context, Hurston's appreciation of the blues charted a path to the center of black culture in Florida. A typical ethnomusical description of Hurston's is included in the Florida guide's depiction of Pahokee on tour 13 (following state highway 25 for 139 miles from West Palm Beach to Punta Rassa): "All night now the jooks clanged and clamored. Pianos living three lifetimes in one. Blues made and used on the spot. Dancing, fighting, singing, crying, laughing, winning and losing love every hour" (475). In Florida she found elements of an African-American culture that she had also encountered in earlier research in the Caribbean. Her appreciation of black music clarified the term dynamic suggestion she applied to black art.

Fundamentally, "dynamic suggestion" was a mode of artistic behavior that attempted to capture the essence of a tradition practiced by the people—getting access to the genuine article—and then transferring that tradition into a more formal medium (fiction, an orchestrated composition, etc.). Hurston's early attempt to work through these issues is her 1934 essay "Spirituals and Neo-Spirituals." There she distinguished between "genuine" spirituals, those black songs sung by a group bent on the expression of feelings and not sound effects, and "neo-spirituals," works by composers or adapters that were based on spirituals and were sung by concert artists and glee clubs. The primary criteria for determining the "genuineness" of a thing (what I refer to as the traditional aura that Hurston felt compelled to seek out and then make available to others through the aegis of the guides) was its degree of ethnocentrism. In the essay, Hurston recognized that the genuine thing, largely overlooked and limited compared to "popularized" versions, is changed into something substantially different when artists like herself adapt the source for different ends:

> Glee clubs and concert singers put on their tuxedos, bow prettily to the audience, get the pitch and burst into magnificent song—but not Negro song. The real Negro singer cares nothing about pitch. The first notes just burst out and the rest of the church burst in—fired by the same inner urge. Every man trying to express himself through song. Every man for himself. Hence the harmony and disharmony, the shifting keys and the broken time that make up the spiritual. I have noticed that whenever an untampered-with congregation attempts the renovated spirituals, the people grow self-conscious. . . . Perhaps they feel on strange ground. . . . This is not condemnation of the neo-spirituals. They are a valuable contribution to the music and literature of the world. But let no one imagine they are songs of the people, as sung by them. (1934, 224)

We can be certain that when Hurston collected blues and folktales from the communities in the Everglades, she knew the eventual product, "a valuable contribution," would nevertheless place her and her sources on "strange ground."

Anyone who has heard the classic Ellington composition "The Blues" sung by Joya Sherill in New York City at a Carnegie Hall concert (and recorded live on the 1944 album *Black, Brown, and Beige*) has an idea of Hurston's sense of ethnic adaptations of a traditional idiom. "The Blues" is an abstraction of the blues idiom—a pyramid effect created by piling on instruments one at a time resolves into a chord infused with a warm saxophone theme played by Ben Webster. The vocalist's second entry into the composition is underlined by a double-time rhythm brought to a dramatic pause, where Sheldon Hemphill provides a coda employing "word painting" or "madrigalism" on the words "Signing . . . Crying . . . Dying."[3]

Hurston's own ethnomusicology asserts that in their lives, black people are constantly invoking a capacity to adapt the source in order to lead lives that are things of beauty. Like the translators of a tradition of written texts, Hurston saw the blues as offering a compelling transcription of experience. In a section of "The Florida Negro" manuscript entitled "The Sanctified Church," Hurston emphasized that the spirituals grew from a native black aesthetic and could only be "twisted in concert . . . into Gregorian chants": They were not "apocryphal appendages to Bach and Brahms" (Hemenway, 253).

The blues as an ethnic phenomenon was also a suggestive cultural metaphor. The blues, whether folksy tunes in the Everglades or sophisticated compositions played in Carnegie Hall—derived from the same vernacular root. As American financiers of the 1920s understood, the blues was a vehicle for displaying the prominence and character of a black artist to white audiences. Houston Baker, Jr., cites the work of Afro-American writer James McPherson to support a claim that the blues, vernacular, and cultural geographies coalesced in the first half of the century to influence a wide economic market for black artist: "A 'race record' market flourished during the Twenties. Major companies issued Blues releases under labels such as Columbia, Vocalion, Okeh, Gennett, and Victor. Sometimes as many as ten Blues releases appeared in a single week; their sales (aided by radio's dissemination of the music) climbed to the hundreds of thousands . . . during their heyday, the Blues unequivocally signified a lucid predominance of the vernacular" (1986, 24).

Though this boom ended abruptly in the depression, Hurston must have been profoundly influenced by the commercial success of the blues tradition as it infiltrated the mainstream culture. Perhaps self-consciously aware that the image of America being disseminated in the guides was subject to romantic illusions, she probably recognized her chance to assert a black nativist tradition for consumption by an increasingly affluent (in the late thirties) white society. In her appreciation for the complex intertextual activities connoted by the blues, Hurston was advancing a cultural position we presently term "Afro-centrism." Hurston saw black art as being a part of "the people," and she promoted a writing style rooted in social realism. At times, this presented an appealing mimeticism where the relation between black art and black life was a direct one. The integration this style implied was attractive to cosmopolitan whites whose own experience of popular culture was increasingly fragmented and disharmonious.

It is important to recognize that Hurston's middling status is not the typical situation of a committed individual whose divided allegiances make her an outsider to both the ethnocentricity she records and the cultural mainstream she wishes to manipulate—she was too professional a writer to be immobilized by difficult choices. Instead, I think she always erred on the side of cultural assimilation. Her efforts to inscribe the black aesthetic into the larger base of American culture always predominated in her work. By placing the regional traditions of Florida into the general sweep of American culture, the social behaviors she described were made intelligible for the ethnologist, the historian, and herself. Hurston's work on the Florida FWP extended racial concerns into the broad mass marketplace. As I mentioned earlier, the economic ideology underpinning the FWP assumed a wide market impact for the American guides.

The materials Hurston collected in Florida provided a regional basis for understanding black culture as a whole. Her intimate glimpse into the culture of the Everglades worked to restore the sacredness of language, a concern with the landscape, an affirmation of cultural identity, and a sense of black solidarity. These values are recorded in the Florida guide's chapter on folklore: It stresses that folk art arises out of community necessity and is replicated because it satisfies a community aesthetic. Even though Afro-American folk art was perpetuated through the most oppressive of circumstances, it was not pathological, but instead became an instrument of survival. Communal need, group artistic expression, a strong ethos in an original social context, a characteristic sensibility—Hurston always maintained that these elements formed the backbone of the African-American experience.

The celebration of the primitive was a "vocational strategy" for Hurston, an occupational prism that enabled her to integrate the different class, educational, and regional backgrounds that she encountered in herself, her sources, and her intended audiences. Basing her professional practice on such a strategy carried the risk that what initially seemed a celebration of ethnic identity might be interpreted as an undesirable conformity to racial stereotypes. As Cary Wintz notes, the relative success of black artists during the Harlem Renaissance placed new dangers in their paths: "Primitivism was a complex issue for participants in the Renaissance. Many whites expected to find it in black writing. Zora Neale Hurston felt very comfortable dealing with it . . . others were hostile to those who seemed to be confining blacks to a stereotype of primitiveness and sensuality that whites had imposed" (183). The Florida materials, in their harkening back to an oral primitivism, define many of the key artistic terms Hurston later defined in her own literature. The years in Florida had their most prominent influence on Hurston's use of the narrative voice. In describing her ability to create a "speakerly text," Henry Louis Gates, Jr., cites the "authentic" quality she distilled from her experiences in black towns in the Everglades:

> The narrative voice Hurston created, and her legacy to Afro-American fiction, is a lyrical and disembodied voice, from which emerges a singular longing and utterance, a transcendent, ultimately racial self, extending far beyond the merely individual. Hurston realized a resonant and authentic narrative voice that chooses and aspires to the status of impersonality, anonymity, and authority of the black vernacular tradition, a nameless, selfless tradition, at once collective and compelling, true somehow to the unwritten text of a common blackness. (1988, 181)

Among other things, Hurston's participation in the FWP was a condition of her economic circumstances. But it is also fairly clear that she could sense the strong integrationist impulses that were building in the years before World War II. I do not mean to suggest that her resurrection of a black vernacular tradition was calculated in the short term to profit herself or fellow black participants in the cultural machinery, but I am saying that Hurston's concern with aesthetics had an overtly political dimension. In opening this chapter, I referred to Walter Benjamin's assertion that stripping a writer from his or her "aura" of tradition served to shift the meaning of art to the overtly political. Hurston's involvement in the Florida FWP problemizes the relationship between her interest in the cultic fabric of the black community and her desire to transpose that understanding for the benefit of a mass audience. If we view the Florida FWP in the most optimistic light possible, "The Florida Negro" and the Florida guide constituted a "pure situation" that used traditional ethnic elements to open a road to new, collective, and democratic art forms. On the other hand, Hurston's role as a professional set her apart and stripped her from her source's aura. The black blues and folklore traditions produce concentration, empathy, absorption, and identification in the audience but, as the climate of the 1930s was geared to a consensual interpretation of the nation and its ethnic enclaves, the sophistication of black culture was often reduced to a supporting role in the larger national drama. Americans, reassured of the vitality of their numerous enclaves in the pages of the American Guide Series, could explain their cultural attitudes by arguing that the larger social dynamic that brings groups together in the first place prevails over any forms of latent racism that occasionally surface. America was the nation of democratic proletarianism, and as the decade progressed the individual achievements of Afro-American artists tended to be appropriated quite easily. The final fifteen minutes of the Marx Brothers' film *A Day at the Races*, which also works off a popularized image of the Florida black, is a classic case of ethocentrism that is folded easily into mass cultural stereotypes and expectations without implying an overt racism.

Works with aura tend to encourage political and aesthetic passivity in the audiences who receive them. The WPA Guide series, for all their "romantic possibilities," were the consummate testimonial to modernity and its technological means of reproduction. No state guide lacks chapters mythologizing a state's transportation, industry and commerce, and newspapers and radio. Indeed the vernacular elements of a state are consistently wedded to the state's economic and technological aspects; the two are merged into a single portrait. Modern mass society invites a disruption of the traditional context of "authentic" forms, confusing the audience's mode of response. Curiously, the preservationist strain exhibited by the FWP's writers and editors unintentionally risked trivializing the aesthetic traditions of the inhabitants and leading to the production of fake authentic productions—the classic roadside tourist trap that has captured a papiermâché "world's largest alligator."

Fake auras do not restore weakened traditions. However, Hurston's earlier embrace of the avant-garde in Harlem caused her to envision her role in the FWP as distinctly modernist in spirit. Given that superadded context, the (mis)appropriation of her Floridian sources was excusable in much the same way that James Agee's use of three poor white families in rural Alabama eventually helped the general class of poor whites by dramatizing the plight of three representative families. The connection between the two cases is not purely coincidental. Both writers' participation in the WPA made available to them the same vocational strategy—namely, each writer, out of a desire to see the regionally specific detail rendered for the benefit of a passive and unknowing public, sought out "genuine sources" and gently exploited them in order to call attention to a lifestyle that traditionally went unrepresented.

As we now know, the families that Agee lived with while he was writing *Let Us Now Praise Famous Men* never received a copy of the book, and many years later they were bitterly disappointed by Agee's portraits, which contained thinly veiled psychosexual urges he projected on some family members. Hurston's involvement with the Florida FWP is much less dramatic, but in professional outlook and methodology the cases are virtually the same. While it is probably true that Hurston maintained a deep respect for her sources (as was probably true of James Agee as well), it is undeniable that her work often merged the public agenda of the Florida FWP with her own ego and perception of the "genuine" in her sources. Hurston can be placed within that tradition of African-American modernism that conceived of "black expressive culture as a reservoir from which a quintessentially Afro-American spirit flowed" described by Houston Baker as "an eternally transformative impulse that converts desire not only into resonant and frequently courageous sound but ceaseless motion" (1988, 5). Her cultural anthropology, expressed in the Florida guide, works to describe the situation of the Florida black with great precision. As Robert Hemenway indicated, Hurston felt that "black lives are universal, and black authors have not transcended but pushed deep into racial experience to prove it" (307).

Hurston's concentration on black culture allowed her to moderate her association with the white cultural establishment. Throughout the 1920s whites were paternalistic benefactors who promoted black artists through literary contest and prizes, as well as the primary consumers of the rediscovered black tradition. The white people in Hurston's life—Fannie Hurst, Charlotte Mason, Franz Boas—fueled her ambitions and infected her work with many of the paradoxes that critics of both races have noticed. As she claimed in *Their Eyes Were Watching God,* "The white man thinks in a written language" while the "negro thinks in hieroglyphics" ([1937] 1978, 158) by which she means word or thought pictures, the basic elements of a dramatic storytelling tradition. Being able to distinguish the essential features of a racial culture and then to manipulate those features in his or her work gives a writer a great deal of social mobility. Hurston's ability to cross racial (and even gender) lines was a hallmark of her literary work. When it suited her purpose, she could inscribe her work in several traditions at once—this too was a conspicuous feature of her involvement with the Florida FWP. Hurston felt that the essence of black experience engaged a notion of revision. She claims, "The Negro, the world over, is famous. [He] imitates and revises, not from a feeling of inferiority," rather "for the love of it" (Gates, 1988, 198). Such an understanding was a major prop supporting her vocational strategy.

Though Hurston probably could not sense the powerful influence black culture would exert on the cultural and symbolic codes of white Americans during her life, popular myths—a definable and unambiguous "American" identity, for instance—have been severely challenged and modified by those cultural characteristics that seemed to be "on the margins" during the 1960s. In fact, her work with the WPA indicates that literature and culture are significantly bound within sociological concerns. It is hard to say with certainty that Afro-American culture was a marginal element in the 1930s; recent criticism argues persuasively that African-American culture consistently escaped social and textual boundaries. Hurston's work was certainly aimed at removing, or at least lowering, the division (real or perceived) between the ethnocentric traditions of Florida blacks and mass culture. That goal has become something of a commonplace reality in recent African-American criticism. Henry Louis Gates, Jr., observes: "Black literature, recent critics seem to be saying, can no longer simply 'name the margin' . . . It is difficult to deny that certain elements of African-American culture are the products of cross-cultural encounters with white racism. No longer, for example, are the concepts of 'black' and 'white' thought to be preconstituted; rather they are mutually constitutive and socially produced" (1990, 20–21).

Hurston's hiatus in Florida was a colonial venture—a profitable (re)discovery of native territory. Like the West Indian natives who made expeditions to Florida ahead of the white man in the belief that the state's many springs held miraculous properties, Hurston probed simplified allegories and generative musical traditions in an effort to stabilize the decline of the communal context of communicable experience.

Notes

1. I borrow the terms extrinsic and intrinsic history from Robert Stepto (1988). In his essay on Afro-American literature, Stepto complains that too much scholarship is devoted to writing extrinsic history that asks questions that invite the melding of mere fact and chronology, and therefore do not risk the acts of narration and fictionalization that is characteristic of intrinsic histories. Herein I hope to establish Hurston's creation and adherence to a "vocational strategy" that helped to remove her from a middling status that one might expect from a black woman writer working in a white, male, officiallly sanctioned work environment. Because she held to this vocational strategy, the work she did for the Florida FWP was faithful to her own sense of self and respectful to the original sources that she adapted.

2. Critics have begun to view Hurston as more than a product of the 1920s Harlem Renaissance. As Robert Stepto argues in *The Columbia Literary History of the United States*: "Hurston wrote of vagabonds and was a vagabond. Harlem was a crossroads, a mecca, but most pilgrims to most meccas travel with round-trip tickets . . . a fuller and truer Literary history (richer in texts, years, and dominion) becomes available when Hughes and Hurston are allowed to journey forth, as they did—Hughes to wherever, and Hurston to her home in Eatonville, Florida" (795). As Stepto indicates, Hurston's tenure with the Florida FWP, though it was a brief episode in a long life, is important to our understanding of Afro-American culture in its reconstituting a version of the black professional writer rather than simply supplementing a literary biography.

3. Andrew Homzy, a musician who teaches at Concordia University, has provided many wonderful program notes pertaining to the album *Black, Brown, and Beige* in a 1988 four-album collection released under the Bluebird label, catalog number 6641-1-RB.

Works Cited

Agee, James, and Walker Evans. *Let Us Now Praise Famous Men.* Boston: Houghton Mifflin, 1941.

Baker, Houston. *Afro-American Poetics: Revisions of Harlem and the Black Aesthetic.* Madison: University of Wisconsin Press, 1988.

Baker, Houston A., Jr. "Belief, Theory, and Blues: Notes for a Post-Structuralist Criticism of Afro-American Literature." In *Studies in Black American Literature: Belief vs. Theory in Black American Literary Criticism,* vol. 2, edited by Joe Weixlmann and Chester J. Fontenot, 5–30. Greenwood, FL: Penkevill Publishing, 1986.

Benjamin, Walter. "The Work of Art in the Age of Mechanical Reproduction." In *Illuminations,* edited by Hannah Arendt, 173–209. New York: Schocken Books, 1969.

Federal Writers' Project. *The WPA Guide to Florida.* New York: Oxford University Press, 1939. Reprint. New York: Pantheon Books, 1984.

Gates, Henry Louis, Jr. *The Signifying Monkey: A Theory of Afro-American Literary Criticism.* New York: Oxford University Press, 1988.

———. "Tell Me Sir . . . What Is 'Black' Literature?" *PMLA* 105, no. 1 (January 1990): 11–22.

Geertz, Clifford. "Thick Description: Toward an Interpretative Theory of Culture." In *The Interpretation of Cultures.* New York: Basic Books, 1973.

Hemenway, Robert. *Zora Neale Hurston: A Literary Biography.* Urbana: University of Illinois Press, 1977.

Hurston, Zora Neale. "Spirituals and Neo-Spirituals." 1934. Reprinted in *Negro: An Anthology,* edited by Nancy Cunard and Hugh Ford, 223–25. New York: Frederick Ungar Publishing Co., 1970.

———. *Their Eyes Were Watching God.* Philadelphia: J. B. Lippincott, 1937. Reprint. Urbana: University of Illinois Press, 1978.

Stepto, Robert. *The Columbia Literary History of the United States.* New York: Columbia University Press, 1988.

Stott, Bill. "Introduction." In *Remembering America: A Sampler of the WPA American Guide Series.* New York: Collier Books, 1985.

Wilson, Christopher. *The Labor of Words: Literary Professionalism in the Progressive Era.* Athens: University of Georgia Press, 1985.

Wintz, Cary. *Black Culture and the Harlem Renaissance.* Houston: Rice University Press, 1988.

CHAPTER FOURTEEN

Text and Personality in Disguise
and in the Open: Zora Neale Hurston's
Dust Tracks on a Road

   KATHLEEN HASSALL

Zora Neale Hurston's autobiography, *Dust Tracks on a Road* (1942), has baffled and dismayed many who admire her and provided an easy target for those disposed to attack. It has long been famous for its erasures, its inconsistencies, its eccentricity of focus, and a tone which has struck some readers as dishonest. To some it has seemed to withhold as much as it reveals: The author conceals her date of birth, for instance, and expunges at least one husband. Some evidence suggests that Hurston silently edited ten years from her account. The most troubling "omission" for many readers, however, has been the book's apparent refusal to document the impact—emotional, intellectual, even financial—of racism on the author's life.

When *Dust Tracks* first appeared, in 1942, Arna Bontemps was tart: "Miss Hurston," he noted, "deals very simply with the more serious aspects of Negro life in America—she ignores them" (3). When the book was reissued in 1969, Darwin Turner scoffed at its implication that Zora Hurston had "never . . . experienced a reportable conflict with a white person"; on the basis of her presentation of herself in *Dust Tracks*, he judged her "desperate for recognition and reassurance to assuage her feelings of inferiority; a blind follower of that social code which approves arrogance toward peers and 'inferiors' but requires total psychological commitment or subservience to one's 'superiors'"(v). Readers notably more sympathetically inclined than Turner have also been troubled. Robert Hemenway, Hurston's biographer, noting that "much of *Dust Tracks* is untrustworthy," explains that the autobiography is in part deformed because it "sacrifices truth to the politics of racial harmony" (1984, xiii–xiv). Even Alice Walker—who has called *Their Eyes Were Watching God* (1937) "as necessary to me and to other women as air and water" (1983c, 7)—has called the autobiography "the most unfortunate thing Zora ever wrote," lamenting its "unctuousness, so out of character for Zora . . . a result of dependency, a sign of her powerlessness" (1980, xvii). "It pained me," she has said, "to see Zora pretending to be naive and grateful" (1983b, 110).

Perhaps there is an important connection between the complaints about the inconsistencies and omissions in the autobiography, the complaints about its "nonconfrontational strategy," and the complaints about its focus: It seems to spend a disproportionate number of pages on Hurston's earliest experiences in Florida, while leaving much of her adult life in shadow. (In terms of organization, the autobiography seems to lose forward momentum and then to deconstruct midway: It begins as a chronological narrative, describing the founding of Eatonville—the author's putative Florida birthplace—and then the courtship of John Hurston and Lucy Ann Potts, her parents. In chapters 2 through 6 it has much to say about the author's Eatonville childhood, but then it begins to telescope time, alternating leaps forward with recursions and digressions. By chapter 12 it has abandoned chronology—and conventional autobiography—altogether, in favor of a series of essays on topics ranging from religion to black intraracial dynamics.) It has little—eight pages altogether—to say about Hurston's career as the author of stories, plays, essays, three novels, and two books of folklore; it has almost nothing to say about her high-energy, high-impact part in the Harlem Renaissance. Again and again it returns to her Florida experiences. Why?

One way to make sense of this problematic text is to recognize it as a series of performances by an actress trained in Eatonville. It might be argued that Zora Neale Hurston was essentially a performance artist: She was a natural actress; a sometimes joyful, often brilliant mimic; a woman inconsistent in many ways and often by choice, but consistent in employing her various media as both message and massage. Alice Walker's choice of the word "pretending" to describe what Hurston does in *Dust Tracks* is telling. *Dust Tracks* seems to be nonconfrontational; it seems to reflect the "powerlessness" of its author. It is possible, however, to read the autobiography differently, to read it as a set of glimpses into the character of an inventive, resourceful, spirited, effective warrior—in disguise. Pretense, misdirection, secrecy, and a deliberate, slippery, unpredictability—all venerable confrontational strategies, and all lessons Hurston learned in Eatonville—direct her performances in *Dust Tracks.*

It might be said that the text itself is in disguise: a direct but encoded response to racism. It only seems to refuse much of the explanation, interpretation, and even inspiration many readers hoped it would provide: These, too, are present in objectified form. Hurston was expected to report and interpret Hurston; instead she *presents* Hurston—or rather she presents an assemblage of fictionalized Hurstons, irreconcilable in some ways both with each other and with the known facts of her life, and yet by their very contradictions revealing her essential strength. Complex, passionate, proud, she was all her life engaged simultaneously in celebrating the culture of her race while thwarting reductive definitions of herself and refusing restrictive choices. The authenticity of her autobiography lies in its performance of the strategies she so often used: Here she reinvents facts, withholds information, blurs the distinction between history and fiction, insists on privacy, changes hats, wears masks, serves her own purposes, and refuses conscription—even in a good cause. She contradicts herself, which prevents closure. She shows her reader how it was possible for her so many times in life to slip through the nets of people and ideas that would have held her. She does on these pages what she did at Barnard, in Harlem, and in Polk County—what she learned to do in Eatonville. Arguably, there is no distortion in her devoting so much of her autobiography to her Florida experiences, because these experiences explain her. They translate a thousand choices she made in her life and in her art.

It has been often noted that Hurston's childhood in Eatonville—an all-black town whose laws were written by her own father, three times elected mayor—goes far to explain both her confidence and her insistence that black culture is not pathological, not merely a reaction to white oppression, but a vital, healthy, *separate* tradition. The poet June Jordan, for instance, has pointed to Eatonville as "a supportive, nourishing environment" which underlies Hurston's ability to convey "a total, Black reality where Black people do not represent issues: they represent their own, particular selves in a Family/Community setting that permits relaxation from hunted/warrior postures, and that fosters . . . natural, person-postures" (6). Jordan's use of the word "postures" is apt: Hurston describes a community which supports, nourishes, and fosters not only relaxation, but performance. Eatonville functions as a stage on which individuals and groups adopt spontaneous, creative poses; they act out courtships and feuds, conversions and triumphs, history and prophesy. In Eatonville, performance, or as Hurston significantly terms it, "lying," is the central creative activity.

The "liars" on the front porch of Joe Clark's store—"the heart and spring of the town" (*Dust Tracks,* [1942] 1984, 61)—generate continuous unrehearsed performances, making and breaking reputations, entertaining themseves and each other, and filling the air with brags, jokes, judgments, and new versions of old tales. Hurston reports that as a child she "could and did drag [her] feet going in and out, whenever [she] was sent there for something, to allow whatever was being said to hang in [her] ear": Over time she heard everything from "sly references to the physical condition of women" and "brags on male potency by the parties of the first part" to confident explanations of various decisions made by God (62).

In 1935, Hurston the anthropologist would present black folklore in *Mules and Men* through vivid representations of oral performances; ten years earlier Hurston the raconteur had mesmerized sophisticated party-goers in New York with performances of her own: "She was a perfect mimic, and she displayed a wide range of storytelling techniques learned from the masters of Joe Clark's store porch" (Hemenway, [1977] 1980, 22). She had learned the lessons of the store porch so well, and come to enjoy oral performance so much, in fact, that some friends worried about her squandering her talent on conversation and never writing anything down. When she did write, whatever she wrote—"autobiography" or "anthropology" or "fiction"—was colored by the "lying sessions" in Eatonville.

In *Dust Tracks,* as in *Mules and Men* and her best novel, *Their Eyes Were Watching God,* she presents oral performance—lying—as both a celebration of individual voice and a positive interaction between the performer and the community. In *Their Eyes,* typically, Eatonville fact informs her fiction. Joe Clark becomes Jody Starks; Eatonville appears under its own name. The performers on the store porch are familiar, and their lying sessions are the center of the community's social and creative life. One of the liars wants to improvise on the subject of "Big John de Conquer"—"Lawd, Ah loves to talk about Big John. Less we tell lies on Ole John"—but then three young women come into view, and the performance glibly changes focus, becoming a "pushing, shoving show of gallantry . . . to the entertainment of everybody. . . . The girls and everybody else help laugh. They know it's not courtship. It's acting-out courtship and everybody is in the play. The three girls hold the center of the stage" ([1937] 1978, 104–5).

Not quite everybody *is* in the play, however: A central issue in the novel is that Jody Starks denies his wife a role—and so denies her both the right to act and the right to play. While the other players on the store porch strut and shout and laugh, Janie is invariably sent inside. Joe has "forbidden her to indulge. He didn't want her talking after such trashy people. . . . [W]hen Lige or Sam or Walter or some of the other big picture talkers were using the side of the world for a canvas, Joe would hustle her off inside the store to sell something" (85). Joe's denial of Janie's right to participate in the play-acting on the store porch finally amounts to a denial of her rights to individuality and community. To use John F. Callahan's phrase, what Joe denies Janie is the opportunity to "survive and thrive in the world as an articulate presence and personality" (106). Janie's frustration and her increasing resentment of Joe's "classing her

off" from the other actors—his imposition of silence or absence—under-
scores the importance of performance as a form of play and as both
participation in and contribution to the creative life of the community.
Significantly, after Joe's death, Janie's happy life with Tea Cake includes
his endorsement of her participation in the lying sessions out on the muck:
"The men held big arguments here like they used to do on the store
porch. Only here, she could listen and laugh and even talk some herself
if she wanted to. She got so she could tell big stories herself from listening
to the rest" (200). For Janie, as for Hurston, performance, power, and
freedom are linked.

"Big stories" were forbidden to Janie until she was forty years old, but
Hurston herself began to act as a child: "I came in from play one day and
told my mother how a bird had talked to me with a tail so long that
while he sat up in the top of the pine tree his tail was dragging the
ground. It was a soft beautiful bird tail, all blue and pink and red and
green. In fact I climbed up the bird's tail and sat up the tree and had a
long talk with the bird. . . . I dashed into the kitchen and told Mama how
the lake had talked with me, and invited me to walk all over it. I told
the lake I was afraid of getting drowned, but the lake assured me it
wouldn't think of doing *me* like that" (*Dust Tracks,* 71). Hurston's grandmother was furious at the child—"Why dat lil' heifer is lying just as fast
as a horse can trot," she said. "Stop her! Wear her back-side out." But
Hurston's mother recognized that she was "just playing," "never tried
to break [her]," and "never seemed displeased" (72).

The grandmother's furious objection was very likely based in part on
a fear Zora's father had also expressed: that the child's exuberant—and
imprudent—"forward ways" might someday draw fire in a white racist
society that expected blacks to remain as far as possible both silent and
invisible. Papa "predicted dire things for me," Hurston remembered.
"The white folks were not going to stand for it. I was going to be hung
before I got grown. Somebody was going to blow me down for my sassy
tongue" (21)—and Papa's fears were not unfounded. His predictions bring
to mind a snatch of autobiography written by a Mississippi woman in
1969: "My parents taught us never to have fear of the white peoples
because they were just people like anybody else and wouldn't harm us.
As long as we be truthful" (Walker, 1983a, 30). Almost certainly, her
grandmother recognized that the child Zora was engaged in a dangerous
activity, presenting fictions as facts, *performing* fictions. She never an-
nounced that she was telling a story; instead she presented herself as an
eyewitness and participant, a child who had just had a conversation with
a lake. Her grandmother wanted the child smacked to knock the lying
out of her—otherwise, Hurston recalled, "I was just as sure to be hung

before I got grown as a gun was iron"—but her mother was adamant: the child's spirit was not to be "squinched" (*Dust Tracks*, 72). The performances went on.

The concept of performance is everywhere in *Dust Tracks*. Again and again Hurston describes the performances of others or reports her own performances. She also performs—and when she does so, she never announces her assumption of a character. As she did as a child in her mother's kitchen—and as the liars on the store porch did before her—she simply begins to talk. The audience—her reader—may take her to be lying or take the lie for truth, and may very well never realize there's a performance going on: This is always the position of the audience in guerrilla theater.

Hurston's descriptions of the performances of others serve to establish by example what she maintains in "Characteristics of Negro Expression": "Every phase of Negro life is highly dramatized. No matter how joyful or how sad the case there is sufficient poise for drama. . . . There is an impromptu ceremony always ready for every hour of life" ([1934] 1981, 49):

> It is said that Negroes keep nothing secret, that they have no reserve. This ought not to seem strange when one considers that we are an outdoor people accustomed to communal life. Add this to all-permeating drama and you have the explanation. There is no privacy in an African village. Loves, fights, possessions are, to misquote Woodrow Wilson, "Open disagreements openly arrived at." The community is given the benefit of a good fight as well as a good wedding. An audience is a necessary part of any drama. We merely go with nature rather than against it. . . . So then if a man or woman is a facile hurler of threats, why should he or she not show their wares to the community? Hence, the holding of all quarrels and fights in the open. One relieves one's pent-up anger and at the same time earns laurels in intimidation. Besides, one does the community a service. There is nothing so exhilarating as watching well-matched opponents go into action. (60–61)

In *Dust Tracks*, writing about Florida, she tells of holding big "lying contests"—with prizes for the winners—in a sawmill camp in Polk County (189), and she describes the particular kind of performance called "specifying," or "putting your foot up on a person": "If you are sufficiently armed—enough to stand off a panzer division—and know what to do with your weapons after you get 'em, it is all right to go to the house of your enemy, put one foot up on his steps, rest one elbow on your knee and play in the family. That is another way of saying play the dozens, which also is a way of saying low-rate your enemy's ancestors and him, down to the present moment for reference, and then go into his future as far as your imagination leads you" (187–89). Having established a context of oral performance, she presents herself as a performer, from childhood on, within that context.

She also makes clear that under threat, the performances could be reactive. Ordinarily celebrations of various kinds of strength—imaginative, verbal, even sexual—the performances could on occasion respond to matters of great seriousness, like the protective performances—pretenses of ignorance, incompetence, affection, compliance—which could and did save the lives of slaves. In the chapter of *Dust Tracks* called "My People! My People!" Hurston writes about curious language she heard all her life: black people telling jokes of which black people—and particularly black women—were the butt; black people telling stories in which they represented themselves as monkeys outright or as men with monkey-size brains; black people questioning the comparative capability and worth of people with dark skins. Then, however, she tells a story about a night during her childhood: It was possible to hear the sounds of a man being beaten, screaming, back in the woods. One Eatonville man was not home yet, and everyone in town remembered things that had happened in Georgia, Alabama, west Florida. With very few words, a dozen men, Hurston's father among them, loaded their guns and went off into the dark. Behind them, the lights went off in Eatonville. The doors were barred, and behind them were ranked the only weapons left, scythes and axes and pitchforks. In the dark houses the women and chidren kept silent and waited. The alarm turned out to be false—the victim was a white man being punished by his neighbors for having written something indiscreet in an Orlando newspaper—and finally Hurston, her sisters and brothers and mother heard "a bubble of laughing voices" coming toward their barn. "Mama," she says, "hissed at us to shut up when, in fact, nobody was saying a thing" (229). The men came home laughing too loud and too long, and telling jokes. Hurston's mother was too unnerved to be able even to light a match, but neither she, nor her husband, nor any of the men acknowledged what they had feared. "[T]hey just laughed," Hurston says. "The men who spoke of members of their race as monkeys had gone out to die for one. The men who were always saying, 'My skin-folks, but not kin-folks; my race but not my taste,' had rushed forth to die for one of these same contemptibles" (231). Both the language before the fact and the laughter afterwards seem to have been performances; the *reality* was the dozen men going quietly into the dark, in the direction of the screams.

Hurston's death in 1960 came too soon, of course, for her to know the recent work of Henry Louis Gates, Jr. His identification of the "Signifying

Monkey" of African-American culture with Esu, the Yoruba trickster figure and messenger of the gods, would have delighted her. Gates has shown that the monkey trope she puzzled over—immovably convinced as she was of the strength and beauty of her own culture—is in fact a *sign* of the persistence of black tradition in the face of white-imposed displacement and the white myth that aboard the slave ships, "the Middle Passage was so traumatic that it functioned to create in the African a tabula rasa of consciousness" (4). Moreover, Gates reports that "[i]n Yoruba... 'monkey' (òwè) and proverb or riddle (òwe) are virtual homonyms" (16): The monkey is both a figure in disguise and a trope for the indeterminate, the ambiguous, the enigmatic. Gates defines "signifying" in part as "repetition and revision": His identification of the monkey's characteristic strengths signifies on both Zora's life and her presentation of that life in *Dust Tracks.*

In *Their Eyes Were Watching God,* Hurston describes another instance of performance as a technique for coping under threat, performance as a disguise under which action is possible. The bigot Mrs. Turner values other black people in direct relationship to the lightness of their skin. She tries repeatedly to convince Janie (whose father and grandfather were white) to break away from Tea Cake, "too black," in Mrs. Turner's estimation, to be worthy of Janie's love. "It's too many black folks already," says Mrs. Turner, with Tea Cake listening. "We oughta lighten up de race.... Ah can't stand black niggers. Ah don't blame de white folks from hatin' 'em 'cause Ah can't stand 'em mahself" ([1937] 1978, 209–10). Tea Cake wants Mrs. Turner gone, as do the other blacks who work with him on the muck: They all know she despises them even as she takes their money in her restaurant.

With payday, then, comes a performance: Two of the men seem to be particularly drunk and to get into a drunken argument at Mrs. Turner's eating place; Tea Cake seems to try his best to break them up, urging them to show some respect for nice Mrs. Turner; the fight seems naturally to escalate, to get out of hand, and to wreck the restaurant. In a matter of minutes the debris is knee deep. The next day the two men who started the fight come by to apologize to Mrs. Turner in the midst of the wreckage; they seem to be profoundly embarrassed about the damage they say they do not remember causing. They give her five dollars apiece; she goes back to Miami. Hurston never overtly identifies this episode as a performance. She establishes a motive for action against the colorist Mrs. Turner; she has her characters express a desire to have the woman gone; then she lets the actions—deliberately innocent in appearance—speak for themselves.

Again in *Dust Tracks* appears evidence that Hurston herself was able to use disguise and performance for various ends from childhood on. When visiting white "ladies," enchanted by the child Zora's ability to read the story of Jupiter and Persephone, held out their "flower-looking fingers" for her to shake and asked her if she loved school, she lied and said she did (50). When her elders praised her for her childhood "devotion to the Bible," which she was *really* reading in order to learn "the facts of life"— all the things "Moses told the Hebrews not to do in Leviticus"—she just said thank you (55). She fascinated her playmates by regaling them with "the real truth of the matter" about an Eatonville man, Mr. Pendir, whom she knew to be able to transform himself into an alligator and walk "the surface [of the lake] like a pavement" (81).

Her telling of the conception of the Mr. Pendir story may itself be a performance. In 1934 she published a piece called "Uncle Monday" in Nancy Cunard's anthology, *The Negro.* Ostensibly the Uncle Monday story is about the folklore surrounding a conjure doctor reported to be able to walk on water and change himself into an alligator. Here Hurston reports various widely believed exploits of Uncle Monday, and especially his defeat of a rival hoodoo doctor, Aunt Judy Bickerstaff. This story is inarguably the Mr. Pendir story, with some interesting differences. In *Dust Tracks* Hurston says she turned Mr. Pendir into an alligator for her own amusement. She talks about how she constructed the story as a child, adding deliciously frightening details for the entertainment of her friends. She explains that when an elderly local woman, Mrs. Bronson, had a stroke and clung overnight, half her body paralyzed, to the edge of the Blue Sink, it was an inspiration: "Right away, I could see the mighty tail of Mr. Pendir slapping Old Lady Bronson into the lake. Then he had stalked away across the lake like the Devil walking up and down the earth" (81). What she describes in *Dust Tracks* in 1942 as Old Lady Bronson's experience, she had described in 1934 as Aunt Judy Bickerstaff's experience—minus any reference to non-hoodoo causes for Aunt Judy's night of horror on the lake, and minus any indication that Uncle Monday's hoodoo powers were given him by Zora Neale Hurston. Perhaps Hurston in *Dust Tracks* presents folklore—community "property"—as her own invention; perhaps describing "Uncle Monday" and "Aunt Judy Bicker-staff," she presents her own inventions as folklore; perhaps *both* presentations are in part fictions. (In *Dust Tracks,* by the way, the Eatonville midwife, never connected with hoodoo, is "Aunt Judy.")

Certainly one of the ways Hurston disguised herself all her life was to deconstruct the borders between various definitions of herself and her work. She produced fictionalized anthropology and anthropological fiction, on the one hand introducing a semifictional version of herself to guide her reader through the world of *Mules and Men*; on the other, weaving traditional black folklore into the fabric of her own short stories. She was collecting—or rather she had absorbed—a great stock of folklore materials before she ever studied anthropology at all; Arna Bontemps, who knew her in New York during the Harlem Renaissance, recalled her performnances then of "exaggerated stories that she called 'lies'": he professed not to be "able to tell where the folk left off and Zora began" (Hemenway, [1977] 1980, 64). She was made in part of the folk tradition, but then she made parts of the tradition herself.

Moreover, her choosing not to be precise about the "ownership" of various parts of her work, her apparent carelessness about attribution, makes sense placed against a tradition that not only endorses, but celebrates "repetition and revision, or repetition with a signal difference" (Gates, xxiv). The performances on the store porch are all grounded in tradition, new tellings—with original embellishments—of old tales. High John de Conquer, Old Massa, Brer Rabbit, and Sis Snail "belong" to the community in general as well as to the particular liar who adds to their stories. The listeners' familiarity with the traditional tales informs and enriches their response to the version at hand. Absolute invention—the idea of a genuinely "original" source—is foreign to such a tradition. "What we really mean by originality," Hurston says, "is the modification of ideas" ("Characteristics," 58).

In the Dust Tracks chapter entitled "Religion," she makes clear both the importance and the traditional nature of performance in the Eatonville church where her father preached. The celebrants' ecstatic testimonies of their "Christian experiences," the "visions" that brought them forcibly to God, filled the church with "tumult" and "high drama"; however, "These visions are traditional. I knew them by heart as did the rest of the congregation, but still it was exciting to see how the converts would handle them. Some of them made up new details. Some of them would forget a part and improvise clumsily or fill up the gap with shouting. The audience knew, but everybody acted as if every word of it was new" (272–74). Again Eatonville presents the model of performance (by both the convert and the congregation) unannounced, traditional materials employed and recognized but unacknowledged. Gates notes in his introduction to The Signifying Monkey that it has long been apparent "that black writers read, repeated, imitated, and revised each other's texts to a remarkable extent" (xxii); the black oral tradition—and both Hurston's performances and reports of performances in Dust Tracks—is similarly grounded in response and revision.

"'Plagiarism,'" notes Madelyn Jablon, "'is an integral part of the transmission of folk." In "Zora as Literary Theorist, or the Zora Aesthetic," Jablon explores Hurston's struggles to speak the language of scientific discourse in the voice of an African-American storyteller, and the difficulties caused by her tendency "to improvise on [her] material," a license at war with Western scientific tradition but essential to the success of the storyteller's performance. Jablon speaks, too, of Hurston's various self-representations, her wearing various disguises—"a white lab coat," "the mask of the devoted student," and a "humble stance"—in order to negotiate with her white mentor (Franz Boas) and her white patron ("God-mother" Mrs. R. Osgood Mason). Mrs. Mason had contracted for absolute control over Hurston's anthropological research (Hemenway, [1977] 1980, 109–10)—and so, perhaps in part to escape the woman's suffocating patronage, Hurston apparently abandoned anthropology for fiction—and yet, as Jablon points out, Hurston's "research" had always born resemblances to both fiction and drama. The pattern of acting-out, performing in person and on the page so that the "real" Hurston was always both present and absent, so pervaded her life that its marking of *Dust Tracks* cannot surprise.

Hurston's first really successful short fiction, "Drenched in Light," published in 1924, is about a little girl named Isie Watts who lives in Eatonville, Florida. Isie's grandmother's name is Hurston's grandmother's name, and Robert Hemenway has pointed out that "Zora's identification with Isie is almost total" ([1977] 1980, 11). He notes that Isie's favorite occupation—sitting happily on a gatepost outside her home and begging rides from passing cars—is a childhood memory Hurston reports not only in *Dust Tracks,* but in a 1928 article, "How It Feels To Be Colored Me." More interesting, however, is his characterization of "Drenched in Light" as "a belligerent, combative statement of independence," his observation that the story reflects Hurston's deliberate choice to focus on strength, to present black experience, and herself, without sorrow, without rage, and without self-pity ([1977] 1980, 11). Hurston put much of herself into her portrait of Isie, but it seems clear that she also put much of Isie into her portrait of herself. She could and did silently, deliberately edit her own life.

Many of the seeming inconsistencies in *Dust Tracks* reflect these emendations. Whole sections appear to be unannounced performances. For instance, there is Hurston's presentation of herself as a naïve little girl who charmed a traveling Gilbert and Sullivan company with her combination of green innocence and spunk. One of the performers took her on as a lady's maid, and the whole company made a pet of her, she says. She was subjected to endless good-natured teasing: The gentlemen, with serious faces, would send her to inquire about the "welfare and condition of [the ladies'] cherries and spangles" (137), and they derived great amusement from Hurston's inability to understand the message she delivered or the answer she received.

This is the same Hurston who *years* before had heard men on the store porch call out to passing women, "Hey, Sugar! What's on de rail for de lizard?" (*Dust Tracks*, 63), the same Hurston whose Uncle Jim was famous because he passed by the store, stopping off to buy a few presents, on his way to see "a certain transient light of love," and then his wife passed by, going the same direction and carrying an ax, and then the wife passed by one more time going the opposite way, still carrying the ax, but also carrying the retrieved presents and her husband's pants (23–24). Hurston's own mother, over the question of Zora's father's affections, had "spoken out" one woman and gone after another with a horsewhip (17). Hurston cannot have been baffled and blushing, years later, over cherries and spangles.

She very much needed that job, though, and she managed to convince the members of the company that she was what they wanted her to be. She successfully maintained the performance day and night for eighteen months: She was clearly far and away the troupe's best actor. Chapter 8 of *Dust Tracks*, "Backstage and the Railroad," provides a small sample of her performance in this role.

On other occasions she presented herself—and presents herself in *Dust Tracks*—in other disguises. There is the matter of the missing ten years: It seems clear now that Hurston was twenty-six, not sixteen, when she started high school, and thirty-four when she enrolled in Barnard College. Yet her autobiography, as Hemenway has pointed out, "gushes with a schoolgirl's enthusiasm" over her high-school experiences. He wonders whether "the mature author [is] creating a teenager who never was or perpetuating a myth created in 1917" (1984, xii). The question seems to be whether she was performing in 1917, in 1942, or both. As for Barnard, "those who arranged for her admission thought her a young, untried coed" (xii); she was in fact not only a veteran of the Gilbert and Sullivan tour, but a grown woman who had worked for years as a domestic and a waitress, and who, perhaps, had already been married. She was able to create a Zora to suit Barnard. Then, discussing her Barnard career in *Dust Tracks*, she creates a Zora who has "no lurid tales to tell of race discrimination" (169). There is evidence that she *did* encounter race discrimination at Barnard, but she doesn't deny that: She simply refuses to tell the lurid tale. This is consistent with her lifelong ability to accept mixed blessings when the unmixed variety were not forthcoming; with her impulse, clear as early as "Drenched in Light," to present herself in terms of health and strength; with her tendency to protect herself by producing Zoras suitable to the occasion at hand; and with her unwavering refusal to assume the posture of a victim. Throughout her career she struggled to make enough money barely to live. She knew that black writers who focused on "the race problem" could and did sell their work, but she scoffed at those who "made whole careers of being 'Race' men and women" (*Dust Tracks,* 218); she insisted she was not "tragically colored" and did "not belong to the sobbing school of Negrohood who hold that nature somehow has given them a lowdown dirty deal" ("How It Feels," 215). Consistently, she refused to define black consciousness as a reaction to white oppression. When she reported her own experiences, she edited out pain; she edited out weakness. She refused to show her wounds.

Hemenway has reported that one difficulty he faced, beginning his work on Hurston's biography, was the contradictory, sometimes nearly opposite memories people had of her, though all the memories were vivid. "Her personality could seem a series of opposites," he notes, "and her friends were often incapable of reconciling the polarities of her personal style" ([1977] 1980, 5–6). Perhaps they were remembering the same actress in different roles, some of which overlapped. Hurston could be a primitive for Mrs. R. Osgood Mason or make her way into the volatile society of a lumber camp by presenting herself as a bootlegger's woman on the run. She could change her age and degree of experience to suit herself and the occasion. She could always produce fiction: When she was discovered, in 1950, working as a maid in Miami, she provided three different people with three different—and irreconcilable—explanations of her situation. Sometimes the performances offered her opportunities for growth or for advantage or even for play. She pretended to be a hot dog vendor because she wanted to study the speech of the hot dog buyers; she smoked on the street for the fun of shocking people. Often the performances offered her protection and disguise. As a black woman artist, she faced a daunting range of threats: opposition, silence, the deforming of her personality and her work. The performances helped her slip through the ropes. By generating enigmatic, inconsistent, multifarious performance Hurstons, she thwarted attempts to define her, and some of her secrets are still her own. Did she feel herself diminished by the acting? She was able to say, "I love myself when I am laughing. And then again when I am looking mean and impressive." There seems always to have been a strong and courageous face behind the mask—and Hurston seems always to have had a powerful appetite and an extraordinary capacity for joy. "When I set my hat at a certain angle," she said, "and saunter down Seventh Avenue . . . the cosmic Zora emerges. . . . How *can* any deny themselves the pleasure of my company? It's beyond me" (quoted in Bloom, 4).

Works Cited

Bloom, Harold. Introduction. *Modern Critical Interpretations: Zora Neale Hurston's "Their Eyes Were Watching God,"* edited by Harold Bloom, 1–4. New York: Chelsea House, 1987.

Bontemps, Arna. "From Eatonville, Florida to Harlem." *New York Herald Tribune,* November 22, 1942, 3.

Callahan, John F. "'Mah Tongue is in Mah Friend's Mouff': The Rhetoric of Intimacy and Immensity in *Their Eyes Were Watching God.*" In *Modern Critical Interpretations: Zora Neale Hurston's "Their Eyes Were Watching God,"* edited by Harold Bloom, 87–113. New York: Chelsea House, 1987.

Gates, Henry Louis, Jr. *The Signifying Monkey: A Theory of Afro-American Literary Criticism.* New York: Oxford University Press, 1988.

Hemenway, Robert E. Introduction. *Dust Tracks on a Road: An Autobiography,* by Zora Neale Hurston. 1942. 2d ed., edited by Robert E. Hemenway. Urbana: University of Illinois Press, Illini Books, 1984.

————. *Zora Neale Hurston: A Literary Biography.* Urbana: University of Illinois Press, 1977; Illini Books, 1980.

Hurston, Zora Neale. "Characteristics of Negro Expression." 1934. Reprinted in *The Sanctified Church: The Folklore Writings of Zora Neale Hurston,* 49–78. Berkeley, CA: Turtle Island Foundation, 1981.

————. "Drenched in Light." *Opportunity* 2 (December 1924):371–74.

————. *Dust Tracks on a Road: An Autobiography.* 1942. 2d ed., edited by Robert E. Hemenway. Urbana: University of Illinois Press, Illini Books, 1984.

————. "How It Feels To Be Colored Me." *World Tomorrow* (May 1928):215.

————. *Mules and Men.* 1935. Reprint. New York: Harper, 1970.

————. *Their Eyes Were Watching God.* 1937. Reprint. Urbana: University of Illinois Press, Illini Books, 1978.

————. "Uncle Monday." 1934. Reprinted in *The Sanctified Church: The Folklore Writings of Zora Neale Hurston,* 41–48. Berkeley, CA: Turtle Island Foundation, 1981.

Jablon, Madelyn. "Zora as Literary Theorist, or the Zora Aesthetic." Manuscript. Stockton State College, Pomona, NJ.

Jordan, June. "On Richard Wright and Zora Neale Hurston." *Black World* (August 1974):4–8.

Turner, Darwin. Introduction. *Dust Tracks on a Road,* by Zora Neale Hurston. 1942. Reprint. New York: Arno Press, 1969.

Walker, Alice. "But Yet and Still the Cotton Gin Kept on Working . . ." *Black Scholar* (January-February 1970):17–21. Reprinted in *In Search of Our Mothers' Gardens: Womanist Prose by Alice Walker,* 22–32. San Diego: Harvest/HBJ-Harcourt, 1983a.

————. "In Search of Zora Neale Hurston." *Ms.* (March 1975):74–79, 85–89. Reprinted as "Looking for Zora" in *In Search of Our Mothers' Gardens: Womanist Prose by Alice Walker,* 93–116. San Diego: Harvest/HBJ-Harcourt, 1983b.

————. "Saving the Life That Is Your Own: The Importance of Models in the Artist's Life." Speech, Modern Language Association, San Francisco, 1975. In *Women's Center Reid Lectureship: Papers by Alice Walker and June Jordan.* New York: Barnard College Women's Center, 1976. Reprinted in *In Search of Our Mothers'*

Gardens: Womanist Prose by Alice Walker, 3–14. San Diego: Harvest/HBJ-Harcourt, 1983c.

———. "Zora Neale Hurston—A Cautionary Tale and a Partisan View." Foreword. *Zora Neale Hurston: A Literary Biography*, by Robert E. Hemenway. Urbana: University of Illinois Press, 1977; Illini Books, 1980.

CHAPTER FIFTEEN

Three Legal Entanglements of Zora Neale Hurston

 KEVIN M. McCARTHY

Toward the end of her life, Zora Neale Hurston was involved in three legal entanglements, one as a defendant, one as a short-story writer, and one as a reporter. The first one was so devastating that she considered suicide in the midst of it, and it affected her writing after that; the second one allowed her to objectively explore the difficulties of a black maid facing a white accuser in a court of law; the third one enabled Hurston to write two long pieces about a black woman who killed a white man, not exonerating the woman but trying to understand the motivations behind such an act. Taken separately, as they usually are, the three legal entanglements seem merely episodic in the life of a writer who had many different experiences. Taken together, as we will do here, they present a different picture of a great writer; at least one of them may help explain why she lost her creative abilities at the end of her life.

In some of her early fiction, Hurston had written about judicial trials, but from a different point of view from that of later in her life. In her 1937 work, *Their Eyes Were Watching God*, Hurston wrote about a black woman going before a jury of twelve white men. After Janie Crawford was accused of killing her husband, Tea Cake, when he was about to attack her in his rabid state, she had to go into court and be tried before a jury of white men. In the courtroom Janie thought about how she would have preferred to have white *women* sitting on the jury instead of white men, but she did not really fear for the outcome. The people who were against her and tried to testify what a bad woman she was were the blacks in the segregated gallery. They wanted to point out that she had had no right to kill Tea Cake, but the judge never let them vent their anger at Janie. In the end, the white jury acquitted her of the crime, and she went free. Hurston wrote that, after the trial, there was nothing for Janie "to do with the little that was left of the day but to visit the kind white friends who had realized her feelings and thank them" ([1937] 1978, 280).

In her 1942 autobiography, *Dust Tracks on a Road*, Hurston also wrote about a trial, but it was quite humorous. In one scene she described how two defendants appeared before a justice of the peace in Maitland:

> The defendant had hit the plaintiff three times with his fist and kicked him four times. The justice of the peace fined him seven dollars—a dollar a lick. The defendant hauled out his pocketbook and paid his fine with a smile. The justice of the peace then fined the plaintiff ten dollars.
>
> "What for?" he wanted to know. "Why, Mr. Justice, that man knocked me down and kicked me, and I never raised my hand."
>
> "That is just what I'm fining you for, you yellow-bellied coudar! Nobody with any guts would have come into court to settle a fist fight." ([1942] 1971, 44).

At the end of the 1940s, Hurston would feel much differently about the legal system and would not write such humorous material again about a trial. Tracing her exposure to the legal establishment from this humorous incident, to her traumatic imprisonment in New York, to her fictional representation of a black woman in a white court, to her presence at the Ruby McCollum trial represents an odyssey from naïveté to hardened realism. It also marked the beginning of the end of a great writer.

Hurston as Defendant

In 1948, at the peak of her career and just when she was collecting material for another work, something happened that brought an abrupt end to Hurston's success. In September of that year, New York police arrested Hurston on the charge that she had committed sodomy with a ten-year-old boy. It turned out to be a trumped-up charge—she was actually in Honduras when the alleged incident took place—but she had a difficult time getting anyone to listen to her. She even offered to take a lie-detector test, but the authorities refused. It turned out that the mother of the boy had resented Hurston's suggestion that the woman take the boy, who was mentally unstable, to Bellevue Hospital for psychiatric testing. Hurston could not believe that the courts would take the word of a ten-year-old over that of an adult. She also hoped that the case would just die and that the newspapers would not learn of it; cases involving children were supposed to be private. However, a black employee of the court informed New York's black newspapers, and a reporter for the *New York Age* asked her about the charges (Hemenway, 1977, 319). A national paper, Baltimore's *Afro-American*, picked up the story and put it on the front page of its October 23, 1948, edition, right in the midst of reports on several sensational crimes. Bold headlines on the other stories ("Police Seeking Bathtub Killer of Young Mother"; "Jealous Woman, 58, Slays Pastor, 68, for Scorning Her"; "Seven Men Held in Sex Orgy Cases Probe") appeared right below the photograph of Hurston. The main headline on that front page, "Boys, 10, Accuse Zora," had as a lead-in right above it: "Did She Want 'Knowing and Doing' Kind of Love?" The secondary headline was "Novelist Arrested on Morals Charge," followed by "Reviewer of Author's Latest Book Notes Character Is 'Hungry for Love'" ("Boys," 1). The newspaper reported, inaccurately, that three boys, not one, were accusing Hurston and labeled the charges "particularly sordid."

Even worse was the reporter's intertwining in that story lines from Hurston's book *Seraph on the Suwanee* (1948). That article reads as follows:

> Zora Neale Hurston, 45, one of the nation's top authors, who in her latest book, "Seraph on the Suwanee," had one of her characters beg for "a knowing and doing love," last week pleaded not guilty to charges of having committed sodomy with three school boys here, and was held for trial in $1500 bail by Judge Saul Streit in General Sessions Court.
>
> The well-known novelist was arrested on Sept. 13 on the complaint of Alexander Miller of the Children's Society, who charged that she committed acts of sodomy with two school boys aged 10 and one aged 11 on Aug. 15 at [a certain address].
>
> The charges brought by Miller against the writer were particularly sordid.
>
> Miller charged that the three boys had stated to him that on Aug. 15 Miss Hurston first committed the act of sodomy with one of the 10-year-old youths in the presence of the other two and that she then committed the act with the other two boys.

Complexity Mirrored in Book

Miss Hurston's plea of not guilty followed by one day a New York daily newspaper's review of her latest book in which the reviewer noted that

"Incompatible strains in the novel mirror the complexity of the author. Miss Hurston shuttles between the sexes, the professions, and the races as if she were a man and woman, scientist and creative writer, white and colored."

In another part of the review the reviewer quoted a passage from Miss Hurston's book, published by Charles Scribner's Sons, in which one of her characters complains about the loving of the central character, Arvay.

Small Satisfaction

The passage reads as follows:

"I feel and believe that you do love me, Arvay, but I don't want that stand-still haphazard kind of love. I'm just as hungry as a dog for a knowing and doing love. You love like a coward. Don't take no steps at all." ("Boys," 1)

The district attorney investigated the case, found that it would not stand up in court, and had it dismissed in March 1949, but great damage had been done to Hurston (Hemenway, 1977, 320). She felt particularly betrayed by the fact that a black employee of the court had leaked the story to the press and that a black newspaper had picked it up and twisted the facts. In a letter she wrote to a friend, she contemplated suicide:

> I care for nothing anymore. My country has failed me utterly. My race has seen fit to destroy me without reason, and with the vilest tools conceived of by man so far. A society, eminently Christian, and supposedly devoted to super decency has gone so far from its announced purpose, not to protect children, but to exploit the gruesome fancies of a pathological case and do this thing to human decency. Please do not forget that thing was not done in the South, but in the so-called liberal North. Where shall I look in the country for justice. . . . All that I have tried to do has proved useless. All that I have believed in has failed me. I have resolved to die. It will take me a few days for me to set my affairs in order, then I will go. (Neal, 1971, xxii)

She did not commit suicide and, in fact, seemed to resume her normal life, but the incident had a great effect on her writing and on her psyche. Robert Hemenway views it as the start of a long dark period of her life, one from which she never did return to the quality of her early writing (1986, 87). The fact that it was a black court employee who leaked the story to the press and that it was a white official who exonerated her reminds one of Janie Crawford's acquittal by a white jury despite the treachery and enmity of her black neighbors in *Their Eyes Were Watching God*.

Hurston as Writer

Two years after the first incident, when she was falsely accused of sodomy, she published a short story entitled "The Conscience of the

Court" in *The Saturday Evening Post* (1950a). Earlier Langston Hughes had written that Hurston's ability to adapt to circumstances was the keystone to her success as an anthropologist (14). The same might be said of her as a writer. One can argue that she transformed her experience of being exonerated by a white official when falsely accused and wrote a story about a black woman who was similarly falsely accused of a crime and exonerated by a white judge. The plot dealt with the plight of a black maid, Laura Lee Kimble, who was accused of assaulting a man who had come to the house where she worked. The man was a moneylender who had gone to the house to take the furniture Mrs. Clairborne, Laura Lee's employer, had used as collateral for a $600 loan. Claiming she had not made payments on the loan, the moneylender arrived to seize the furniture while Mrs. Clairborne was away on a trip. Laura Lee attacked the man in order to prevent this.

The courtroom scene is puzzling and threatening to Laura Lee. To answer the charges, she had to enter a world totally alien to her. Laura Lee's innocence and naïveté moved the people in the courtroom, especially the judge:

> This unlettered woman had called up something that he had not thought about for quite some time. The campus of the University of Virginia and himself as a very young man there, filled with a reverence for his profession amounting to an almost holy dedication. His fascination and awe as a professor traced the more than two thousand years of growth of the concepts of human rights and justice. That brought him to his greatest hero, John Marshall, and his inner resolve to follow in the great man's steps, and even add to interpretations of human rights if his abilities allowed. No, he had not thought about all this for quite some time. (1950a, 23)

Laura Lee explained to the judge how she happened to be in Jacksonville, the scene of the story. When Laura Lee's husband, Tom, had died, Mrs. Clairborne had borrowed $600 from a moneylender in order to take Tom's body back to Georgia for burial. Mrs. Clairborne and Laura Lee had returned to Jacksonville after the funeral, and then Mrs. Clairborne had gone to Miami Beach for a vacation. When the moneylender showed up to cart off Mrs. Clairborne's furniture, Laura Lee defended her house and beat off the man. It turned out that the moneylender had lied to the court, that in fact the loan was not due for another three months. In the end the court found Laura Lee not guilty, and the judge said some kind words to her. After she was exonerated, Laura Lee retreated to the safety and security of the home she had so faithfully guarded.

Some critics criticized the story for its image of the subservient black woman, a figure quite different from those in Hurston's other stories. Laura Lee is almost the stereotype of the loyal family maid, but she is not totally passive, as she does attack the man trying to take her mistress's furniture. In fact, she takes a kind of pleasure in confronting the man: "'All I did next was to grab him by his heels and frail the pillar of the porch with him a few times'" (122).

The other problem with the story is its strange ending. Laura Lee returned home from the trial and performed a strange ritual:

> Back at the house, Laura Lee did not enter at once. Like a pilgrim before a shrine, she stood and bowed her head. "I ain't fitten to enter. For a time, I allowed myself to doubt my Celestine. But maybe nobody ain't as pure in heart as they aim to be. The cock crowed on Apostle Peter. Old Maker, please take my guilt away and cast it into the sea of forgetfulness where it won't never rise to accuse me in this world, nor condemn me in the next."
>
> Laura Lee entered and opened all the windows with a ceremonial air. She was hungry, but before she would eat, she made a ritual of atonement by serving. She took a finely wrought silver platter from the massive old sideboard and gleamed it to perfection. So the platter, so she wanted her love to shine. (122)

That ending raised some hard questions, such as: What was Hurston trying to reveal with her main character and the maid's blind loyalty to her mistress? As Robert Hemenway points out in his biography (1977, 327), one factor may be that the editorial staff of *The Saturday Evening Post* may have heavily edited the story.

The story might have been autobiographical to some extent since both Laura Lee and Hurston were middle-aged when they were accused of a crime, and both were abandoned by their friends and had to defend themselves alone. Both women refused to let marriage tie them down and restrict their growth, both ended up working as a maid, and both had a close, personal relationship with a white woman who paid their wages.

What is important about the story is that it reveals the feelings and motivations of a black woman. This story was published the same year as Hurston's essay entitled "What White Publishers Won't Print." In that article she wrote that white people have no curiosity about "the internal lives and emotions of the Negroes, and for that matter, any non-Anglo-Saxon peoples within our borders, above the class of unskilled labor" (1950b, 85). It is true that the protagonist in "The Conscience of the Court" was a servant, but it was an attempt to see the situation through Laura Lee's eyes. If, as Hurston claims, the ordinary reader has a stereotype in his mind of the foot-shuffling, eye-rolling black picking up a banjo and singing away, her black protagonist in "The Conscience of the Court" does not fit that stereotype. Laura Lee shows a loyalty to her mistress that epitomizes great virtue.

Hurston as Reporter

Three years after "The Conscience of the Court" was published, an event happened in Live Oak, Florida, that involved Hurston once again with a judicial proceeding, but this time as a reporter for a black newspaper. On August 3, 1953, a black woman named Ruby McCollum shot and killed a white doctor in the small north Florida town. The doctor, who had recently been elected to the Florida legislature and was thought by some to be preparing to run for the governorship of the state, had apparently had a long affair with McCollum, had fathered one of her children, and had impregnated her again.

For whatever reason, either because she was tired of being harassed by the doctor or in self-defense or in anger, Ruby McCollum shot and killed the doctor in his office. She then drove home with two of her young children, prepared a meal for them, changed her dress, and calmly waited for the police to arrive. After they arrested her, neighbors informed her husband, Sam, about what had happened. He rushed home, gathered up the children, packed as much as he could in a short time, including some $85,000 in cash from his bolita racket, and drove to Ruby's mother's home near Ocala. The next day he died of a heart attack.

The all-white jury that heard the case against McCollum found her guilty, and the judge sentenced her to the electric chair. After several appeals, she was eventually committed to the state mental hospital in Chattahoochee and spent twenty years there. In 1974 she was released from the hospital after being declared innocent by reason of insanity.

Hurston may have become interested in that particular case because white reporters were ignoring it, but also because Ruby McCollum was a black woman who did not fit the stereotype of black southern women. Besides covering the trial for a black newspaper, Hurston finally interested one of the South's most famous antisegregation writers, William Bradford Huie, in the trial. In an article he wrote for *Ebony* magazine, Huie claimed that Hurston wrote to him in 1953 that "there was truth that needed telling in Suwannee County, Florida, and that I, as a conservative white Southerner of many generations, might be able to break down the walls and tell it" (1954, 16). For his knowledge of the trial Huie relied on Hurston's coverage printed in the *Pittsburgh Courier* in 1952 and 1953. Huie eventually wrote a book about the trial: *Ruby McCollum: Woman in the Suwannee Jail.*

More important than the day-by-day court proceedings that Hurston reported was the long account of Ruby McCollum that she wrote, partly to try to understand the woman behind the gun. Ironically enough, McCollum's early story was like that of Hurston herself and of Laura Lee in "The Conscience of the Court": a young black woman who had dreams of bettering herself by leaving her small town, making her way in the world, and attaching herself to someone who could improve her life in material ways. Hurston did not try to prove that Ruby was innocent of the killing, because that would have been impossible. But she did try to explain the motivations behind such an act whereby a black woman would commit a crime that would destroy the unity of her own family and imprison her in a mental hospital for many years.

Hurston wrote the following about Ruby McCollum in the *Pittsburgh Courier*, and it might just as well apply to herself: "Whatever her final destiny may be, she has not come to the bar craven and whimpering. She has been sturdy and strong. . . . She had dared defy the proud tradition of the Old South openly and she awaits her fate with courage and dignity" (1953, 2).

In the remaining years of her life, Hurston never regained the creative success she had had with *Their Eyes Were Watching God*, *Dust Tracks on a Road*, and *Seraph on the Suwanee*. Like Florida's other great female writer of the 1940s, Marjorie Kinnan Rawlings, who never regained her writing success after she was tried in 1946 for invasion of privacy (Acton, 143), Hurston never wrote much after her run-in with the law in 1948. She spent much time working on a novel, *Herod the Great*, but publishers rejected it. She did publish an editorial about another legal case, the 1954 Supreme Court decision about desegregation (1955, 10), but she did not support the decision, arguing instead that the U.S. government should enforce compulsory education for southern black children as it did for white children.

As Mary Jane Lupton has pointed out, in all three legal entanglements the black woman, whether Hurston herself or Laura Lee or Ruby Mc-Collum, survived, as did many of Hurston's characters; but the women were certainly deeply affected by what happened in the courts of law. Hurston had come a long way from her early humorous depiction of a trial and had experienced something that made her angry and bitter, especially in her own encounter with the law. How deeply she was affected may never be known, but she never published works comparable to her earlier ones. Her legal entanglements marked the beginning of the end of a great career.

Works Cited

Acton, Patricia Nassif. *Invasion of Privacy: The Cross Creek Trial of Marjorie Kinnan Rawlings*. Gainesville: University of Florida Press, 1988.

"Boys, 10, Accuse Zora," *The Afro-American*, October 23, 1948, 1.

Hemenway, Robert E. "That Which the Soul Lives By." In *Zora Neale Hurston*, edited by Harold Bloom, 83–93. New York: Chelsea House, 1986.

———. *Zora Neale Hurston: A Literary Biography*. Urbana: University of Illinois Press, 1977.

Hughes, Langston. "Harlem Literati in the Twenties." *Saturday Review of Literature*, June 22, 1940, 14.

Huie, William Bradford. "The Strange Case of Ruby McCollum." *Ebony*, November, 1954, 16.

———. *Ruby McCollum: Woman in the Suwannee Jail*. New York: Dutton, 1956.

Hurston, Zora Neale. "The Conscience of the Court." *Saturday Evening Post*, March 18, 1950a.

———. "Court Order Can't Make Races Mix." *Orlando Sentinel*, August 11, 1955, 10.

———. *Dust Tracks on a Road*. 1942. Reprint. Philadelphia: Lippincott, 1971.

———. "The Life Story of Mrs. Ruby J. McCollum!" *Pittsburgh Courier*, May 2, 1953, 2.

———. *Seraph on the Suwanee*. New York: Scribner's, 1948.

———. *Their Eyes Were Watching God*. 1937. Reprint. Urbana: University of Illinois Press, 1978.

———. "What White Publishers Won't Print." *Negro Digest*, April 1950b, 85.

Lupton, Mary Jane. "Zora Neale Hurston and the Survival of the Female." *Southern Literary Journal* 15 (1982):45–54.

Neal, Larry. Introduction. *Dust Tracks on a Road*, by Zora Neale Hurston. Reprint. Philadelphia: Lippincott, 1971.

Contributors

Rosalie Murphy Baum teaches early American literature, southern literature, and black literature at the University of South Florida, Tampa. She has published on eighteenth- and nineteenth-century American authors as well as Martha Ostenso, Margaret Laurence, Alice Munro, Anne Tyler, and Toni Morrison.

Alan Brown teaches at Livingston College, Livingston, Alabama, where he is also director of the Writing Center. He has published essays on Ernest Hemingway and presented papers on Ralph Ellison, Richard Wright, and Zora Neale Hurston. He has received a grant from the Alabama Humanities Foundation to develop a program entitled "The History and Literature of Racism."

Warren J. Carson is an assistant professor at the University of South Carolina, Spartanburg, where he teaches courses in Afro-American literature and southern literature. He has presented papers on Afro-American science-fiction writers, Zora Neale Hurston, and Ralph Ellison and has written essays on James Baldwin, Paul Lawrence Dunbar, and James Weldon Johnson.

Margaret M. Dunn is coordinator of English and humanities at Rollins College's Brevard campus in Rockledge, Florida. She has published articles on Kate Chopin, William Faulkner, Gertrude Stein, and H. D. She presented a paper on Hurston at the Zora Neale Hurston Festival of the Arts (1990). With Ann R. Morris, she is currently at work on a manuscript entitled "Femmage: Quilted Fictions by American Women."

Christopher Felker is an instructor at the University of New Hampshire, Durham, where he is also a Ph.D. candidate in American studies. He presented a paper on Hurston to the Popular Culture Association in 1989. He also has published essays on Roger Williams and on male protagonists in Native American fiction.

STEVE GLASSMAN is an associate professor of humanities at Embry-Riddle Aeronautical University, Daytona Beach, Florida. He has published articles on Florida history, Flannery O'Connor, and William Faulkner and a historical novel, *Blood on the Moon* (1990), set in Florida during the Seminole Wars.

KATHLEEN HASSALL is an assistant professor at the University of North Florida, Jacksonville, where she teaches fiction writing; African-American literature and literary theory; and southern literature, particularly the work of southern women writers. She has published eight short stories that attempt to present the South as it is.

DAVID HEADON teaches in the Department of English at the Australia Defense Force Academy at the University of New South Wales. He has written articles on Australian poetry and fiction, convict literature, and blacks and whites in the literature of the northern territories. He is the editor of *Looking Beyond Yesterday: Social Responsibility and the Artist* (1989).

BEULAH HEMMINGWAY is an associate professor at Florida A & M University, Tallahassee, where she teaches African-American literature. She has published essays on Gwendolyn Brooks's women, on sex and race and the use of slang, and on Faulkner's black characters.

JACK LANE is Weddell Professor of American History at Rollins College, Winter Park, Florida. He is the author of three books, including two on the history of Rollins College, and coeditor, with Maurice O'Sullivan, of *The Florida Reader* (forthcoming).

ANNA LILLIOS is an assistant professor at the University of Central Florida, Orlando, where she teaches postmodernism and modern American literature. She has published essays on Lawrence Durrell and nineteenth-century British travelers to Greece. Her presentations include talks on Zora Neale Hurston, *Oedipus Rex,* and Lawrence Durrell. She coordinates the World Writers Series at the University of Central Florida.

KEVIN M. McCARTHY is an associate professor of English at the University of Florida, Gainesville. He has edited *Florida Stories* (University of Florida Press, 1989), *Florida Lighthouses* (University of Florida Press, 1990), and *Nine Florida Stories by Marjory Stoneman Douglas* (University of North Florida Press, 1990).

ANN R. MORRIS is professor of English at Stetson University, DeLand, Florida, where she holds the Nell Carlton Chair. She has published essays on Kate Chopin, black women writers in the Caribbean, sexuality in fantastic literature, and writing. She is working on a manuscript entitled "Femmage: Quilted Fictions by American Women," with Margaret M. Dunn.

MAURICE J. O'SULLIVAN is a professor of English at Rollins College, Winter

Park, Florida, and chair of the Department of Irish Studies. He has published essays on Amiri Baraka, John Dryden, and Jonathan Swift, and is coeditor with Jack C. Lane of *The Florida Reader* (Pineapple Press, forthcoming).

DANA MCKINNON PREU is a professor at Florida A & M University, Tallahassee. She has published papers on black and white authors of the Harlem Renaissance and on Zora Neale Hurston's *Mules and Men.* She is also an actress, having played Matt in the film *Gal Young Un* and Marjorie Kinnan Rawlings in *A Tea with Zora and Marjorie* by Barbara Speisman, in twenty-five performances sponsored by the Florida Endowment for the Humanities.

KATHRYN LEE SEIDEL is associate professor of English and associate dean of arts and sciences at the University of Central Florida, Orlando. She has published essays on Kate Chopin, Ellen Glasgow, and William Faulkner and presented papers on Zora Neale Hurston, Toni Morrison, and Alice Walker. She also has written *The Southern Belle in the American Novel* (University of South Florida Press, 1985).

BARBARA SPEISMAN is an associate professor at Florida A & M University, Tallahassee. She is the author of three plays about Hurston, including *A Tea with Zora and Marjorie,* which was sponsored by the Florida Endowment for the Humanities and has been presented in more than forty Florida cities.

MARY KATHERINE WAINWRIGHT is an associate professor of English at Manatee Community College, Bradenton, Florida. She has published essays on Zora Neale Hurston and the black community and has given papers on Hurston's narrative structure and aesthetics. Her 1989 dissertation compared the aesthetics of community in the works of Hurston, Toni Morrison, and Alice Walker.

Selected Bibliography

Books

Jonah's Gourd Vine. Philadelphia: J. B. Lippincott, 1934. Reprinted, with introduction by Larry Neal. Philadelphia: J. B. Lippincott, 1971.

Mules and Men. Philadelphia: J. B. Lippincott, 1935. Reprint. New York: Negro Universities Press, 1969. Reprinted, with introduction by Darwin Turner. New York: Harper and Row, 1970. Excerpted in *I Love Myself...*, 82–122.

Their Eyes Were Watching God. Philadelphia: J. B. Lippincott, 1937. Reprint. Greenwich, CN: Fawcett Publications, 1965. Reprint. New York: Negro Universities Press, 1969. Reprint. Urbana: University of Illinois Press, 1978. Manuscript in James Weldon Johnson Collection, Yale University Library.

Tell My Horse. Philadelphia: J. B. Lippincott, 1938. Excerpted in *I Love Myself...*, 123–49. Manuscript in James Weldon Johnson Collection, Yale University Library.

Moses, Man of the Mountain. Philadelphia: J. B. Lippincott, 1939. Reprint. Urbana: University of Illinois Press, 1984. Excerpted in *I Love Myself...*, 219–45. Manuscript in James Weldon Johnson Collection, Yale University Library.

Dust Tracks on a Road. Philadelphia: J. B. Lippincott, 1942. Reprinted, with introduction by Darwin Turner. New York: Arno Press, 1969. Reprinted, with introduction by Larry Neal. New York: J. B. Lippincott, 1972. Reprint. Urbana: University of Illinois Press, 1984. Manuscript in James Weldon Johnson Collection, Yale University Library.

Seraph on the Suwanee. New York: Charles Scribner's Sons, 1948. Reprint. Ann Arbor, Mich.: University Microfilms, 1971. Reprint. New York: AMS Press, 1974. Manuscript in Hurston Papers, University of Florida Library.

I Love Myself When I am Laughing ... and Then Again When I Am Looking Mean and Impressive: A Zora Neale Hurston Reader, edited by Alice Walker. Old Westbury, New York: The Feminist Press, 1979.

The Sanctified Church: The Folklore Writings of Zora Neale Hurston. Berkeley: Turtle Island, 1981.

Spunk: The Selected Stories of Zora Neale Hurston. Berkeley: Turtle Island, 1985. Contains "Spunk," "Isis," "Muttsey," "Sweat," "The Gilded Six-Bits," "Cock Robin Beale Street," "Book of Harlem," "Story in Harlem Slang," "Glossary of Harlem Slang," "Herod on Trial."

Other Publications

"Spunk." *Opportunity* 3 (June 1925): 171-73. Reprinted in *The New Negro,* edited by Alain Locke, 105-11. New York: Albert and Charles Boni, 1925.

"The Eatonville Anthology." *Messenger* 8 (September, October, November 1926), 261-62, 297, 319, 332. Reprinted in *I Love Myself* . . . , 177-88.

Color Struck: A Play. Fire!! 1 (November 1926), 7-15.

"Sweat." *Fire!!* 1 (November 1926), 40-45. Reprinted in *I Love Myself* . . . , 197-207; Reprinted in *The Norton Anthology of Literature by Women,* edited by Sandra Gilbert and Susan Gubar, 1639-49. New York: Norton, 1985. Reprinted in *Spunk: The Selected Stories of Zora Neale Hurston.*

The First One. Play. In *Ebony and Topaz,* edited by Charles S. Johnson. 1927. Facsimile reprint. Books for Libraries Press, 1971.

"How It Feels To Be Colored Me." *World Tomorrow,* 11 (May 1928), 215-16. Reprinted in *I Love Myself* . . . , 152-55. Reprinted in *The Norton Anthology of Literature by Women,* 1649-53.

"The Gilded Six-Bits." *Story* 3 (August 1933), 60-70. Reprinted in *I Love Myself* . . . , 208-18. Reprinted in *Spunk: The Selected Stories of Zora Neale Hurston.*

"Spirituals and Neo-Spirituals." In *Negro: An Anthology,* edited by Nancy Cunard, 359-61. London: Wishart, 1934.

"Race Cannot Become Great Until It Recognizes Its Talent." *Washington Tribune,* December 29, 1934.

"Fannie Hurst." *Saturday Review,* October 9, 1937, 15-16.

"Star-Wrassling Sons-of-the Universe" (review of *The Hurricane's Children,* by Carl Carmer). *New York Herald Tribune Books,* December 26, 1937, 4.

"Stories of Conflict" (review of *Uncle Tom's Children,* by Richard Wright). *Saturday Review,* April 2, 1938, 32.

"My Most Humiliating Jim Crow Experience." *Negro Digest* 2 (June 1944), 25-26. Reprinted in *I Love Myself* . . . , 163-64.

"Crazy for This Democracy." *Negro Digest* 4 (December 1945), 45-48. Reprinted in *I Love Myself* . . . , 165-68.

"The Transplanted Negro" (review of *Trinidad Village,* by Melville Herskovits and Frances Herskovits). *New York Herald Tribune Weekly Book Review,* March 9, 1947, 20.

"Ruby Sane." *Pittsburgh Courier,* October 11, 1952.

"Ruby McCollum Fights for Life." *Pittsburgh Courier,* November 22, 1952.

"Bare Plot against Ruby." *Pittsburgh Courier,* November 22, 1952.

"Trial Highlights." *Pittsburgh Courier,* November 29, 1952.

"McCollum-Adams Trial Highlights." *Pittsburgh Courier,* December 27, 1952.

"Ruby Bares Her Love." *Pittsburgh Courier,* January 3, 1953.

"Doctor's Threats, Tussle over Gun Led to Slaying." *Pittsburgh Courier,* January 10, 1953.

"Ruby's Troubles Mount." *Pittsburgh Courier,* January 17, 1953.

"The Life Story of Mrs. Ruby J. McCollum." *Pittsburgh Courier,* February 28, March 7, 14, 21, 28, April 4, 11, 18, 25, May 2, 1953.

[The Trial of Ruby McCollum]. In *Ruby McCollum: Woman in the Suwannee Jail,* by
    William Bradford Huie, 89–101. New York: Dutton, 1956.
"Hoodoo and Black Magic." *Fort Pierce Chronicle,* July 11, 1958–August 7, 1959.

Unpublished Materials

"Eatonville When You Look at It." 2 pp. In "The Florida Negro."
The Fiery Chariot (1935?). Play. James Weldon Johnson Collection, Yale University
    Library.
"The Florida Negro." Manuscript prepared by ZNH and others for the Florida
    Federal Writers' Project. 183 pp. Copy, Florida Historical Society.
Herod the Great. Novel, 269 pp. Hurston Papers, University of Florida Library.
"Maitland." 2 pp. In "The Florida Negro."
"The Migrant Worker in Florida." 7 pp. Hurston Papers, University of Florida
    Library.
Mule Bone: A Comedy of Negro Life (1930, with Langston Hughes). Play. Mimeo-
    graphed copy in Howard University Library. Act 3 published in *Drama Critique*
    (Spring 1964): 103–7.
"Negro Mythical Places." 3 pp. In "The Florida Negro."
"Negro Religious Customs: The Sanctified Church." Folklore, 8 pp. Florida His-
    torical Society.
Polk County: A Comedy of Negro Life in a Sawmill Camp, with Authentic Negro Music
    (1944). Play. James Weldon Johnson Collection, Yale University Library.

Biography

Hemenway, Robert. *Zora Neale Hurston: A Literary Biography.* Chicago: University
    of Illinois Press, 1977.
Howard, Lillie P. *Zora Neale Hurston.* Boston: Twayne, 1980.

Bibliography

Hemenway, Robert. Appendix, *Zora Neale Hurston: A Literary Biography.* Chicago:
    University of Illinois Press, 1977.
Newson, Adele S. *Zora Neale Hurston: A Reference Guide.* Boston: G. K. Hall, 1967.

Index